Community Visioning for Place Making

Community Visioning for Place Making is a groundbreaking guide to engaging with communities in order to design better public spaces. It provides a tool kit to encourage and assist organizations, municipalities, and neighborhoods in organizing visually based community participation workshops, used to evaluate their existing community and translate images into plans that embody their ideal characteristics of places and spaces. The book is based on results generated from hundreds of public participation visioning sessions in a broad range of cities and regions, portraying images of what people liked and disliked. These community visioning sessions have been instrumental in generating policies, physical plans, recommendations, and codes for adoption and implementation in a range of urban, suburban, and rural spaces, and the book serves as a bottom-up tool for designers and public officials to make decisions that make their communities more appealing. The book will appeal to community and neighborhood organizations, professional planners, social and psychological professionals, policy analysts, architects, urban designers, engineers, and municipal officials seeking an alternative vision for their future.

Anton C. Nelessen Tony is the inventor of the Community Visioning Process using the Visual Preference Survey and Vision Translation workshops. He has applied it in nearly 400 communities across the country and world. He is a trained architect and urban designer, professor, author, film and multi-media producer, painter, sculptor, and visioning facilitator. He has led an award-winning urban planning firm since 1989. He has been Undergraduate Program Director for Planning, Public Policy and Public Health at Rutgers University. Currently, he is Professor of Urban Planning, Design and Visioning at Rutgers. He and his wife live in downtown Princeton, New Jersey.

"The Visual Preference Survey process in an exemplary tool involving and educating the general public about the impacts of development and the choices that they have for improving their community."

—*Jim McKensie, Executive Director of Metroplan, Little Rock, Arkansas*

"The Vision Planning Process by Tony Nelessen is an exciting new planning technique that allows people to become the planners and architects of their community's future."

—*Gordon Linton, Federal Transit Administrator, US Department of Transportation*

"While there are many 'specialists' in land planning, it is hard to find true leadership and methodology to bring the energy and determination of an entire community together towards the success of development. Tony Nelessen has proven his ability to do this very successfully."

—*Richard Sharpe, President of Sharpe Architecture, Wilmington, NC*

"This is the most innovative and engaging process for community participation and generating a vision that I have ever experienced."

—*Andy MacCabe, Redevelopment Authority, City of Bayonne, New Jersey*

"The Visual Preference Survey Process is an original and effective way for citizens to actively engage in the planning process. The Visual Preference Survey and the documentation of the results are both strong educational and involvement tools. They embody the bottom-up approach of trusting the public to intuitively know what makes communities desirable and safe places to live and work."

—*Gretchen Karfour, Commissioner, City of Portland, Oregon*

Community Visioning for Place Making

A Guide to Visual Preference Surveys for Successful Urban Evolution

Anton C. Nelessen

Routledge
Taylor & Francis Group
NEW YORK AND LONDON

First published 2021
by Routledge
605 Third Avenue, New York, NY 10158

and by Routledge
2 Park Square, Milton Park, Abingdon, Oxon, OX14 4RN

Routledge is an imprint of the Taylor & Francis Group, an informa business

Library of Congress Cataloging-in-Publication Data
A catalog record for this title has been requested

ISBN: 978-0-367-62284-8 (hbk)
ISBN: 978-0-367-62283-1 (pbk)
ISBN: 978-1-003-10871-9 (ebk)

Typeset in Adobe Garamond
by codeMantra

The **Visual Preference Survey**™ (VPS) referred to in this book has been trademarked to A. Nelessen Associates, Incorporated, since 1989.

The **Vision Translation Workshop** (VTW) has been used with the VPS as a component of the Nelessen Community Visioning Process since 1989.

All images and maps used this book are provided by A. Nelessen and were used in multiple VPSs. Unless specifically sourced to others, all images are attributable to Anton "Tony" Nelessen and A. Nelessen Associates. Inc.

This book is dedicated to the current and future generations who must live, work, play, and survive in the positive or negative world we build.

Armed with a workable Community Visioning process, using the results of VPSs; the Demographic, Policy, and Market Questionnaire; and VTWs, participants can generate positive and negative visual and emotional data to help plan, design, zone, and then build safe, healthy, sustainable, and equitable future for everyone and every place on this planet. Implementing Community Visioning can assist in the preservations of a historic and natural area; transform negative places; and build positive places and spaces that are healthy, loved, cherished, and cared for.

All of us are in some small way responsible for the short- and long-term future. We all live on one small planet where everyone and everything is connected. We are part of the urban evolutionary spiral. Negativism through increased inefficiencies, pollution, depression, frustration, and apathy with the places we live must be overcome. Positive places must be visioned and emulated to build a positive world and guide successful urban evolution.

Contents

Preface

Declaration of Independence

"We hold these truths (visions) to be self-evident."

The images, narratives, and recommendations in this book have been generated by thousands of individuals who have participated in a Vision Process using the Visual Preference Survey™ (VPS), combined with a Demographic, Market, and Policy Questionnaire and a Vision Translation Workshop (VTW). Visual images transcend age, income, profession, gender, social status, race, and language. You see a picture, and you instantly react to it. Do you like it? Would a place or space like here presented be appropriate in your neighborhood? No images displayed in this book, including existing (before) images are staged or styled; they were all photographed as they were seen with the normal human eye and captured with standard lenses. Most images were captured as people would experience them as a pedestrian or seen from a moving vehicle. The simulated (after) images are the results of listening to participants and transforming the existing (before) image, using Photoshop and other computer programs, into a place or space people told us they wanted. Once completed, the images were presented and evaluated to determine the response values. It was only then could we determine the differences between the response to the existing and new proposed image(s).

Individuals Possess an Innate Positive or Negative Sense of Place and Space

The VPS results present a phenomenological approach for evaluating places and spaces by generating numerical values to quantify the emotional responses to images and videos. The interactive visual and graphic content of Community Visioning allows everyone to participate. Language is no barrier because it is visually and graphically based. The accompanying questionnaires are translated, when needed, into various languages. The Demographics, Policy, and Market responses from each person are recorded and compared to the demographic profile of the entire community in order to determine trends and consensus issues. The majority of participants were not architects, planners, engineers, or politicians. Most were concerned residents across a spectrum of ages, incomes, professions, genders, social statuses, and races from a range of locations within and outside the study jurisdiction. People feel at ease participating. Everyone reacts to places and spaces: They know the streets, buildings, parks, neighbors, and neighborhoods in their communities by experience as pedestrians or from cars, or by memory of places previously experienced or genetically embedded in their minds. Determining responses, through peoples' own perceptions, beliefs, and programming, then quantifying emotional responses for all participants facilitates a consensus understanding of the essential value of places and spaces.

Through Participation by Large Numbers of Individuals, Positive and Negative Visions of Places and Spaces Emerge

This book reveals the visual preferences and aspirations of the citizens who want to correct neglected streetscapes and neighborhoods. Neglected streetscapes and neighborhoods will not do. Participants also want to preserve and enhance natural and rural environments, and improve the value and livability of suburbs, towns, and city centers.

Thousands of images and reports were edited down to select three hundred images that could most contribute to the **basic minimum preference standards** for natural, rural, suburban, small town, and the cores of larger urban cities.

Acknowledgements

I am forever grateful for each and every participant, estimated at over 150,000, for sharing their feelings and emotions about places and spaces that impact their lives now and in the future. Without their input and trust, their community vision would not result in positive recommendations and implementation.

Thanks to the hundreds of communities and organizations that commissioned Community Visioning, along with the participants who felt empowered to become part of the future of their communities. Specific thanks to the citizens of Milwaukee, Wisconsin; Orlando, Florida; Midtown Atlanta, Georgia; Princeton, New Jersey; Jersey City, New Jersey; Overland Park, Kansas; and the many hundreds of other communities and organizations that used the results of their public participation process to adopt master plans, redevelopment plans, and zoning ordinances and building codes. These legal documents were instrumental in approving new construction that brought people's visions to fruition.

I want to posthumously thank Professor Willo Van Moltke, Director of the Harvard Graduate School of Design, Urban Design Program, and Masey Lawrence, Director of Imageworks School of Photography and Media Arts, who allowed me to pursue the postgraduate research and application of this visioning process. Both men provided the resources to research and test place response presentations, formats, and feedback mechanisms. Thank you to the many student interns and colleagues who helped construct and test image formats, projection techniques, and soundscapes. The encouragement, equipment, and space allocations remain truly appreciated. Because of them, I was able to beta test formats, present multiple existing and proposed visual contexts, and evaluate participants' responses.

Typical Community Visioning Sessions   Typical Vision Translation Workshop

I especially want to thank Mayor John Wiley; Borough Council; and residents of the Borough of Metuchen, New Jersey, where the first VPS was used as an urban planning tool to guide the future redevelopment of their downtown. That vision is still being built to this day, some 40 years later, as a testament to the lasting power of visioning.

Many more people have been involved in the evolution of the visual and graphic forms. I want to particularly acknowledge the staff of A. Nelessen Associates (ANA), who, over a period of more than 35 years, helped facilitate Community Visioning workshops that resulted in interesting and innovative urban design plans and codes. Most staff members at ANA were recent graduates of Rutgers or other leading universities. They provided an enormous amount of energy and ideas to the ongoing research and application—most interestingly, the first use of photo simulations. Their contributions helped shape and facilitate the public participation visioning process and, most importantly, the resulting urban form that was built and is yet to be built. It was a very heady, productive, and exciting time for public participation for quality urban design. These now professional planners and architects have continued the use of the VPS in their careers in government and as consultants on the betterment of landscapes, towns, and cities worldwide.

I want to thank my wife, Francoise, who has been there through it all, the ups and the downs, the successes and failures, since 1974, tolerating the long days, nights, and weeks with me and the staff, as we devoted so much time and energy to understanding people's visions and translating

these into reports, urban design plans, and codes. She has been my consummate travel companion as we filmed locations all over the world to capture many of the images and videos used in research and application. We assembled millions of images and hundreds of hours of video. Her photographic skill is amazing. Thank you for your generosity, understanding, and critiques. Equally to be thanked are my three sons, who lived in the office most of their young lives and tolerated a "workaholic" father who was pursuing Community Visioning in lieu of attending their soccer games and crew races. Here's a debt that will never be able to be repaid.

As a final acknowledgment, I want to thank Dean Dona Schneider, Joann Visicaro, Karen Cacy, Carlos Rodrigues, FAICP, and particularly Ron Tindall, AICP, for their most constructive comments and edits. These were invaluable in the completion of the manuscript and selection of images.

Community Vision Becomes Reality

The desire for a Downtown Market was expressed in the VPS and VTW. The community vision was quickly realized as one of the early catalytic projects in downtown Milwaukee. The architecture, urban design, and streetscapes have transformed the location. Early implementation of people's visions is critical as a catalyst for long-term change.

Introduction to Community Visioning

ID Number_____

ENVISIONING DOWNTOWN PRINCETON
Sponsored by the Greater Princeton Chamber of Commerce

Demographic, Policy and Marketing Questionnaire
to accompany the Visual Preference Survey ™

This portion of the survey complements the 80 images in the Visual Preference Survey™. Mark your answers to the questionnaire on the **Red Form**. Please mark only one answer, whichever is the most appropriate. You will be given instructions regarding the ID number on this form at the beginning of the survey session.

This survey is not intended to be a scientific sample, but a gauge of perceptions and preferences of interested residents, property owners, business owners, visitors and other users of downtown.

Thank you for your participation. Your time and this information is extremely important. It is your option to print your name on the response forms. All personal information and answers will be kept confidential.

Demographics
Please tell us about yourself

1. When were you born?
   1. before 1920 3. 1940 to 1944 5. 1968 to 1980
   2. 1920 to 1939 4. 1945 to 1967 6. After 1981

2. Gender
   1. Male
   2. Female

3. Ethnicity
   1. Mexican American 5. Latin/Hispanic
   2. African American 6. Native American
   3. White/Caucasian 7. South or Central American
   4. Asian/Pacific Islander 8. Other (Specify) _____

4. Gross Household income
   1. under $24,999 5. $75,000-$99,999
   2. $25,000 to $34,999 6. $100,000-$149,999
   3. $35,000 to $49,900 7. $150,000-$200,000
   4. $50,000 to $74,999 8. Above $200,001

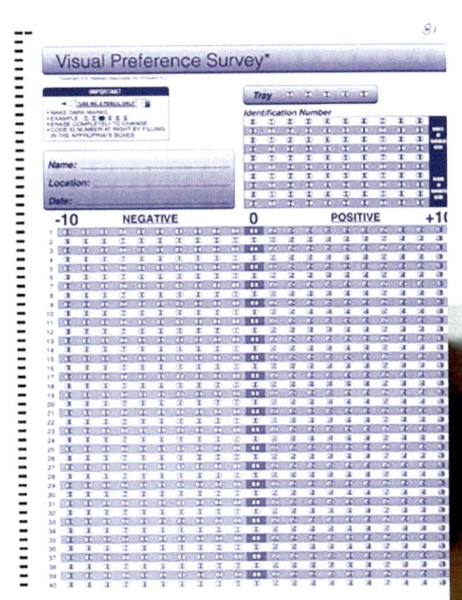

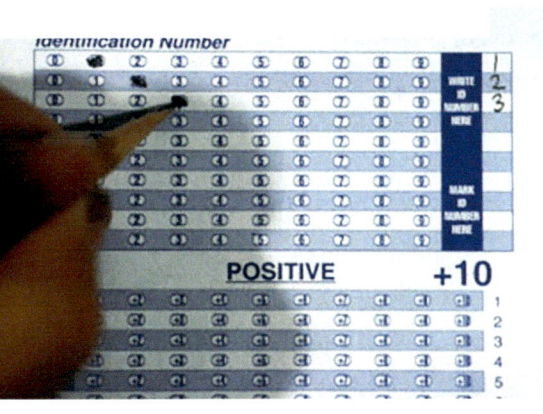

Using Visual Preferences and Vision Translation Workshops for Place Making

One of the early books I read as an architectural student was *Autobiography of an Idea* by Louis Sullivan. I read it again later on in my career as I worked on the early phases of Community Visioning. Sullivan's description of vision is compelling. He wrote,

> *Now think of the power we call vision; that inner sight which encompasses the larger meaning of its outer world, which sees humanity in the broad, which beholds the powers, which unifies its inner and outer world, which sees far beyond where the eye leaves off seeing, and as sympathetic insight finds its goal in the real.*

That last phrase, *"as sympathetic insight finds its goal in the real,"* is why consensus vision translated into the actual building of places and spaces is both powerful and necessary.

Using the gift of sight and emotions to guide the future of urban evolution is powerful. Tapping into expectations, experiences and memory is crucial to guide the future of positive urban evolution. Everyone has hopes for the future. Giving form to those hopes is the challenge and great opportunity that community vision provides.

Early in my professional years as a consultant to local planning boards, it became apparent that too many people on the board, as well as the general public, attorneys, and many planners, simply could not envision a place from a two-dimensional site plan. Nor could they say with certainty what they liked or disliked about

The vast majority of people have similar positive or negative responses to the same places and spaces. A key to a positive physical future is determining those places and spaces that resonate positively in most peoples' minds and then translating these into plans and codes that are built.

the proposed development. When the public and members of the boards couldn't see the proposed three and four dimensional form from a two dimensional plan and elevations, the reaction was typically negative. These experiences have led me to the belief that the mind's eye of most human brains is unable to imagine being in a new place, or moving around or through a building, space, or place, when this is presented in two dimensions alone. More was needed for them to make a rational decision. Most decisions defaulted to attorneys and the existing zoning regulations, mostly written by attorneys with no visual training. Three-dimensional models were not required or affordable for site plans or sub-division approvals. Sophisticated computer modeling and three-dimensional printing had not yet been invented. However, board members and the public could and **did respond to renderings and photographs**. Was this the key to planning and constructing buildings and spaces that will improve the quality of life along with the health and welfare of communities.

Images are the more important component of any Community Visioning process. Images used in Visual Preference Surveys (VPS) are best captured by three- and four-dimensional representations of spaces and places using still and video cameras. Additional information and techniques will be presented later in this book.

Images generate emotions, stir imagination, trigger intuition, and inspire people to want a positive form and character of place, or to see positive change when a place or space is perceived as negative. When images are evaluated and stored in your memory, they create a powerful gestalt. **When many people envision the possibility of a place transformed from negative to positive, change becomes possible**.

As an Assistant Professor of Urban Design at Harvard's Graduate School of Design (GSD) and later as Director of the Multi-media Lab at Imageworks School of Photography and Media Arts, I researched and then developed a variety of photographic and projection techniques, along with response forms that tested the public reaction to a variety of rural and urban spaces and places. It was apparent from early beta tests, using projected slides and movie/video imagery, that people could more easily orient themselves and evaluate places and spaces. The positive results of these experimental techniques led to the development of the more simplified VPS.

The images in a typical VPS use many images of an existing location. These are supplemented by images of places and spaces that have been built in communities of similar size, character, and geographic location. In addition, there are renderings or computer simulations of places containing visual characteristics revealed during focus groups. The emotional response to these images answers the question:

How appropriate or inappropriate are these spaces and places now and in the future for this community?

A numerical scale response ranging from −10 to +10 is used. The minus numbers, from −1 to −10, measure the intensity of negative emotional response and inappropriateness of an image. The plus numbers, from +1 to +10, indicate a positive emotional response and appropriateness.

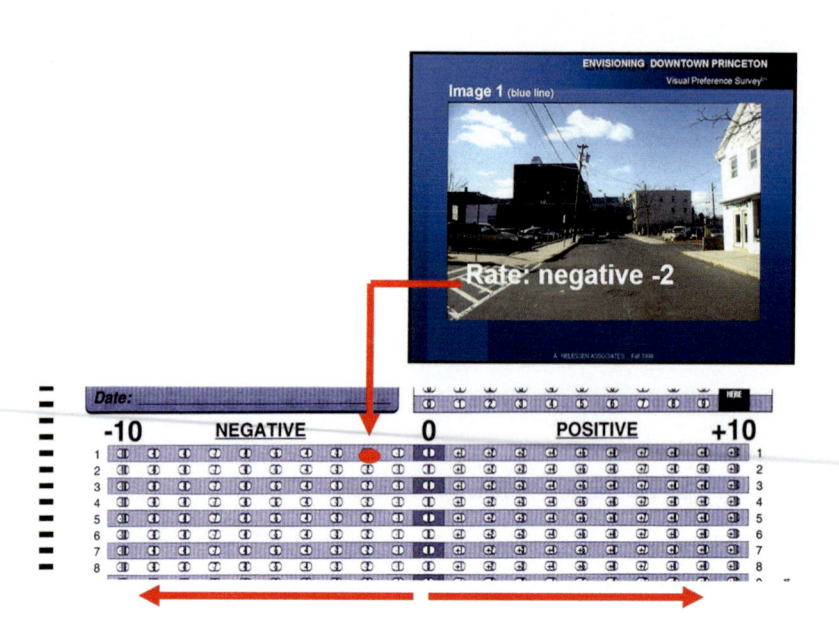

Response Form (Blue Sheet)

The response form is divided into 21 possible responses. In this case, the image above the form was given a –2 response value.

The center "0" referred to no positive or negative response, or indicated that people were not emotionally moved either way.

One item on the questionnaire handed out at all visioning sessions asked, "When you gave an image in the VPS a negative response rating which of the following describes the emotion you were experiencing?" The other asked, "When you gave the image a positive response rating which of the following describes the emotion you were experiencing?"

From a summary of hundreds of questionnaires, the responses to the negative question had the following responses:

Depressed	46%
Hopeless	10%
Threatened	7%
Anxious	4%
Fear	4%
Rage	3%
All the above	**26%**

Additional responses can be found in Appendix III – Book of Public Comments

The responses to the positive question were as follows:

Hopeful	25%
Joy	16%
Happiness	19%
Safe	9%
Pride	6%
All of the above	**25%**

"Depressed" and "Hopeful" seem to be the two strongest emotions, with many participants responding to "all of the above." To further understand these responses, focused discussions with participants, social workers, psychiatrists, and religious leaders were conducted over many years in an attempt to understand why certain images generated these reactions. As you page through this book the response values, whether collectively positive or negative, are notated above the images alongside a brief description of their negative or positive qualities, some including recommendations. Most negative responses generate a feeling of depression and hopelessness in contrast to the hopefulness, happiness, and joy felt when experiencing positive visions of places and spaces. As visual response testing has evolved, results have indicated that many of the places and spaces people rated as positive reflected the physical design and land use elements expressed in the natural and rural landscapes, and traditional historic cities. For example, buildings from the City Beautiful Movement, Jane Jacobs's type streets, and early examples of Neo-traditionalism rated very positive. The visual and spatial characteristic inherent in the positive images are what people want now and in the future. Unfortunately, what they wanted was not what they could expect in development. In many cities, zoning regulations would not allow these places and spaces to be built without variances.

Most features of urban deterioration, functionalists' buildings, and commercial and residential sprawl generate negative responses. The ubiquitous exurban sprawl model was planned to accommodate the single-family home, strip commercial development, and an auto dependent lifestyle which became the norm after World War II. Once they were codified in the 1950s' comprehensive master plans and zoning, exurban sprawl was subsidized, built, and heavily marketed. With millions of units being built in the late 1940s and 1950s, it is difficult, if not impossible, to reverse this trend, and it continues to this day. Most buyers have limited choices. Units were cheap to build, the land was plentiful and zoned for sprawl, and highways were subsidized. The prerequisite was that to live in suburbia, must have a car, or two or three. A massive consumer economy emerged. This land use pattern impacted most new development and spawned negative thinking about the livability and viability of cities. When tested by many Community Visioning sessions, suburban roadways, parking lots, strip commercial buildings, and most higher density suburban residential development are value rated as negative, as were deteriorated cityscapes, open parking lots, and unmaintained buildings and streetscapes.

The preponderance of negative responses led to the realization that barriers to the continuous creation of negative places could only be broken if there were positive consensus visions of alternatives. Thus, the evolution of Community Visioning was developed through a feedback loop of visual responses by many participants.

"If anything, the human story affirms that we have become what we are because we learned how to survive by intellectually and *physically adjusting to environmental change."*

Before Atlantis: 20 Million Years of Human and Pre-Human History

by Frank Joseph

Positive and negative images, surviving many years of evolution, are embedded, or "filed," somewhere in people's memories. Current experiences, beliefs, attitudes, and expectations add more complexity. It is extraordinary that the human mind can evaluate in fine detail what is seen, as well as whether it is positive and good or negative and bad. Unfortunately, results generated in Community Visioning sessions conducted in a broad range of cities and regions have revealed **that negative images dominate**.

This book presents many negative images that make communities feel depressed, balanced with many positive images that could ameliorate these negative conditions. The collective positive visions generate hope for a more positive visual, spatial, emotional, and sustainable short- and long-term future.

Reviewing over 40 years of Community Visioning, the positive and negative image responses have been extraordinarily consistent over the years. People know what they want if given choices. The goal of the visioning process is to identify negative places and spaces, and then enact some variation of the positive visions in

building new positive places. To accomplish this, positive community visions need to be illustrated and written into updated comprehensive plans, existing codes, and zoning. They must be translated into two-, three-, and four-dimensional development and redevelopment plans for people to understand.

There are too few "well designed" places that meet the collective, desired, and imagined positive experience of place. Where these places exist, or have been transformed from negative to positive, people feel more happiness, and the economic value of place and efficiency increases. There **need** to be many more positive **places**. There need to be more explicit visions of what people want that can induce hopefulness and get built.

To capture a holistic vision of places and spaces, surveys have revealed that an optimum of fourteen (14) image categories must be probed separately and then combined. To accomplish this, many images have to be photographed and evaluated. A Visual Preference Survey typically contains between 30 and over 240 images, combined with a selected number of stop action videos. This smaller number of images is typical of an online Community Visioning session or probing a specific visual and spatial feature or location.

Each positive or negative image in this book has been extensively tested, with its collective response values expressed as the mean or average of all responses, and its standard deviation. We have found mean and standard deviation to be the most understandable for the public when presenting results. On the other hand, the median or middle value, with half of the responses above and half below, and the mode, the number most often used, are often found to be confusing.

There are many positive and negative consensus visions in this book, intended for a wide range of land use, places, spaces, and mobility options. The selected images in each chapter present a collective positive or negative emotional response, along with recommendations for implementation to improve unacceptable places.

This book also contains value rated images of negative, unacceptable places and spaces which generate depression, hopelessness, fear, and anger. When places become unbearably negative, escape may result in anger, health disparities, and augmented reality using drugs, alcohol, internet and video games. When people encounter too many negative places, the images are embedded into their memory, then hopeless sets in, leading us to imagine even more negativity and fear while repressing the positive scenes we encounter.

A disturbing article in *Harvard Magazine* titled "How Depression Lingers," published by Professor Jill Hooley of Harvard in 2016, states,

The brains of recovering patients (depression) still show distinctive activity patterns – even though

the subjects report feeling normal.

When additional negativism of place is focused on these brains, relapse could occure. This made me think seriously about those people who repeatedly experience negative places, with resulting inescapable negativism and depression, day after day. The Community Visioning sessions have also clearly demonstrated that negative places provide the greatest opportunity for potential change. Most people want these negative-rated places to change for the better. Unfortunately, there are many who prosper from places remaining in their negative conditions. Think about the suburban and urban commercial and urban residential slumlords.

Selecting the final set of images for the book was extremely difficult given the vast number of images and places that have been evaluated over nearly 40 years and 400 vision sessions.

Many images in this book were evaluated in multiple vision sessions, in various locations, and to a wide demographic, thereby providing a large cross section of responses to specific images of ubiquitous land uses, like strip commercial developments or low density subdivisions. The multiple responses that were generated by participants from various communities generated a broader consensus of the most acceptable and unacceptable visual and spatial characteristics in their towns and yet to be built neighborhoods. These visioned places impacted recommendations for development, redevelopment, preservation,

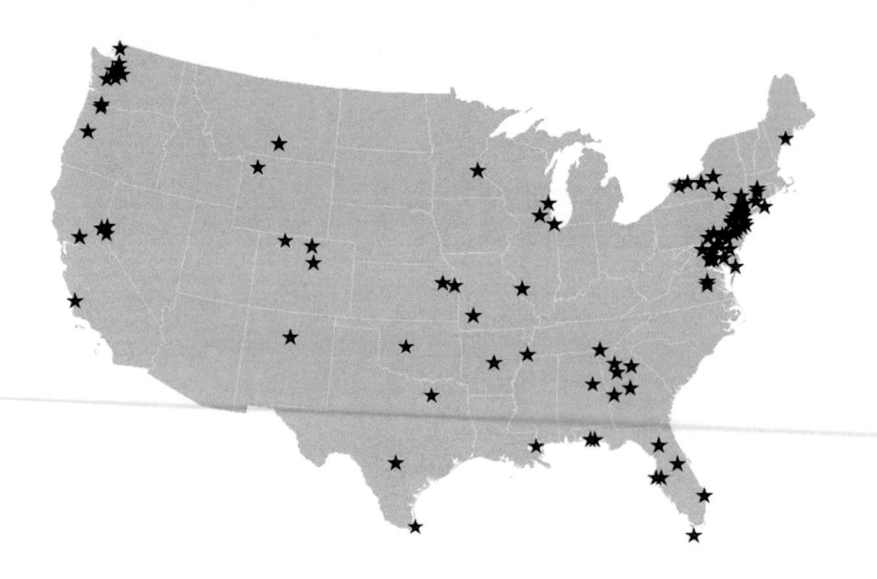

Location of Community Visioning Sessions

Distribution of locations across the United States where responses were generated.

The images, response values, and recommendations in this book were generated in 397 cities across the United States. The list of these locations by state can be found in Appendix II. This does not include those in Canada or other locations worldwide.

or removal. The accumulated collective feelings about these images, experienced by a large number of people, are a validation of the universality of the emotional and physical reactions. Positives are to be promoted; negatives are to be redeveloped.

all Community Visioning sessions are compared, results share positive and negative values, and attributes across multiple categories.

The collective visions from each community are unique but share an incredible number of commonalities. When images from

One overriding commonality is the intense desire for places and spaces that generate positive feelings. These images portray places that are healthy and sustainable for living, working, playing, procreating, and retiring. Community Visioning participants want places that integrate nature, provide a sense of community, are safe, are cost effective, and sustainable. They must also have buildings and streets built on a human scale, promote walkability, and have easy mobility connections to other places via transit. **Everything needed should be available within a reasonable 10- to 15-minute walking time, a maximum 2 ½ mile bike ride or a 20-minute transit ride.** These are the most desired time distance relationships. The participants expressed a need for healthy food and water, and jobs; perhaps most importantly, they wanted to be part of a greater vision to make their communities more positive, livable, human-scaled, safe, and affordable.

Two Community Visioning Sessions

Public meetings are typically well attended. There is an intensity of interaction when there is a meaningful visual and oral exchange to which everyone can respond.

The participants in the vision sessions represent a broad and diverse range of individuals. The following is a general profile of participants.

Age	
70 or older	19%
50 to 69	34%
26 to 49	**35%**
18 to 25	12%
Gender	
Male	51%
Female	49%
Income	
Less than $24,999	7%
$30,000 to $74,000	**39%**
$75,000 to $99,999	24%
$100,000 to $200,000	28%
Greater than $201,000	2%
Habitat	
Home owners	**82%**
Renters	18%

Gender distribution suggests an almost equal balance of men and women. The age of participants indicate that the survey responses are skewed to the older generations, with 53% of participants ranging from 50 to 70+, in their mature years when they have the most power, control and financial capability. They are concerned about the present and the future of their children and grandchildren. The largest cohort, 35%, ranged from 26 to 49: People who are in the highest consumer positions and have the most invested in the existing condition and immediate future.

47% ranged between 18 to 49 years, the most aggressive, concerned, and consumer-based cohort.

The vast majority of participants are home owners, with 18% renters.

63% of participants have a household income range of $30,000 to $99,999, with $30,000 to $74,999 being the household income of the most participants. Therefore, the visions are more for the middle class, with further good input from those in upper-income households. When the positive and negative responses of all groups are combined, a consensus vision emerges: A catalyst for change.

Fundamental to Community Visioning is the belief that **no one knows a community better than the people who live, work, play, and are educated there**. The greater the number of participants, the more successful the results. When the collective vision presented at the completion of the process becomes embedded into the memory and imagination of those who participated, they become advocates for the implementation of the vision and work toward small and large successes.

People have unconscious desires, and these are utilized best when reinforced by hope of implementation and future happiness recalling positive places that they have visited, lived in, or imagined before. This is **what people want**, but can it be realized?

Such use of the word "people" does not have the political meaning of representing "the people," as in the political "I was elected and therefore I am the voice of the people." A politician's vision still comes down to their personal wants and desires, what their donors want, or whatever corporate interest or profits they are protecting. It also does not represent the visions of the engineers or architects who think they know what people want or what is best or safest for them. Sometimes they do, if they have had sufficient exposure to positive alternatives, which can also inspire their imagination. Most of the time, however, officials and developers create negative places following inappropriate zoning, with their consultants acquiescing to the regulations or seeking variances.

There is often confusion between a positive vision and a mission statement. Mission statements, captured in words, can be internalized to have many different meanings. These are typically debatable or sometimes purposefully vague. Words have multiple meanings based on individuals' experiences and memories, e.g. what is the meaning of a "good place to live"? In everyone's mind, there are multiple mental images of what this could mean. However, none of us, as yet, can see inside others' minds or transpose their emotions and feelings into places without assistance.

Communities that have conducted Community Visioning and adopted the results in whole or in parts are flourishing as their visions become

reality. The consensus visual results portray a higher quality of life, pride of place, economic success, and better opportunities for sustainability. When there is acceptance, adoption, and implementation, positive change is assured.

For this to be achieved, we need a positive, humanistic hope for the natural areas, farmlands, villages, towns, and cities on our planet. This book is about a process and applications that can be used to influence and build positive physical and emotional places and spaces to live in now and in the future.

Successful community vision results in most positive places have been generated from partnerships of political, professionals, businesses, and neighborhood residents. As we pass through current sustainability, economic, health, political, and climate crises, recognize that natural ecology and the positive, hopeful, caring character of humans will triumph. The earth has existed for over four billion years. Humans have been only been here for a tiny amount of that time, and much of that has been destructive, with times of extraordinary positive contributions. It is my sincere hope that Community Visioning can make a positive contribution. It is a bottom-up process incorporating a wide variety of participants. The process is most successful when sanctioned by administrative and political approval. With sanctions and support, the results are more likely to be implemented. When the administration is minimally or not involved, the likelihood of implementation decreases. If participants form a political movement and advocate for the collective vision, they can work to get a Vision Plan approved. If political and administrative powers do not approve of the consensus vision, participants can work to have them removed from office. The attitude displayed by "I have been elected by the people and therefore I am their voice and vision" has proved to be false and unproductive, frustrating and depressing to participants, particularly when the vision of the rich and powerful differs from the consensus of a broad range of people.

These proverbs are particularly appropriate:

Where there is no hope, the people shall perish.

> **Plans succeed when councilors are many and fail when councilors are few.**

The planet is undergoing rapid and dramatic changes. Every living organism will have to adapt to changes, as has been done since human species formed communities of hamlets, villages, and cities. With a positive consensus vision, the ability to adopt to a healthier, sustainable short- and long-term future will be easier, thanks to a solid understanding of negative and positive visions, and the realization that places, spaces, and attitudes are undergoing constant change.

Notes on Contents

Very little information contained in this book is currently in the public domain, except as contained in the recorded presentations, videos, or professional reports commissioned by clients. The totality of what is presented here is being revealed to the general public for the first time. I hope that some of the positive and negative visions contained herein are already held by you, and these visions reinforce your thoughts and actions. It is my further hope that more people can be influenced by the resulting knowledge.

Please use the Community Visioning process in your academic and professional career; as a member of a neighborhood organization or professional service organization; or as a member of your town's governing body or planning or zoning commission to ensure that the positive and negative images of place are generated by your citizens and implemented by you.

2

The Progression of Urban Change

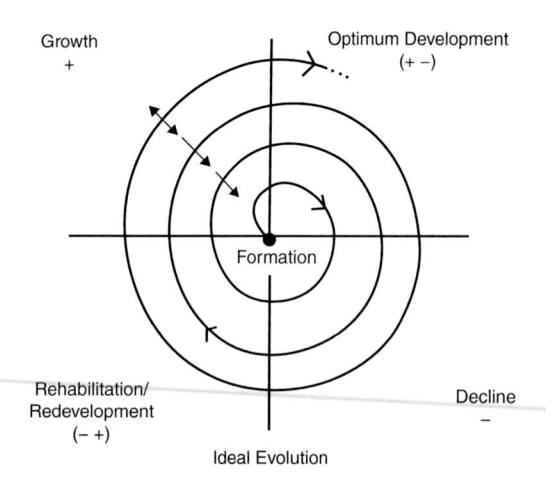

Growth
+

Optimum Development
(+ –)

Formation

Rehabilitation/
Redevelopment
(– +)

Decline
–

Ideal Evolution

The Urban Evolutionary Spiral

Places and spaces are never static. They are in a constant state of change, some more rapid than others. The diagram above was generated to help people understand the continuum of urban change. This diagram allows them to determine where their block, neighborhood, town, or city is on an urban evolutionary timeline; how it evolved; and possibilities for its future.

The Urban Evolutionary Spiral was generated from the study of the history of cities, architecture, and archology. It provides a graphic representation of how places evolve and the current and expected changes in urban morphology as it passes through four basic quadrants, representing the phases or lifecycles of urbanism. This diagram makes this complex evolution of urbanism more understandable and predictable to people. The Urban Evolutionary Spiral has variables of time with some urbanism staying in designated phases for longer or shorter periods of time. The time spent in each phase of the spiral will distort the geometry but nonetheless the evolution continues from phase to phase.

Every space or place, city, town, or natural area, no matter how small or large, is in some phase of this spiral. Everything and everyone has a lifecycle, including your car, computer, and cell phone, which become obsolete over time. We, as humans, also pass through this spiral. Unfortunately, after we deteriorate, we die. Most urbanism continues on. Streets and roads are the most lasting.

The evolution of urbanism is complex. Here, it is represented simply by a graphic spiral, an urban timeline/path passing continuously through four fundamental quadrants or phases. This is an important simple graphic for participants in a Community Visioning session to see and comment upon. Most participants can mark the condition or phase of their community on such a simple spiral.

All urbanism begins with the formation of a hamlet or village which, in some locations, grows into a city. Early formation is located in the center X and Y axis of this spiral. Its growth and evolution are represented by the line radiating along the spiral over varying times. In early urbanization, a hamlet or village optimizes based on the available technology, financing, sociology, climate, war, religion, resources, and so on. As the optimum condition changes, older areas begin to decline. Deterioration of physical form follows, leading, inevitability, in most places, to redevelopment, growth, and then optimization once again. Some urbanizations terminate at the end of the optimization phase, but most continue through the spiral. Some retain the best of the early optimization period and combine it with redevelopment and new growth. Having participants determine where a community is on this timeline is critical to Community Visioning of the place.

Many communities that have commissioned a Community Vision have areas that have reached the lowest level of deterioration on the Urban Evolution Spiral but have hope for future growth and optimization. In some locales, the social and physical deterioration is so negative that it would take massive physical, emotional, financial, and educational capital to heal. Unfortunately, too many of these communities have dysfunctional governments and individual leaders lacking the vision needed to see a positive future. These towns are typically too poor; too disorganized; or too caught up in fear, mistrust, and neglect, making them seemingly incapable of reaching out for a new vision. The most disheartening comment I have ever heard was "We cannot generate a vision plan because it will raise undue expectations." Keeping places dysfunctional and deteriorating is immoral. No place is beyond hope. Where there is a positive vision there is always hope. It might take time and changes to leadership, but the spiral does not lie!

Where communities have negative levels of deterioration and character, determined by the community itself in its negative responses, these locations are prime for redevelopment and for a new vision to be built and lived in. Positive visions must always be filtered through realistic financial feasibility analysis, but that cannot be the only measure. Financial feasibility without positive design vision (potential market) has historically led to places that are, at best, neutral, functional, and not perceived as positive or enjoyable.

Because negatively rated places are so ubiquitous, a premium value is set on places designed and planned appropriately. Why do well planned, designed, and maintained places cost so much more? Because a short supply of positive places has created a pent-up demand for the most desirable places. Excluding natural and rural locations, the most beautiful, well proportioned, human-scaled urban places are pedestrian oriented, with proven urban design features, including walkability and the integration of greenery. Greater value and profit to developers seems assured with the development of the positive places. Savings to the user, taxpayer, and environment are also assured.

Places determined to be negative have a high cost of physical and emotional health among individuals and the community. Maintenance is deferred, and services are minimized. The real costs of emotional and physical health, and lost opportunity in negative places is very high. When places are inclusively renewed to be visually, spatially, and emotionally positive and full of life for existing and new users, they regain greater social, financial, emotional, and visual values. Once the new vision is constructed, the character of the new place and the positive experience it generates will be the catalyst for a sense of positive accomplishment which, in turn, can be used to create more positive places in more cities and towns.

In the same way that positive or negative experiences condition people to the current character of place, a new vision generated through a community vision applied over time, provides the greatest potential for continuous positive change. Implementation and application of consensus vision through local codes can translate the visual image into new streets and quality buildings with great spaces and places.

Vision is the companion of our most powerful emotional senses. It can be used to influence urban evolution.

Obviously, there is no single positive or negative consensus vision that fits all places. There are different solutions to the needs that are appropriate for different locales. Although they may share some common spatial features and architectural elements, each will have regional differences.

In the coming decades, according to the Urban Land Institute, the U.S. is going to develop and redevelop places to accommodate 60 million additional residents. At the same time, a new generation will become the dominant cohort, and their vision for the future will begin to gnaw at the sprawl and city deterioration approved by previous generations. Of all the possible locations for the application of the vision process, the redevelopment and rehabilitation of existing urban areas are the most critical. Nonetheless, sprawl will continue, despite the high costs in terms of ecological, environmental, natural resources, and human well-being. Many of the newer generations will succumb to living in sprawl away from cities and higher density if and when their incomes and lack of environmental consciousness permit.

An article published on June 5, 2017, by NBC News, titled, *"Who's Powering the Housing Market? Surprise! It's Millennials,"* says that millennials are fueling the housing market and purchasing four-bedroom homes that they term "forever homes." They are also buying larger SUVs. But, the article asks, do they realize the long-term costs?

Community Visioning provides the opportunity to express preferences for a wide range of places and spaces, enhancing existing places and specifically **creating markets for new places**. The construction of places people want will, in turn, generate even greater investments, improved quality of life, and a greater joy of living with positive emotional responses. The larger the number of participants in Community Visioning sessions, the greater the probability for more compelling and visually positive results. As more towns, cities, and rural areas use a public participation visioning process, the probability for the creation of a healthy, sustainable future will increase, with buildings, spaces and spaces which people will cherish and maintain in the long term, thereby ensuring a more positive progression of change.

People want places and spaces better than standard construction generated from current zoning and market studies, which typically indicate what certain demographic groups have recently purchased from a limited range of possibilities. The logic follows that future purchases by a similar demographic cohort will be similar or slightly improved. Community Vision helps determine what people really want in their living, working, and playing environments, if such things were made available at a price they could afford and in a location that made sense. Participants factor these into their preference responses. These **preferences impact urban evolution over time**. Realistically, what if what people want cannot be built based on current zoning? What if negative or, at best, neutral place responses continue? Then zoning needs to be changed when a community is locked in the timeline at the end of the optimization phase.

On the other hand, what if zoning implemented the consensus visions, allowing developers and bankers to finance and build the vision? What is positive, acceptable, and most appropriate, or negative and unacceptable for the specific locations and for the largest number of people? Once all the image values; the results of the Demographic, Market, and Policy Questionnaire; and overlays maps are collected and carefully analyzed, an illustrated vision plan and recommended zoning code reflecting the collective positive visual value and acceptability of specific recommendations can be realized.

The positive images can be used to illustrate a graphic and image form-based zoning code. Once completed, the visual code must be promoted and adhered to. But, first and foremost, implementing a short-term project generated from the vision process is critical. Participants must be assured that their vision has value and that this short-term implementation is the first step toward implementing the longer-term vision. It is sometimes referred to as "tactical" urbanism. The visioning process is the only planning tool in which the desired form and "feeling" of a community can be generated by public participation, before two

and three dimensional plans are generated. These plans effect value, future marketability, safety, and a feeling of well-being. It has also revealed that attendees generated wonderful, unpredictable solutions that enhanced the vision and advanced change.

It is critically important to accurately prepare for and interpret the response values given to all the images. The notion that the town planner, urban designer, engineer, traffic consultant, and architect know best is inaccurate. What the professionals need to respond to is the consensus vision of the people as their foundation; then they must add their special talents and skills to complete the project form and character.

Community Visioning (C Vis) participants are more sophisticated, realistic, and forward-thinking than most professionals understand. C Vis releases the ingenuity of the public; it encourages innovation and taps alternative energies. When positive preferences are built and lived in, they positively impact physical and emotional quality of life, resulting in joy and contentment! Positive places generate a sense of well- being, safety, wealth and happiness, and can impact the progression of change. The desire for a better future is a basic human desire.

Realized the Community Visions

Images of buildings, places, spaces, and the new light rail that were built after the visioning sessions in downtown Milwaukee, When many people who have been through the Community Visioning experience their preferences as reality, confidence grows in their preferences, and even more positive places and spaces are built!

Images of buildings, places, and spaces that were built after the visioning sessions for Robbinsville, Town Center.

Research, Development, and Results

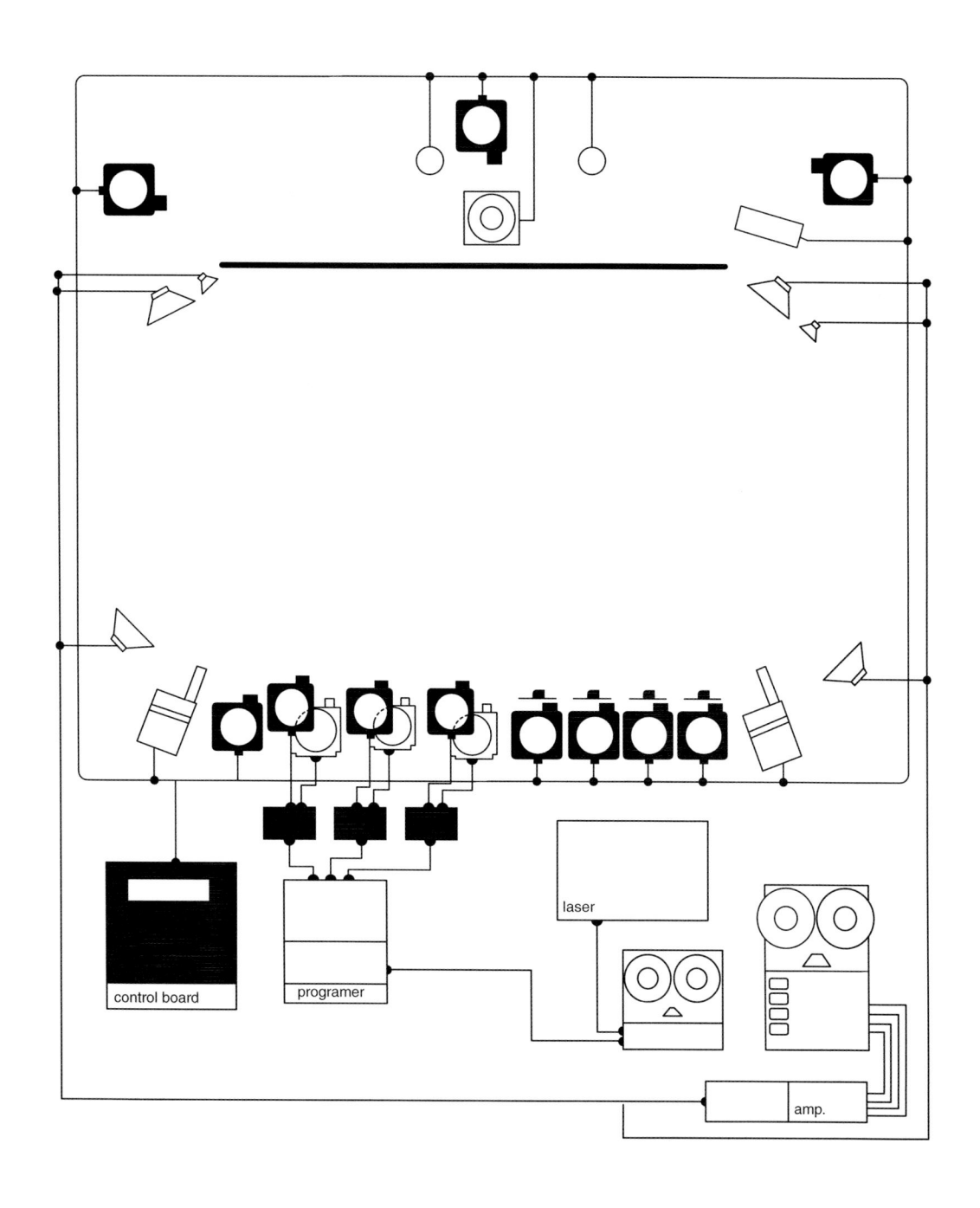

I bought my first used Nikon in 1965 with the belief, borrowed from Fred R. Barnard, that *"One picture is worth a thousand words."* As a newly minted architect, I primarily photographed places and spaces. I began to build a large collection of 35 mm colored slides which could be projected, measured, and used as inspiration for designing. I was always most interested in places and spaces, less so in individual buildings. My interest in the process started early in 1966 when I was working in Los Angeles for Victor Gruen Associates and was influenced by the work of Walt Disney using a projection technique call Circle Vision –360. This technique used nine 35 mm projectors that surrounded the viewer and an odd number of screens with projectors at their intersections. For the first time, a viewer could be in a place or moving through it, then turn around and experience the "full" impact. It was used in Expo 67 in Montreal in the U.S. pavilion. I also experienced it in Moscow at a military exposition. Here, the technique used 11 screens. What an extraordinary planning and design tool that could be used to test people's reactions to places and spaces. I wondered if it could be reduced to seven screens and use slides and super 8 film.

But first, images of places and spaces needed to be photographed. Images on seven screens, shot in a circle on a tripod with a special perspective correction lens, was possible within my budget and technical capability.

After receiving my Master of Architecture in Urban Design from the Graduate School of Design (GSD) at Harvard, I had the opportunity to work on a new town of Louvain la Neuve and travel in Europe and Asia, where I photographically captured hundreds of the most important and historic public spaces and places in 360 degrees, with a goal to use these in teaching urban design and place making. That opportunity came after photographing Expo 70 in Japan when I was asked to return to Harvard to teach in the Urban Design program.

All of my early urban imaging testing was completed at Harvard's GSD and Imageworks School of Media Arts. The years between 1967 and 1975 involved testing multiple screen formats with multiple slide projectors. The first major production with seven screens was the walk-through Expo 70 Japan. Seven slide projections and three 8 mm projectors were accompanied by a questionnaire which provided profiles of the participating viewers a response forms necessary to register their positive or negative reactions and a map for their sequential responses. The primary research questions were "What was your emotional response to these projected images in 360 degree?", "Could they orient themselves along the sequence through the Expo?", and "Did it enhance their understanding of urban form and spatial sequencing?"

The responses to the format and images was very positive, providing initial answers to the research questions. Yes, they could orient themselves through the sequence. The places and spaces projected impressed the participants, and further, the characteristics of the places and spaces presented enhanced their understanding of urban form and design. But would other formats be as effective?

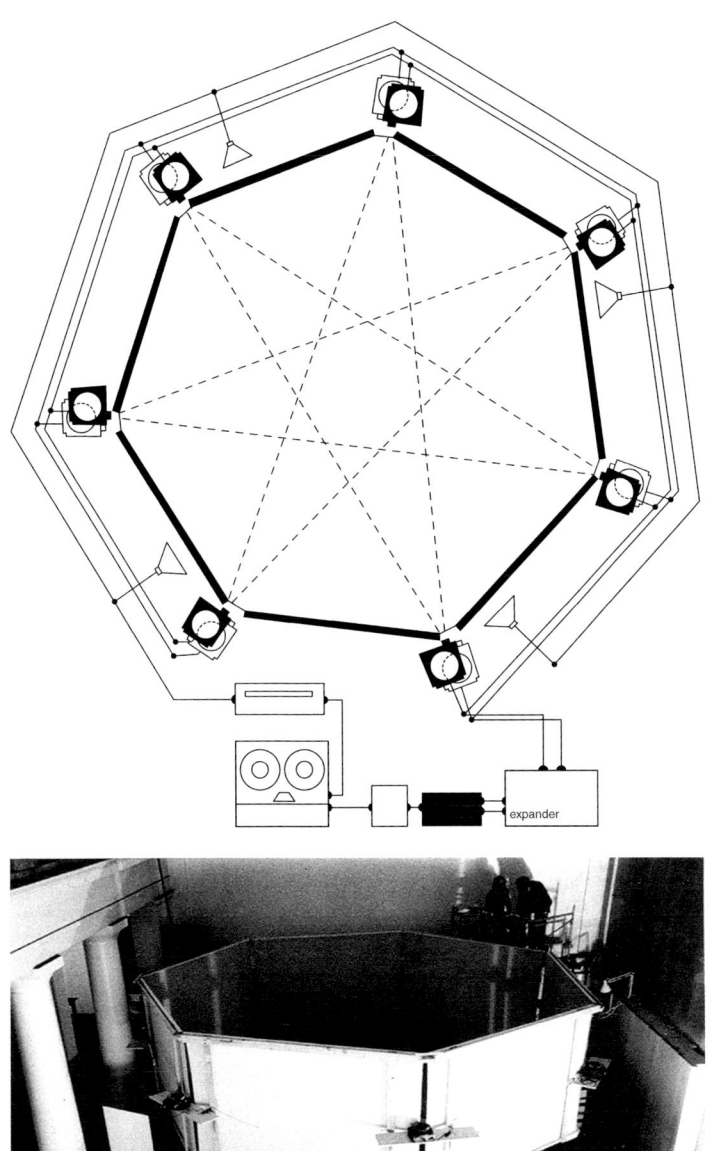

360 Degree Image Capture

Above, the plan of the visual Simulation Machine with seven screens. On the right, the construction of the first 360 degree Urban Design Simulation Machine using ten projectors. It was built in the courtyard of the GSD Robinson Hall at Harvard in 1971. It employed seven slide projectors and three super 8 projectors. Participants sat in the center and were surrounded by continuous and fractured images. The film walked the viewers through the space, and when it paused, the full 360 image of the place appeared. Participants tracked the movement (walk-through on maps) and provided valuable feedback on its effectiveness. This was the beginning of my vision quest. It was completed with Roger and Lena Transik with a grant from the Harvard's Milton Fund.

While I was teaching Urban Design at the GSD, I was invited to become the Director of Multi-Media at Imageworks School of Photography and Media Arts. Here, in addition to teaching, I had unlimited freedom with great facilities and equipment to complete a series of research projects, and continue the search for multiple projection and screen format methods to use in exposing and testing people's responses to a range of places and spaces. I wanted to test their emotional reactions and search for the format that best approximates how the mind visualizes and remembers. The research simplified the screen format but increased the number and types of projectors in order to capture multiple images that the mind normally remembers. This refers to an idea proposed in the late 1700s by Etienne Candillac: ***"Sensations are to be found through the analysis of compound ideas and images. Everything in the end, was sensory."***

To stimulate visual memory by experiencing places and spaces in a new format with multiple

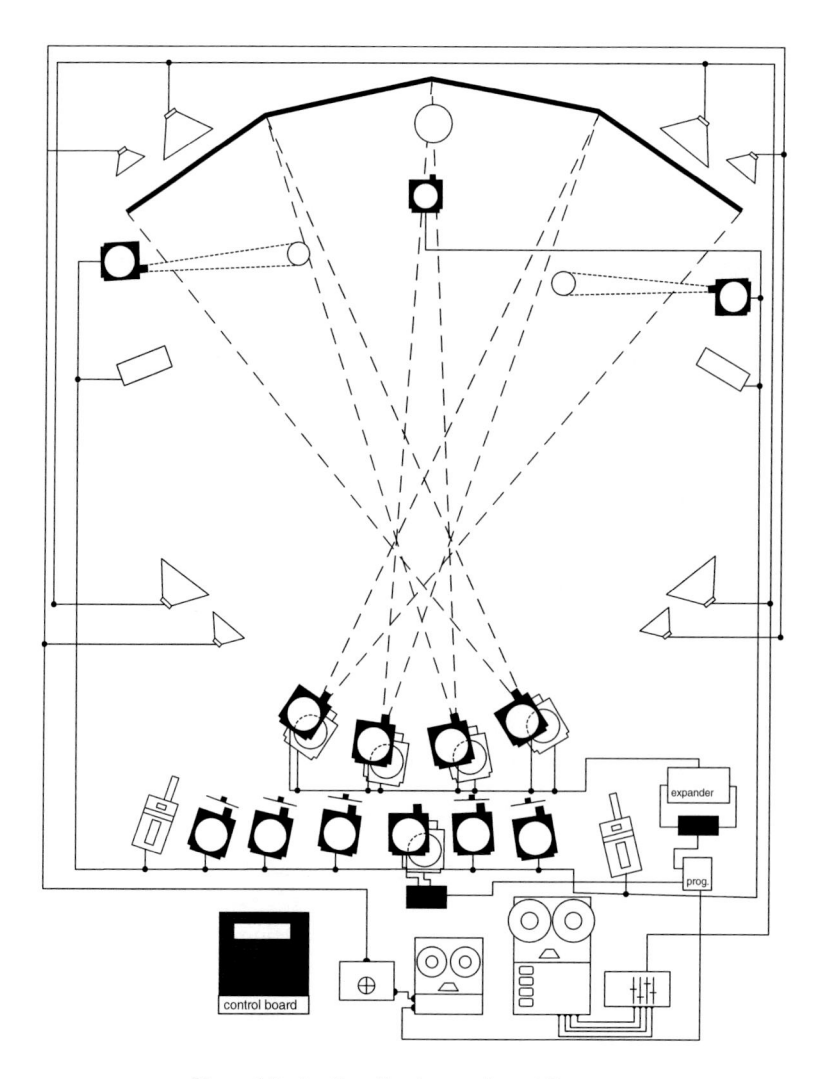

Plan of Projection Equipment and Screens

Semicircular Screen Format

One of the multiple place projection research projects at Imageworks School of Media Arts, Cambridge, Massachusetts, 1972. On the previous page, the screen and seventeen projector plan for Simulation Machine 2. Above the four screens with a continuous pan of a skyline of Boston. The presentation format was used for productions called "Night Journey" and "Memory of an American City Fair," which tested a partial enclosure (front curve of your brain when imagining) to elicit visual responses. We used a similar format for the staging of the ballet "Where the Wild Things Are" by the Boston Ballet to great success.

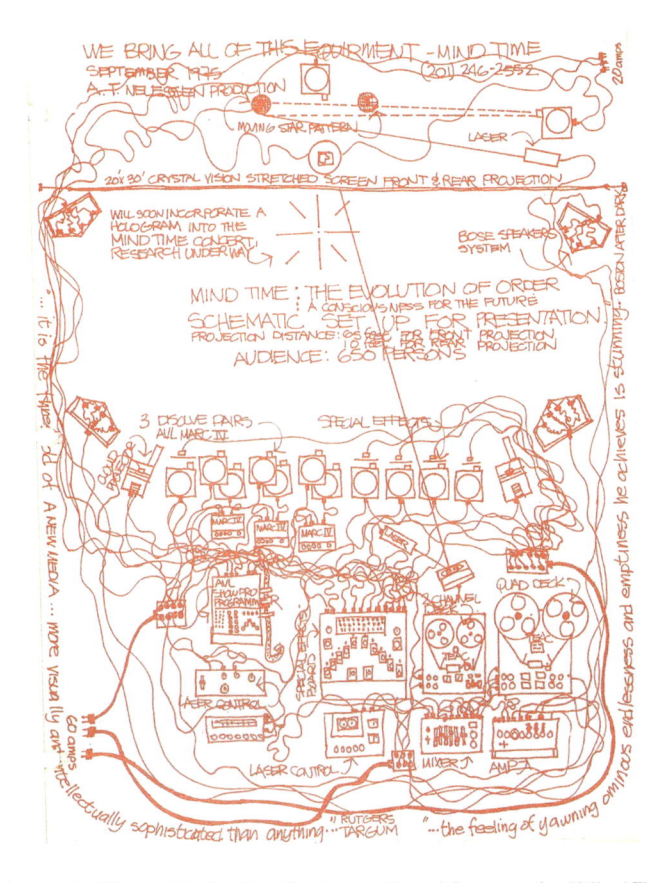

Schematic Plan of Projection Equipment and Screens for "Mind Time"

Source: Bill Ravanesi.

Tony Nelessen in front of a Double Sided Stretch Screen

In 1973, the culmination of these visioning research projects generated a production called "Mind Time: The Evolution of Time Through Space." It used a single screen with front and back projection; 15 projectors; and multiple light effects, including lasers and quadraphonic moving sound. It explored the mental capacity of participants to not only experience a range of places and spaces but to project places and spaces through a time continuum. Using a large, two-sided stretch screen and 30 optical devices, including moving star projectors, linked to audio tape-driven computers, the audience was enveloped in the massive images and could experience time travel and places only generated by the subconscious. The production tested whether it could "take" people mentally to and through uncommon spaces and places, and back again.

images could enhance their memory visions and influence what gets built. Fundamentally, the purpose was to implant great positive places into the memories of those participating. To that end, the experiments at Imageworks played a critical step in the research and development. Five urban planning visual research experiments were completed at the GSD and Imageworks using various presentation formats.

Refining the Community Visioning Process took many years of work, beginning with photographic and psychological fundamentals , including a labyrinth of techniques and technologies, testing, and

> ## "takes their mind to another otherworldly place and time"
>
> *Boston Phoenix*

field trials. As with most things in life, generating results was a slow process, revealed through observations, deliberation, reading, and employing every evolving advance in projection and computer technology. Through it all, there was always a single driving motivation to identify positive images of place that would "stir their souls" and determine ways of implementing **the best features of the desired positive place**. Implementation would generate more positive, healthy, and sustainable towns and cities for everyone participating in the Visual Preference Survey (VPS) process, which is now one of the major techniques used in Community Visioning for Place Making.

The conclusion of all these early multi-media experiments was that participants became emotionally involved. By combining images, movement, and sound while expanding their periphery vision onto larger screens or multiple screens of various sizes, created the greatest experience impact. It was remembered because it was spatial and multisensory. Since that time, using what I learned, I was commissioned to prepare projection presentations for live theatre productions, including the Boston Ballet and Crossroads Theatre, a black theatre company with presentations in London, New York, Los Angeles, and the Caribbean. Projections I designed were used in nine live stage productions; the most awarded was "Colored Museum" by George Wolf, which won a Hollywood Drama Logue Award for Projection.

The Visual Teaching Alliance has reinforced my research, testing, and teaching. Their findings determined that *"Of all the information transferred to the brain 90% is visual,"* that *"Visuals are processed 60,000 times faster than text or words,"* that *"40% of nerve fibers are linked to the retina,"* and that *"visual stimuli and emotional responses are linked."* The visual preference survey technique was the key planning and design instrument in facilitating potential changes for the better in places and spaces in the urban future.

In 1973, I accepted an assistant professorship at Rutgers, the State University of New Jersey, in the Department of Urban Planning and Policy Development. I wanted to continue my research and production capacity by providing a more practical, inexpensive, and easily applied technique of presenting, testing, and implementing visual and emotional responses to images of places. Everything had to be simplified so that it could easily be moved and set up. The projected images used a single screen and one slide projector with no computers or soundtrack. A simple positive (+) and negative (–) response form was used. This was the simplest response format and the easiest to understand. The early VPS focused primarily on the redevelopment of existing small towns or potential new communities in the emerging suburban landscapes. The first beta test VPS was conducted in 1975 during graduate urban planning and design studios at Rutgers. The first professional VPS was conducted in 1976 for the planning and design of the Central Business District of Metuchen, New Jersey, used to involve the residents, merchants, and businesspeople in downtown Metuchen early in the planning and design process. Participants were invited to evaluate images of existing conditions in the downtown as well as images from other locations that emulated the potential building form, height, scale, and proportions, along with streetscapes and building walls that might be appropriate for this small town. Many of the images were new infill from historic downtown Philadelphia. We wanted to determine whether participants considered these appropriate scale and character for their downtown now and in the future.

The first response sheets used a simple (+) for "I like it and find it appropriate" and (–) for "I don't like it and find it inappropriate." The +'s and –'s were tabulated. It was startling to the members of the studio and town that the images of their existing downtown received the most negative (–) responses. The positive image portrayed the scale and character of the buildings, streets and spaces the citizens of Metuchen wanted, leading to 40 years of positive redevelopment, which continues to this day.

During the early beta years at Rutgers, using the simplified format, five sample groups with over 600 participants provided their visual responses to a broad range of spaces and places.

Participants included:

- Undergraduate students of Urban Studies at Rutgers University
- Graduate students in the Urban Design Studio
- Students in the course Introduction to Design and Site Planning
- Participants in the 1982 Planning Conference of the New Jersey Chapter of the American Planning Association
- Members of the Planning and Zoning Board, Municipal Council, and Environmental Commission for Washington Township, Mercer County, NJ
- Citizens groups concerned with the revitalization of Main Streets
- Participants in several speaking engagements

For these Community Visioning Sessions, the numerical scale of +10 to –10 was introduced. Images were valued on the 21-point scale from +10 to –10, with 0 as the neutral score. Only the mean or average responses from all participants were used in the early VPS sessions.

For each image, the question asked was:

How appropriate or inappropriate is the image you are seeing now and in the future for you and your location?

Conclusions from Early Community Vision Sessions

1. There was consensus on images there were positive and appropriate and those that were negative and needed to change.

2. There was a remarkable coherence of positive and negative responses. When an image was perceived as negative or positive, 94% of participants gave that image a plus or negative value, within a tight range. The largest difference occurred for images that received a neutral value response where there was a wider range of responses. When an image received a very positive or negative response value, the responses by most participants were similar. For example, for one positive image in four difference surveys, the following average values were typical: +6.4, +7.0, +6.9, and +6, representing very tight range. A similar grouping of the negative aver-

ages to one specific image was also typical: –5.5, –6.8, –4.6, and –3.6. These response values to these images in multiple surveys leads to an understanding of specific visual and spatial characteristics that make the place or space perceived as positive (acceptable) or negative (unacceptable) to most people. What is more important is if these images are generic land uses like strip commercial development or a beautiful, tree lined mixed-use street. Creating new places, preserving existing places or redesigning places value rated as negative using the positive characteristics provides exciting design opportunities. Once implemented, they give people a positive sense of pride and well-being as they feel responsible for the positive change.

Images of What People Found Acceptable and Unacceptable

The following images, selected from that initial sample, contain the fundamentals that can be referenced for future planning and design decisions. Many of the negative images represent the development trends and zoning at that time, and were in the deteriorating phase of the Urban Evolutionary Spiral. A negative value response by enough people reinforces the need for change, but the positive places they want might not be developed for some time, if at all, since their development depends on market and financial conditions. Nonetheless, the visions will be filed in the people's memories. As a rule, the most positive images that they wanted were ahead of

their time. Because of political and zoning ineptitude, many visions were not realized. However, in towns where the political structure was astute, and zoning was amended, many came into being because of the belief in the group's vision.

The following images from Community Visioning sessions using the VPS **contain fundamentals that can be referenced for future planning and design decisions**. At the first Congress for the New Urbanism, held in Alexandra, Virginia, in 1989, the first presentation of the initial beta tests of the VPS was made with value rated images of places and spaces that people wanted and despised. Most of the images reinforced the principles that were to emerge from the New Urbanism, which is now a major planning and design movement. Over time, these images have proven, through actual construction, that the VPS process identified visions that are positive, marketable, and loved.

Most Positive Images from the Initial Visual Preference Surveys

The following images from the original set best represent fundamental preferences. These land uses, places,

A view along the sidewalks in Back Bay, Boston.   A view of a café under an arcade in Paris.

Positive Urban Places and Spaces

and spaces, both positive and negative, have influenced planning and design, development, and redevelopment as well as Master Plans and Zoning codes

Note that the images only include the mean response values from all participants.

The standard deviation was added later with the realization that there could be a large range in responses from individuals to some images. The standard deviation assisted the understanding of the range of acceptance and a better understanding of the physical characteristics that the image contained.

Comment: These two images in the urban category received the highest response values. They are intensely urban. The Back Bay of Boston has a density estimated at 80+ dwelling units per acre. The buildings are four to six stories high with a classic streetscape, including wide brick sidewalks, street trees, pedestrian-scaled lighting, parallel parking, enclosed semi-private front yards with the first floor elevated above grade with stairs and stoops, bay windows, brick and stone, and façades of different architectural treatments within the same Design Vocabulary.

On the right, the tall arcade is a semi-enclosed, partially protected café but still has a narrow pedestrian walkway. It is full of people, tables, and movable chairs, enhanced by plants, umbrellas, etc. These are places people want to walk and experience. Arcades are best when filled with activity while still allowing pedestrians to pass. This one is approximately 22 feet wide. The height to width proportions are almost perfect.

Design response: Incorporating the many urban design characteristics inherent in these two images into any urban area will create positive urban places, ideal for living and spending time. A few important design characteristics are the articulation of the façades, the consistent use of materials and colors, the proportions of the pedestrian realm, and the treatment of the semipublic yard.

Emotional response: Beautiful, dignified, safe. A place people want to experience and live

Response Value +5

Farm

View across fields to a cluster of farm buildings surrounded by productive fields.

Comment: This image portrays active farms with their out-buildings in a rural-forested setting. The farms are assimilated into the slightly rolling landscape with large trees. This is not an agribusiness farm with vast open fields but rather a small family farm with its collection of primary and secondary buildings. This type of small farm, particularly for organic produce, is slowly returning. In this form, it is very appropriate to all participants.

Design response: We must preserve open "rural" character and the agricultural functions of the land through zoning where good soils and agricultural food production exists or could exist, now an in the future. Land for food production

will become cost-effective and valued rather than another sprawled subdivision. Preserve long vistas (view sheds) in which rural character is dominant through Master Plans and zoning. This image could represent a farm, rural cluster, or agricultural hamlet—an opportunity for some limited development surrounding the cluster of buildings is a positive opportunity. Transfer of Development Rights (TDR) should also be considered for the preservation of rural character and viability.

Emotional response: "Provides a sense of peace and quiet," "feels right," "integrated with nature," "healthy," and "reinforces our nature-based past" were some of the comments from participants. The strength of this image is the thousands of acres that have been preserved in New Jersey using publicly voted Open Space Preservation Bonds. An estimated 230,000 acres have been preserved as farmland in New Jersey through this process or TDR where this photograph was taken.

Response Value +5

Rural Agricultural Estate

View of a single-family house in an agricultural landscape. One housing group on 10 to 20 acres of land.

Comment: This image portrays a new, simple, gabled two-story house, framed with existing landscaping, surrounded by agricultural land, and enclosed with a split rail fence. This form of development is desired by all participants in a rural areas. Tax breaks are allowed if the property in New Jersey is over six acres and generates a small revenue to the owner. Many argue that six acres is not enough property and that real food should be produced on the land, not just Christmas trees or hay.

Design response: Amend zoning to only allow very large lots in rural/agricultural areas, but not on the most productive Class I soils, which should be preserved in perpetuity. On all other land, require a minimum lot size of 10 to 20 acres. Approval must be contingent on producing an agriculturally based product, e.g. food, animals, etc., for sale or barter.

The footprint of the building must have a very large setback to farm the front and side yards. Define the edge of the lot with a rural-type fence. Keep rural roads narrow. This Rural Agricultural Estate is ideally located beyond walking distance of a rural hamlet or village.

Emotional response: Openness, sense of prosperity, safe, integrated with nature.

Response Value +4.8

Attached Buildings on a Historic Main Street

Historic colonial Main Streets resonate positively with many people. They have a human scale and positive architecture, and building wall character with the use of materials, building modulations and differences in height.

Comment: Classic small downtown in a historic village. This features a row of attached mixed-use buildings, many with retail on the bottom level and housing or offices above. Building front on a streetscape with wide, walkable textured sidewalks; street trees; street furniture; and parallel parking. There are a variety of attached building types, widths, and heights, with various facades and roof treatments. All share common materials and color palettes. The more prominent building is expressed by its size, enlarged window, and details. This form of development is desirable by all participants. People like to walk here.

Design response: Because it has been well maintained and supported by the community over the years, it is a viable, well-liked downtown form. Unfortunately, many small town Main Streets have been decimated by zoning for suburban arterial strip commercial on their edges, big boxes with bigger parking lots and now internet shopping. It is very important to maintain and retain existing functional town centers. Many are transforming into destinations for restaurants, services, and specialty shops. The scale and details (not necessarily mimicking the colonial architecture) can be used as inspiration when retrofitting suburban strip commercial areas for a walkable mixed infill. Use a similar massing; simple and classical architectural forms and proportions; and two- and three-story buildings, with a continuous but undulating building-wall containing a variety of attached structures that share similar scale, materials, and colors as well as wide sidewalks. Provide well-designed street landscaping with textured sidewalks, street furniture, and trees. These places have stood the test of time.

Emotional response: Beautiful, has dignity, provides a sense of community, safe, walkable, historically nostalgic.

Response Value +4

Row Houses on a Very Narrow Street
View down Elfreth's Alley in Philadelphia. Buildings and street circa 1750.

Comment: These three-story colonial attached row houses on this very narrow street are individually articulated and range in width from 14 to 18 feet, with little or no landscaping but a very well-designed shared streetscape. The street accommodates only one car in one direction. Each house is different but shares a common Design Vocabulary of brick, vertical windows with shutters, and entrances raised off the street. The space in the center is more of a public space and pedestrian sidewalk. This form of walkable, narrow street development is desirable by all participants. It was never designed for cars, just narrow carts or people on horseback or walking. Cars and the need for parking would not appear for 150 years destroying the opportunity for more narrow streets. Today, private cars are excluded, except for taxis and service vehicles. Residents with cars park in a nearby parking structure, an excellent adaptions and lesson for today's planners and designers

Design response: Zoning for three- and one-half-story townhouses with classic fenestration, facade variation, and changes in color that modulate the street view should be allowed and encouraged. Allow narrow distance between facades, approximately 25 feet. Require intensive streetscapes, including brick or paving blocks textured from building to building. Keep streetscape pedestrian areas scaled with low decorative street lights, bollards, and wheel paving stones that distinguish the vehicular path from the pedestrian flow. Pedestrians feel comfortable on this street. Provide remote parking within an optimum five-minute walk. Allow cars access for deliveries, drop-off, and pickup. Most people don't know that this form and character violates current street standards while it has functioned well for the past 200 years. Although it has great appeal, it would be nearly impossible to build this again based on existing zoning which needs to be changed to accommodate this positive rated place.

Emotional response: Beautiful, has dignity, provides a sense of community, safe, unique. Positive pedestrian experience. Some feel it lacks privacy.

Most Negative Images

The most negative images were of deteriorated urban areas and suburban arterial sprawl. Understanding what is negative, unacceptable, and most depressing to people begins a discussion of the impact these characteristics have on people and what can be done to change negative values to positive. What are the characteristics?

Deteriorated and Neglected Urban Areas

On the left, an urban street in Newark, New Jersey. On the right, a boarded-up, mixed-use building. Litter and lack of maintenance are always perceived as negative. Plywood over windows and doors is equivalent to <u>urban cancer.</u>

What are the policies that must be considered when so many negative places and spaces are continuing to be built? Is it disinvestment, lack of maintenance, and improper zoning, or are these negative rated places well into the phase of deterioration, waiting for redevelopment? What are the positive visions and opportunities? What revisions or standards of planning and policy/zoning must be made?

Comment: Urban neglect, disinvestment, and abandonment generate the most negative responses. In the urban evolutionary spiral, they are in the deterioration phase, near the bottom. These places **generate fear and depression**. Whenever streets and sidewalks are not cleaned, litter prevails, buildings are not maintained, and metal security curtains are present with no perceived human activity, places are unacceptable. Boarded-up buildings in urban areas always elicit a negative response. These conditions are unacceptable to everyone who took the survey. They are prime targets for redevelopment and reinvestment if planned and designed well.

Design response: Despite their urban conditions, places must be cleaned and litter-free. Street maintenance is both a municipal and a private obligation. The plywood will protect the interior of the building from destruction but sends the signal that these areas are in serious trouble economically, socially, and psychologically. Is it better to leave the building in this state or demolish it?

Emotional response: Depression, fear, anger, hopelessness.

Strip commercial developments when seen from the car or from a parking lot always elicit very negative response values of –7 or lower.

Above is an early example of a 1940s-type strip commercial development that has evolved over time into a very negative place. It has a shallow asphalt parking area attached to the street and one-story single front buildings, poorly maintained, with many billboards, overhead wiring, and high-way-scaled signs.

Above is 1950s-type strip commercial development in a haphazard pattern of multiple frontage with multiple signs and overhead wiring. Even with a green center planting strip between lanes and a small strip along the frontage, it still generates a very negative response.

Comment: Older and more recent exurban commercial sprawl along arterials are always value rated as negative. The response values are typically lower when in rural settings. The image on the left has a lower negative value than the strip commercial development in the image on the right, which has more lawn, planting, etc. Despite the "landscaping," both are extremely negative. The unfortunate truth is that this is often the only visual amenity required by zoning. Every building here is an auto and surface parking-dependent commercial establishments built at the same time as residential sprawl.

Design response: No one really wants to shop or spend time here. Because of multiple ownerships, little can be done except for some additional landscaping and/or building and sign modification as the uses change. As market and shopping patterns change, as the internet becomes more popular, gas prices increase significantly, and/or incomes do not increase to meet inflation, many commercial buildings will go vacant. There is also a possibility for mixed-use redevelopment, provided that there is a market demand with the necessary vision and a well-thought out urban design plan and zoning code to allow redevelopment to occur. Perhaps many of these places will simply continue to deteriorate and be reclaimed by nature.

Emotional response: Depression, confusion, and seeming hopelessness.

Conclusions and Summary

These ten images, extracted from a sample of 160 used in the first VPSs in the 1980s, are still relevant today. The highest- and lowest-rated images were of urban areas. The most negative images were of deteriorated, littered urban streets; landfills; boarded-up urban housing; refineries; mono-form suburban subdivisions; and old and new strip commercial development along arterials. Much of the suburban building and street forms built since 1945, including all strip commercial developments in various stages of decay, with empty parking lots, dysfunctional signing along highways, and local arterials, are value rated negative. Deteriorated buildings and streets in urban areas were perceived as very negative, ugly, inhumane, inefficient, and psychologically harmful. **Until people put a declared negative value on places, they will never be curtailed**.

The most positive images were of healthy urban settings; cafés; streets of Back Bay, Boston, and classic Main Streets; narrow streets with townhouses where people like to walk, complemented by farms; and large single-family homes on very large lots, along rural roads.

These images were the earliest numerically quantified Visual Preferences based on participants' response values to images of the places and spaces being evaluated. The revelation of these response values was extraordinary at the time and impacted all my urban design thinking and teaching for rural areas, small towns, and suburban development. These positive values had a profound influence in multiple places and spaces we were designing that were inevitably implemented. The design recommendations were instrumental in setting forth a positive approach to the preservation of farmlands, limiting the growth in suburbia to hamlets, villages, and town centers, and the need to re-landscape, rehabilitate, and infill urban areas. This set of images catalyzed a land use spatial distribution model for future growth and redevelopment.

Policy Recommendations from Initial Visioning Session

1. Preservation of the open "rural" character of the land where farms and their adjoining forest, lakes, streams, and wetlands exist.

Farmland preservation programs have been successful in many states. Agricultural farmlands and grasslands reduce and delay rain runoff and downstream flooding. Farmed land for local, healthy food production is becoming more important as population increases, and there is a demand for more organic healthy products. Every day, many young people are taking up this vocation. Keeping the rural agricultural land was critical not only for its ecological importance and emotional benefits but also as a way to restrict more suburban small lot residential land uses and their corresponding auto-oriented strip commercial and office/services development.

- In rural areas, only allow farming or very large lot zoning, with a minimum of 10 to 15 acres that must also be used for gardening and food production.
- Allow and build agricultural hamlets of 10 to 20 units on small, 1/8 to 1/4 acre lots with a small community center and/or common, preserving a minimum of 60% of the parcel dedicated to gardening and food production.
- Preserve all-natural areas, streams, creeks, ponds, forests, and wetlands within the rural areas.

2. Redevelopment of deteriorating city and town centers as first priority.

   - Infill existing vacant and underutilized lots, surface parking lots, and remove and infill deteriorating buildings.
   - Rebuild deteriorated neighborhoods and their community centers back to real neighborhoods. Focus design on beautiful streets and spaces with attractive, pleasing, and well-designed buildings and street-walls.

3. Restrict additional strip commercial development and redevelop or demolish when these are deteriorated or vacant.

   - Redevelop or demolish all the land uses along thoroughfares that receive negative response values. Limit the time for which they can be vacant and/or unmaintained.
   - If suburban commercial development is allowed, it should become part of a regional or community mixed- and multiple-use town center with a balance of housing, workplaces, recreation social services, and education.

4. Design for mixed-use buildings with higher urban residential densities.

   - Most favored are dense attached townhouses, apartment buildings at various heights, with a range of mixed-use buildings that create interesting street walls and urban spaces within walking distances.

5. Design nature into the urban setting

   - Landscaping/nature is critical to the look and feel of an urban area; include street trees, semipublic spaces, public greens, plazas, water features, green roofs and walls, and dynamic pedestrian realms like sidewalks and other walkways devoted to pedestrians.

6. Develop a growth and redevelopment pattern that reflects all the recommended actions.

It has been reassuring as the years have passed to have so many people and organizations, armed with these positive and negative images, producing codes, transects, new neighborhoods, and regional centers that embrace these policies and principles. They have succeeded because they have intuitively or cognitively tapped into this positive vision and the emotional desire of people to be happy and safe, surrounded by beauty, delight and comfort.

Implementing just these six policy recommendations from the initial VPSs could transform many rural and urban areas. There are many negative strip commercial

and sprawled
auto-dependent
subdivisions and too
many deteriorating
urban places that
need transformation
to be sustainable
and inclusionary.

Any place once
it has a negative
community
consensus value
rating, the possibility
of transforming to
positive is
manifest.

Measuring Visual Responses for Place Making

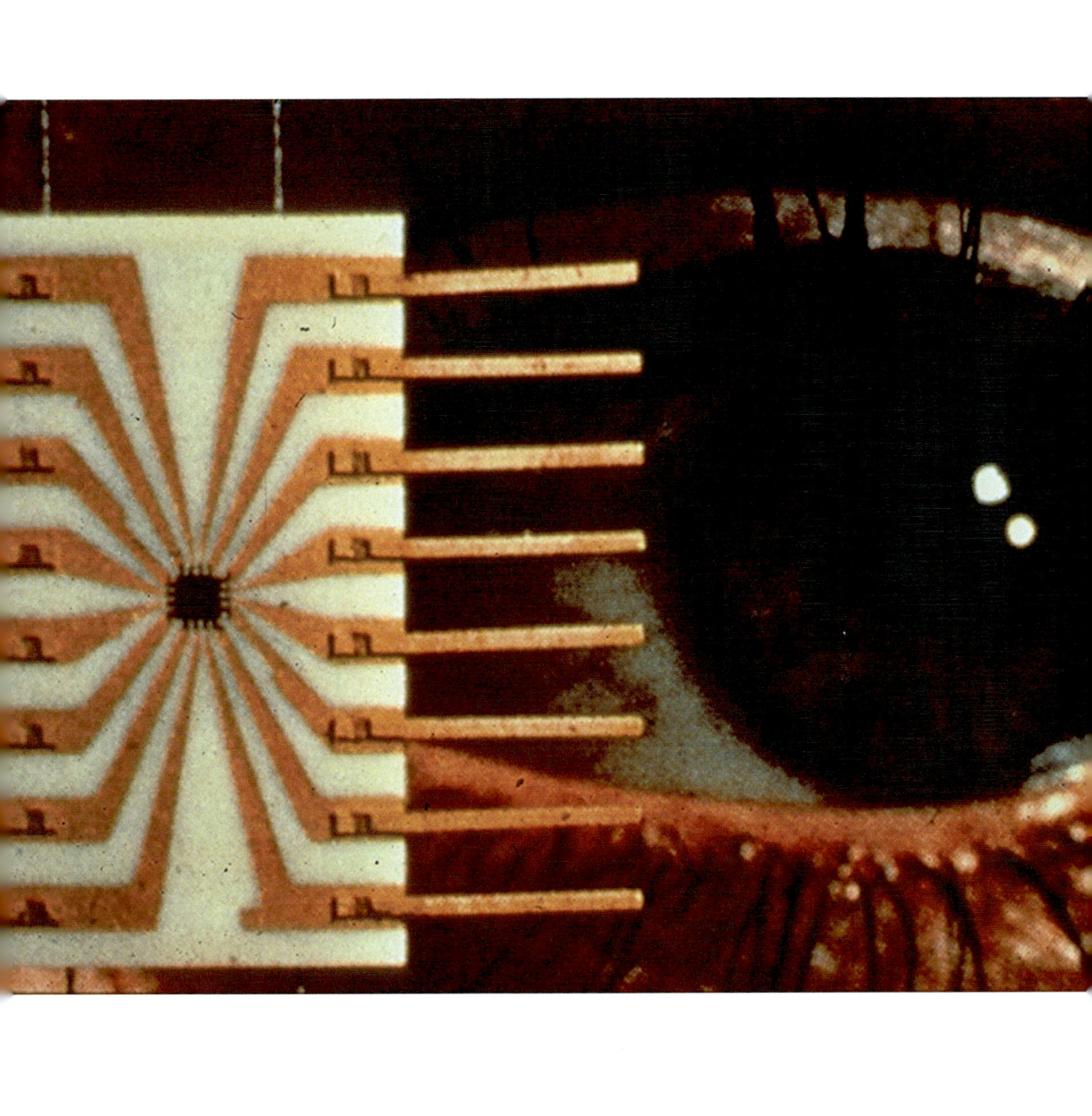

Understanding What Influences Your Responses to Places and Spaces

This chapter presents the background thinking and method used in the Visual Preference Survey (VPS) portion of Community Visioning sessions.

Since my first exposure to it in the early 1960s, I have had a specific fascination with psychology. Early texts like *Reading for an Introduction to Psychology* by Richard King (1961), *Reading in Attitude Theory and Measurement* by Martin Fishban (1967), and *Human Behavior and Environment* edited by Irwin Altman and Joachim F. Wohlwill (1976) were seminal in my early research, as were so many other books and papers. As an urban planner and designer, understanding motivations, how people think, and decisions they make regarding spaces and place making is critical to potential implementation and building in years to come.

In a *Clinical Psychology Review* of February 2013, in an article by David G. Pearson et al. entitled "Assessing Mental Imagery in Clinical Psychology", the authors write, "mental imagery is an under explored field in clinical psychology."

Human beings are equipped with an extraordinary brain, akin to a cyber/biological supercomputer that absorbs external stimuli, attitudes and beliefs from in-vitro to the very moment you are reading this sentence. At the same time, it is regulating emotions and actions, and running bodily functions. The mind is constantly radiating and receiving cyber energy responses and absorbing behavior, attitudes, learned responses, data, images, experiences, and expectations, all of which are stored in the memory. Memory combines life experiences with previous ancestral programming. All experiences of the past, present, and programmed future reside in memory, which has the capacity to retain and retrieve the impressions we receive on a daily basis; this becomes complicated when these impressions are combined with previous ancestral experiences and programming. The past, present, and programmed future interact in photographic memory. This parallels the thinking of Carl Jung in his paper *"Concept of Collective Unconscious."*

Probably as important for me as a trained architect was the writings of architect Louis Sullivan. This quote is particularly poignant:

> Decoding people's responses to places and spaces can be an extraordinary tool for designing and building the future.

And it is even so as we forget that each of us was once a child; even as we banish the thought as crude, that out of that very child we have grown inevitably to be what we are; that the thoughts, the feelings, the emotions, the reactions, the waking dreams of that child have governed and determined us, willy-nilly, through the course of our lives and careers with compelling power – that what the child accepted we accepted; what that child rejected we reject.

Memories can be positive or negative, seriously impacting one's psyche and vision for the present and future. If you have had a bad or a good experience in a city, it will impact the way you think about cities. If you always loved driving, you might not like public transit. If you loved trains as a child, you might really like streetcars. If you had a great time in nature and parks, you will probably think positively about having more parks close to where you live or would like to live. Could this be why the baby boomers who were teenagers in the 1950s, at the height of auto culture, still love their cars and the sprawl that forces them to tolerate driving every day?

Then there are all the memories inherited genetically from our ancestors. These memories, emotions and impressions are retained in some "file" in our brains. Some are easily accessed; some are filed away in other files, etc. They may be difficult to access, but they are always there waiting for some synapse to trigger them. An eminent psychiatrist suggested that the human brain still contains 2% of our Neanderthal programming, developed well before Homo sapiens evolved. Does this trigger the positive response to natural settings? Does it trigger survival mode and a possible justification for gangs and armies, the survival of the fittest? Is this why so much of our current culture is generating fear—of terrorism, local crime, murders, disease, or people different from ourselves—or is this media's persistence in presenting the negative and the sensational or both?

Will the influences, impressions, and memories of younger generations impact the decisions they make in the future? When children today are in their leadership years, when they are around 50 years old, will their past psyche and exposure to negative and positive places and spaces, real or virtually imagined, impact preservation and urbanism? I don't think there is any questions about this. The current influences are very strong and are required to be understood to truly grasp the meaning and physical characteristics inherent in the response values to the images.

What influences condition your expectations?

There are **18 basic influences** that have strong impacts on present decisions and future aspirations and **which impact the responses values to spaces and places**.

There are probably others, but these are the most familiar:

1. Historic Evolutionary—the milestones of human evolution, from the beginning to the present
2. Influence of Family and Generations
3. Influence of Religion
4. Influence of Media
5. Influence of Population Growth and Change
6. Influence of Climate Change
7. Influence of the "Free Market"
8. Influence of Brands and Franchising
9. Influence of Personal Wealth and Financing
10. Influence of Protest
11. Influence of Political Power and Lobbying
12. Influence of "Bigger" or "Smaller" is Better

These chapters had to be eliminated from the book. They are available as a download from tony@nelessen.com.

To synthesize the enormous amount of data—influences, feelings, dislikes and likes, acceptances and disapprovals, beliefs and attitudes, emotions, motivations, and programming—a single positive, neutral, or negative number with a standard deviation was indispensable to assist people in responding and in order to determine results and direct planning and design decisions. A final average number could be produced when thousands of participants responded to an image of places and spaces, each with their own standards. The question asked of each participant is "How appropriate or inappropriate is the image you are seeing now and in the future for your —neighborhood, community, region?" "Rate it from a +10 appropriate and makes me feel good to –10 totally inappropriate and makes me feel very bad; or any number in between." "If you have no feelings, it is neither appropriate nor inappropriate, give it a 0 response based on the strength of your feelings – what is your brain telling you?" What has been the most remarkable observations is that for most participants the response value was made seconds after seeing an image. I find it remarkable considering all the influences on the human brain that are being processed to make such a determination. The human brain is extraordinary.!

It is the mind, with its collective influences, some stronger than others, that molds the way we think and directs how we want to live.

It is the brain that generates and absorbs the "spirit of place," one of the definitions of Genius Loci. The memory holds these impressions. Depending on its genetic and life experiences, the human mind can, under normal circumstances, perceive the differences between negative and positive influences. It also has the ability to probe beyond itself for guidance, inspiration, and love. Some people seek self-assurance and thrive on their own inspirations. Others, however, are insecure and must reach out for guidance. Others have combinations of both of these traits.

It is currently impossible to comprehend what is going through the minds of participants, although there are currently amazing studies and research of the human brain being conducted to better achieve artificial intelligence (AI). The VPS, in order to be effective, needs a single positive or negative number to determine results and make recommendations. This simple single positive or negative number, the heaven or hell, life or death, yin or yang, like or hate, allowed two sides of the moral compass to be activated in response to places and spaces. When individual response values are collected from all participants the final collective value (CV) expressed as means and standard deviation provides extraordinary visual, spatial and emotional information to determine the future quality and character of urbanism and the environment.

The prerequisite to determine peoples' responses to places and spaces was reinforced after exposure to *Reading in Attitude Theory and Measurement,* by Martin Fishban. It totally reinforced my approach and the responses we were receiving from the VPS.

The visioning "formula" that emerged begins to express the complexity of the mind as follows:

$$CV = \sum[B + A(nb + mc)]m$$

Although this reads like a formula, there are, not presently numerical values to insert into each of the factors in the formula. Perhaps in the future, each factor will be able to quantify by the number of synapses activated. Observing participants' responses, when values are determined in nanoseconds you can almost feel the current/energy emanating from the brain. I am confident that AI scientists, who are making extraordinary progress understanding the brain and transforming it to supercomputers, will be able to do this calculations in the future.

CV = Collective Values

The CV of an image is the totality of all participants' responses, generated after reviewing an image or video of places and spaces. The CV is the summation of all responses manifested in a positive or negative value on an image of a place expressed as a mean and standard deviation. For example, if an image received an average response value of +5 with a standard deviation of (3), this means that the response range is roughly from +8 to +2. Assuming that 600 participants evaluated the image, everyone agreed that this particular image was positive and appropriate for their community. Although mode and median are helpful, they are not as well perceived or understood by the public.

B = Belief or Values

Beliefs or Values, good and bad, are learned from early experiences; teaching; and the actions of our parents and religious leaders as well as a myriad of influences and genetic programming. They are ingrained and engender confidence without facts or proof. Faith might be a substitute. Consider the classic religious tenant "to belong you must believe without proof." You may believe that cities, towns, places, and spaces are nominally good or bad, ugly or beautiful, well-proportioned or non-descript, or places you would live or not live.

A = Attitude

Attitude is the psychological acceptance or rejection, promotion or demotion, of behavior codes and policies. Your feelings of security and protection, rejection or accommodation, rich or poor, etc. contribute to your attitude and the way you act toward other people and places. Attitude is the positive or negative behavior in response to your feelings about your physical surroundings and your resulting actions within them. Attitude is modified by two additional forces, normative behavior and the motivation to comply.

nb = Normative Behavior

Shared behavior manifested by demographic groups. This factor includes their expected or deviant behavior in certain places or spaces.

mc = Motivatiobn to Comply

Trying to consume, respond, look, dress, act and live like everyone else in your peer group. Essentially to to feel included. It generates they following responses: "They have it, I want it." They hate, I hate." "They have this type of house, I want the same." "I want to belong because they belong." These are but a few of the statement of motivation to comply.

m = Mood

Mood is your emotional state of being at the time of placing values. It modifies beliefs and attitudes.

Participants during Feedback Session

Participants at a feedback session, revealing their response values to certain images. This allows many to experience what the group is feeling. The question was "How many of you gave this image a value between +1 and +3?"

This is the most complex and varies from positive to negative. In most Community Visioning sessions, mood is courteous, curious, positive, polite, quiet, and eager to participate.

The Community Visioning is a planning tool for people to express their complex feelings about places and spaces.

Participants Responding to Images

It is extraordinary to watch participants respond to the range of images. There is a great deal of seriousness, pondering, and truthfulness in a few seconds.

Despite or because of the mind's complexity, participants are able to respond to a projected image in a Community Vision session in one or two seconds. Observation of hundreds of public sessions reveals that participants will automatically move their pencils towards the positive or negative side of the response sheet and then pause for internal introspection—"is it +4 or +5?"—before they mark their response value. It is remarkable how the human mind-computer evaluates and decides!

Having the ability to create positive or negative preferences can translate into creating a positive change or result in exploitation of the negative, which is destructive and harmful. If the response reaction is positive, vision and actions for implementation can create places of great humanity and beauty. They can create places that make life worthwhile or make it a living hell.

The highest valued images in a VPS and the category which it they located provide the most powerful insight into the conscious and unconscious desires of the participants. Achieving or preserving this visual and spatial quality is the top priority. All the highest-rated images in each category combine to define the type of places and spaces that participants want most.

The most negative-rated images and the category which they are in are the places and spaces that participants find the most depressing and unacceptable, and want to see changed: infilled, rehabilitated, and/or redeveloped.

One single image with the highest value and lowest standard deviation

emerges in every Visioning Session, representing the highest aspirations of the community.

Participants Responding to Questionnaire

The questionnaire provides valuable demographic data with market and policy questions. The last page of the questionnaire is a written section for additional comments which is saved into the "Book of Public Comments."

Quantifying Emotional Responses

Along with the VPS, a parallel demographic, policy, and marketing questionnaire probes with a series of questions on the emotional responses to the positive or negative images. There are a critical set of questions embedded in the questionnaire which have been asked at every Community Visioning session, revealing the emotional content of the participants' decisions. The questions asked were:

When you gave an image a positive response, which of the following describes the emotion you were experiencing? Next, when you gave an image a negative response, which of the following describes the emotion you were experiencing?

The following are the average responses from all the VPSs included in this book.

The emotional responses to positive images:

Hopefulness	**25%**
Happiness	**19%**
Joy	16%
Safe	9%
All of the above	25%

The emotional responses to negative images:

Depression	**38%**
Unhappiness	**33%**
Threatened	4%
Rage/anger	3%
All of the above	22%

As a note of caution, every image that is completely negative e.g., −6 with a standard deviation of 3, is unacceptable emotionally and physically depressing. We, as planners, designers, and community leaders, have failed in our duties and are causing emotional harm and unhappiness. Look to the positive images for hope and happiness in place making.

Ten Steps for a Successful Community Visioning Process

How much would you support additional walking related amenities provided in the area?*

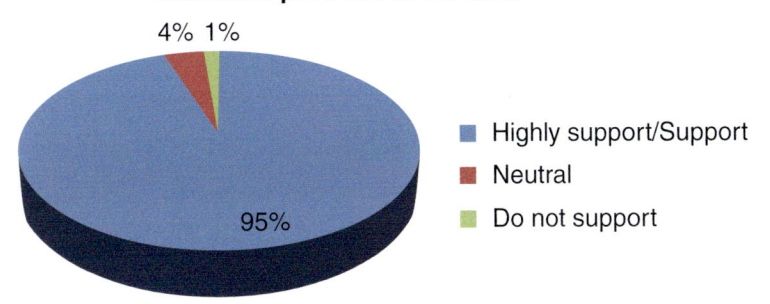

4% 1%

95%

- Highly support/Support
- Neutral
- Do not support

I particularly like this old biblical proverb: *"Plans succeed when counselors are many and fail when counselors are few."* I have quoted it at the beginning of most of my Community Visioning, and it has resonated.

There are ten steps to successfully completing a Community Visioning process for any location, be that a single block, neighborhood, hamlet, village, town, city, county, parish, or region. All are potential locations/clients for Community Visioning, resulting in a strategic Vision Plan.

Community Visioning is a planning technique proven effective in generating a three- and four-dimensional vision plan for the short- or long-term future of a location. The functional and visual character of spaces and places are typically generated piecemeal from ideas generated by a small group of individuals who believe they know what is appropriate for the people of their municipality. This neo-liberal philosophy thinks that current market desires are the most appropriate. In most cases, their decisions express specific self-interests. The most effective and sustainable vision is generated by many people and supported by the political structure.

To be accepted, those visions must tap into the subconscious desires of many people when determining what is the most appropriate. This can be achieved by completing each of the ten steps. When a consensus vision is generated by many participants, they become the major promoter of the vision. When generated by a few, a major public relations campaign exposing the results will be required in order to gain public support.

As a cautionary note, no matter how extensive public involvement, not everyone will be in accord. There will always be a percentage of the populous who view things negatively, no matter how good your intentions. Many of these people are negative about everything all the time. My research indicates that 11 to 14% of participants in most Community Visioning Sessions fall into this category. It is in their psychological makeup and perhaps in their genes to be negative or have a "bone to pick" with a mayor or councilperson. In our experience, the few negative participants have tended to support the positive vision for their towns once early phases have been implemented.

Once the ten steps are complete, a Consensus Vision Plan will be generated. To be implemented, it must be approved by the political structure and then translated into Master Plans, Redevelopment or Rehabilitation plans, and zoning and form-based codes which are the legal mechanisms that allow places to be built in accordance with the vision. The ten steps will best assure that future development and construction take into consideration the vision which will best respond to ecological conditions, economic and political fluctuations, new materials, and construction techniques. Once a community has decided to embark on a full participation consensus vision, the following multiple step process is recommended. This can be amended or modified if these steps are deemed unnecessary.

Step One

Inquiry

Basic questions that must be answered before embarking on a Community Visioning process by the town staff, stakeholders, and committee that manages the Visual Preference Survey (VPS) contract.

1. What are the study limits? How large of an area will be included in the vision plan? This could range from a downtown with a limited number of blocks and buildings, a highway corridor, or a larger community with multiple districts and neighborhoods to a county or a much larger region.

2. How many existing community representatives and neighborhood committees might participate in the visioning process?

3. What is the number of people that you anticipate might participate in the vision process? Do not put a limit upon attendance during the Community Visioning process.

4. Do you anticipate this being accomplished through private and public meetings only, through public meetings supplemented by Internet support, or through Internet alone? How intensively do you plan on using other social media? Will you contract an outside consultant or public relations firm as part of the consultant services?

5. Are there current Geographic Information System (GIS) and other base maps available for the study area which include a quality aerial photo on the same scale as the maps, with streets and roads, lots, building footprints, ownership, value of land and improvements, current zoning, and any redevelopment plans? Larger study areas would include existing land uses, watershed areas, environmentally sensitive lands, flood plains, farmlands, contaminated sites, transportation studies, and recent traffic documentation.

6. Are there current capital improvements or redevelopment plans approved, anticipated, and/or funded? Who are the developers of these approved projects? Should they be included in the Visioning Process? Will your staff invite them?

7. Will your city/county/state staffs participate in the preparation, review, facilitation, and participation of the vision plan? If so, which departments? How many staff persons? What are their titles and responsibilities?

8. When do you wish to begin and end the project?

9. Once the VPS is completed, do you want to facilitate Vision Translation Workshops (VTW) which will help generate recommendations for changes in land use and zoning codes? This is highly recommended. The results of the VPS process provide city officials and citizens with a consensus vision developed by the people.

10. Will you use your own public relations firm to promote the meetings and future public promotions effort in print, public presentations, and social media, or is that expected to be part of the consultant's contract? Ideally, the town should be responsible.

11. What is your anticipated budget for the visioning process and the public relations effort?

These questions must be asked because the answers are important to customize the process for each diverse community. Every visioning process is tailored by the response to these initial questions. The budget, participation by the public, and public relations are the largest considerations. Past experiences demonstrate that the larger the number of working committees and citizens participating in the VPS and VTW, the more successful the visioning process and the resulting implementation of the citizens' vision. People then become advocates for the plans they generated. Participants in the Visioning Processes have been as small as a managing executive committee of 10 to 12 and as large as multiple thousands. The average is about 500, including the managing group of the mayor, council, and planning board.

Step Two

Pre-Visioning Focus Groups

Pre-visioning helps quantify and qualify the existing character of the place being visioned and begins to probe the character of the desired transformation. Pre-visioning requires historical research of the site, understanding of demographic shifts, market changes, and focus groups. Pre-visioning focus groups are extremely helpful in determining the perceived problems and potentials, identifying places that are susceptible to change and places that are considered the most positive and negative, and helping to understand the communities' desired vision in the present and the long term. It helps identify the types and scale of maps needed; what images or videos should be used in the VPS; and what questions should be included in the Demographic, Market, and Policy Questionnaire.

Determining what images or videos are used is one of the biggest challenges. Images to be used in the VPS are charged with physical attributes and emotional value. They must be carefully vetted through interaction with multiple groups, including the city council and planning board members, the steering committee of major movers and shakers, neighborhood and business groups, developers, and student councils. To achieve this, a predetermined set of questions and images, combined with basic mapping exercises, is used. Feedback from the initial focus group members is used to determine the potentials and limitations, and the positive or negative character of place, and, more importantly, to understand aspirations for the short-term future. These focus groups help determine what is "on the drawings boards," the types of development the planning boards are reviewing, and what they have recently approved. All this input is used to prepare the VPS presentations, the Questionnaire, and the VTW.

Here are some of the specific questions asked at these pre-visioning focus groups:

1. How would you describe the study area to someone who has never been here before?

2. What are the characteristics of the area you like most?

3. What characteristics do you like least?

4. What is the largest problem in the area?

5. What is the most positive location in the study area?

6. Which is the most negative?

7. What changes do you want to see in the short-term future?

8. Describe a place you have visited that you wish this community could be like.

9. If this area was to be transformed, what is your ideal vision of what you would want it to become? Imagine the possibilities. Describe the desired changes in as much detail as possible.

10. What changes would you want to see happen in the next six months? One year from now? Five years from now? Twenty years from now? Fifty years from now?

11. Do the places you imagined have some of the characteristics of places you have visited or seen in books, in magazines, or on television? What are their visual and spatial characteristics? Where are they located?

Responses to these questions provide an extraordinary amount of information and frame the format for the entire visioning process. The data informs what visuals are needed and the policy and marketing questions that will be asked.

The next step in the pre-visioning process is a basic mapping exercise. On a prepared base, typically an ortho photograph, we ask participants to locate their home or business. They then outline the locations of the most positive and negative places in the study area and finish with a **Susceptibility to Change (STC) mapping exercise**. This exercise defines the study area in more detail and locates problem areas and opportunities for short-term future intervention for the area. The combination of the response to the questions and the STC mapping exercise provides the foundation of possible design interventions needed for the VPS and the VTW.

Step Three

Image Capture

After evaluating the responses, field visits and photographs are taken for all those places described as positive and negative by the focus groups in the study area. In addition, you must research those places that were imagined, through images from an image library using simulations, traveling to those places and photographing them, or searching the internet. Remember: If you use images other than your own, you must receive permission for their use and provide credits.

To capture in still images and/or video the current character of the community and determine what people think of it as it currently exists, an extensive photographic tour of the focus area and surrounding region is required. To be consistent with the images, the lighting and sky conditions should be the same for all images. Images should focus on what people normally see and experience. No image should be framed for character to make it look either better or worse that it is normally perceived. Because so many places are seen by car, many of the initial images are through the windshield or windows of a car. We call images captured in this way "drive by shootings." Images seen from a pedestrian vantage are the most often used. The angle of the images is the normal view, no wide angels or telephoto views. A 50-degree cone of vision is ideal. Use a standard lens that replicates human eye range and speed when capturing places with video. Avoid wide angle and telephoto images or time lapses. Remember, the VPS is a tool to engage many people to respond to options for the short- and long-term future, not to provide a single solu-

tion. Finding the negative images in the study area is easy. We carefully take note and record the responses from the focus groups, and travel to those locations to photograph or capture video. Video is an ideal media with which to capture a sequence. Using a still frame from the video focuses attention on a specific aspect of the sequence for evaluation.

Finding the most appropriate visual representations of the positive desired places and spaces is challenging and time-consuming. First, we filter through our library of positive place images that might best fit to the scale and character of the community being visioned. Our image library is divided into the 14 visual and spatial characteristics categories that typically comprise the components of place. Streets is one basic category within which there are over 30 sub-types. If we do not find appropriate images that match desires, we travel to those locations suggested by the focus group sessions, or we create visual simulations.

In 1991, A. Nelessen Associates was the first to use Photoshop and portions of images from our library to create an "after" image using the "before" or existing image as a base. Using this simulation technique, an existing negative place can be transformed to a positive place based on descriptions generated from the pre-visioning focus groups. Simulations have become a significant feature of recent VPSs because image transformation technologies are continually improving. As an example, we can easily test for the reaction to increased street landscaping, infill buildings, transit, and building densities.

A typical VPS contains 12 to 16 categories of images or video clips that holistically encompass the visual and spatial characteristics of place. Site photography focuses on specific locations and features that include:

- Landmarks
- Streets—cartway widths, curbs, parkways, tree plantings, intersections, and formation into blocks
- Landscaping
- Edge conditions along streets and highways for various land uses
- Parks, natural areas, and other open spaces
- Pedestrian environments called the "pedestrian realm," including pedestrians on sidewalks, pedestrian streets, cafés on sidewalks, etc.
- Movement paths and facilities, including pedestrians, bicycle, scooters, transit stops, connective linkages, and automobile circulation
- Transit/Mobility—existing and potential options, including bus, light and heavy-rail, taxi, on-demand, shared car, bicycle, scooter, moving sidewalks, escalators, horizontal elevators etc.
- Housing types of various scales, forms, and architecture
- Historic buildings, districts, building details, and heights
- Commercial/retail, offices, mixed-use buildings, scale, types, frontage, entrances, windows, form and character of office parks, multi-story offices, big box stores, strip malls, mixed-use, hotels, etc.

- Main Streets—traditional and historic character
- Civic spaces, plazas, and public buildings, including fire stations, police stations, libraries, community centers, schools, city halls, etc.
- Parking lot location and configurations
- Signage
- Street fixtures and furniture, including lighting, planting, and seating
- Additional locations and spatial issues as generated by the early pre-visioning sessions

Images representing each of these categories are critical in any VPS to best understand holistically how participants evaluate their community character in total. Including images of what could be or what is desired allows policies to emerge as to the value of current and future visual and spatial conditions.

It is also possible to ask people to photograph great places, streets, and public facilities when they travel, to be added to the pictorial design files for future site and land use plans.

Step Four

Assembly of a Visual Preference Survey

The final selection of the VPS images and/or video clips in the various categories requires the most professional judgement. A first critical question is: What is the number of images that can be used? This depends on the area of study; the number of locations; the presentation method (Internet or public); and, quite frankly, the budget. More images are used in a public meeting setting than in an online survey. Between 80 and 160 images are used in a typical public meeting format. An online survey may use from 25 to 45. People are willing to evaluate more images at a public meeting setting than on their PC or cell phone.

A community-wide or regional survey may contain 12 to 16 categories of images or video clips that holistically encompass the visual and spatial characteristics of a place. The actual number of these categories depends on the focus group responses and the size and character of the focus area.

In selecting the actual images to be presented in the VPS, first divide the images into categories as indicated in Step Three.

The selection of the final images is a process that starts with many images, continuously eliminating from this list until the appropriate range and number are reached. It takes hours of professional judgment to select the right images in each category and to assure a comprehensive analysis of existing conditions as well as locations for short- and long-term future options. The final selection of images for inclusion into the VPS is a demanding professional responsibility, requiring the sensitive understanding of the people, habits, location, and cultural anomalies, revealed through the initial interviews, focus groups, interactions with people when photographing in the field, and initial beta tests.

Each image must be reviewed and analyzed for content, color, clarity, responsiveness to the research, visual descriptions, and mapping generated from the focus groups and initial meetings with stakeholders and staff.

When selecting the images to be used in the first beta test of the VPS, the typical ratio is 20:1, that is, 20 images /videos are shot for the 1 that is used. The initial photographic recognizance for a large Community Visioning session could generate up to 1,000 images or 40 to 80 video clips. Choosing which images can provide the greatest amount of visual and spatial information and generate important recommendations requires a careful review of every image. Images and videos must portray existing conditions, along with a range of potential viable solutions in various categories.

It is highly recommended that the initial VPS be fine-tuned using one or more beta tests. The results and feedback discussion from the beta tests are extremely helpful in refining image selection, eliminating redundancies, and even reducing categories. The numerical values of the images that received the highest, lowest, and zero values in each of the categories with the lowest standard deviation are prime images to be included in the smaller Internet VPS. Digital files will then be prepared for presentation using PowerPoint and/or video, or they will be transferred to the project web page through a range of survey instruments.

The number of simulations has ranged from 1 or 2 to over 20. The production of architecturally accurate and potentially implementable and "after" simulations, using an existing "before" image is one of the most expensive, technically challenging techniques and time consuming steps/task in the Community Visioning Process.

Once this image selection is complete in each of the categories, the "before" and "after" simulations must be prepared. In early discussions/meetings and focus groups, there are multiple occasions in which to imagine the future via verbal description, then determine where these new visual and spatial features could be located on a map or aerial of the area. The best way to help translate these thoughts into images is to create, from an existing "before" conditions image, an "after" image that digitally represents these future visions. This is done using an existing image in the study as the background image. This background image is always evaluated in the VPS. A new image of place can be created by incorporating buildings, streetscapes, activity, mobility options, landscaping, etc., generated from other images or created using other graphic imaging programs to "build" photorealistic images with photo-imaging software, like AutoCAD, SketchUp, Maxwell, Ryno, and other virtual reality programs that can add or subtract desirable or undesirable components.

For example, we can visualize what a street would look like with additional trees or buildings, different streetlights, widened and/or enhanced sidewalks, or a change in buildings' forms and locations. Ensuring that these simulations are perfectly completed takes time and talent as well as computer processing power and memory, along with the appropriate computer graphic programs. This is a labor-intensive step in the process. Before and after images must be included in the final selection of VPS images and must not alter the seasonal or light condition. They also must not be placed one after another in the VPS but should instead be separated by multiple images.

Simulations are a powerful visioning technique that allows people to visualize options for the future transforming of negative places and spaces. Most people cannot visualize these alternatives for transformation, but are immediately able to recognize places and spaces that are visually and spatially negative and would like to see changed—but to what? Providing possible options allows people to select realistic ones. If an image is value rated high, many participants ask, "Is there a market for this change in the immediate future?" History has proven that the answer is yes, except that there is an undetermined timeline before implementation. Many urban visions have taken 6 months to 42 years to implement. Nonetheless, after a period of time, and when the financial marketing and political conditions are conducive, many visions have been implemented in a similar form as in the positive simulation.

Response Value –7

Existing condition

Response Value –0

Simulation one

Response Value +3

Simulation two

Response Value +7

Simulation three

The above simulations represent the potential evolution of this arterial as this state highway has been re-placed by a parallel federal freeway. The simulations test the visual acceptability of transforming the highway into a boulevard while adding a positive pedestrian realm and new mixed-use buildings over time. As it be-comes more of a walkable, landscaped boulevard, the positive consensus value increases from a –7 to a +7. The big question raised in this set of simulations is contained within simulation two: "is the response value of 0 good enough, or can the final simulation be achieved?"

The above four images illustrate simulations using the existing "before" image of place and three potential "after" images used in the VPS. The "before" image is photographed with the horizon in the center of the image, as are the other compo-nents, e.g. trees, cars, sidewalks, street furniture, buildings, etc. Testing a phased implementation was one of the goals of this corridor Community Visioning project.

The images were created using Photoshop, illustrating three possible changes in the character and design that were generated through the focus groups and Susceptibility to Change mapping exercise. What the Community Visioning process determined was that the existing condition was negative and steadily improved in value and accept-ance as more of the area was redeveloped through phased implementation.

Step Five

The Demographic, Policy, and Market Questionnaire

The Visual Preference Survey™ is supplemented with a questionnaire that includes Demographic, Market, and Policy Questions.

A "full" questionnaire for public meetings may contain between 40 and more than 80 questions. It is typically divided into four sections.

Section One is the demographics of the person participating. This is located in the beginning of the questionnaire.

Section Two is a series of market-based questions, like "What types of new retail would be appropriate for the area?" and "How often do you shop in the area?"

Section Three focuses on policy questions, like "Should the community provide more affordable housing?"

Section Four is a write-in section that allows a participant to pose comments or add information not covered. This is usually the last page of the questionnaire, which is then removed and assembled into a "Book of Public Comments."

The large public meetings have a more comprehensive questionnaire. An Internet-based survey uses fewer more focused Demographic, Market, and Policy Questions. The questionnaires provide statistically accurate data to correspond to the visual data. Demographic questions are critical to provide a profile of those who participate and how they respond to the images.

The policy and market questions include: demographic changes, housing and shopping patterns, economic development conditions, traffic and commuting patterns, ratings of public facilities, neighborhoods and housing, urban design, downtown development, economic development, community facilities, recreation, historic preservation, open space, and any other critical issues that the client deems relevant. Policy questions help identify and focus on the important policy issues to be included in the plan. It is extremely helpful and informative for the questionnaire to not only be tailored to the entire study but also focus on sub-areas when part of a larger visioning area.

An additional blank sheet is added onto the back of the questionnaire for participates to make any additional public comments. This is removed, read, and incorporated into the vision, and placed in a "Book of Public Comments." See Appendix III for a sample of these comments.

Before these questions are finalized, a preliminary and final draft must be prepared for review and comment by the client. The questionnaire typically goes through one or two revisions and client approvals. Once completed and beta-tested, the final questionnaire is printed and becomes part of the package that each participant receives at the public meetings.

After the Community Visioning session, the questionnaire responses are determined and cross-tabulated with other questions-based demographics, responses to policies, and responses to various images in the VPS. Generating demographic and locational data is critical. All the data on the VPS and the questionnaire can be cross-tabulated. Survey data can compare responses based on age, income, education, employment, location, etc., providing a complete profile of participants and their responses.

The response to the questions used at a public meeting are notated on a standard Scantron red sheet. An ID number on the Scantron sheet is assigned to each participant, which allows the responses from the questionnaire to be linked to the responses from the VPS, e.g., does a person 18 to 24 respond differently to an image than a person 65 or older? Therefore, a wide range of cross-tabulations are possible. Using the internet response to questions included on the website, the process of determining results is simplified and easier using a response-based program to determine the answers to the online questionnaire.

The public meeting is the preferred form of Community Visioning. For participants, it is a more deliberate act, a more intense, memorable, and committed reaction. Participants can publicly respond during the hand-raising response sessions. The response sheets require more time to scan and become a permanent reference record.

Results of the questionnaire are incorporated with the image results into a "Did we get it right?" presentation, the preliminary and final project report, and the recommendations for short- and long-term implementation.

Step Six

Administering the VPS

Two formats of VPS are most common. One format with the largest number of images is prepared for public meetings, the other typically with with fewer number of images for the Internet. Most communities use some combination of public meeting and Internet application to reach more people. Towns may add a video sample of the VPS on their local TV stations to encourage participation. Other communities have used a "pin up" presentation for public events, like community fairs, where participants can place a value on a printed pictorial image as they walk by.

A typical public meeting using a comprehensive Visual Preference Survey™ consisting of 60 to 100 images in multiple categories and takes between 30 minutes to 1 hour to administer. Completing the Demographic, Market, and Policy Questionnaire, which typically follows the VPS, takes an additional 10 to 30 minutes. The total length of these two applications of the process depends on the duration of the public discussion during the feedback session, which is typically lively, interesting, and highly encouraged.

For public meetings, it is critical to secure venues that are conveniently located and conducive to participants being able to see the images and mark their responses. The larger the room, the larger the screen and projection equipment needed. Chairs and tables are required. Lighting in the room is critical for both seeing the images and filling in a response form. Hotel or convention centers with dimmable lighting are preferred, providing there is focused light for the facilitator.

A lighted podium with a sound system is needed for larger meetings. The images for the VPS are stored in a laptop at the podium. It is important for the facilitator to introduce the various categories and the number of the image being evaluated, e.g. "in the streets category this is image 23." Some of the best visioning sessions are those with hardly a sound in the room as people concentrate on the response values to each of the images and questions.

The Internet survey consists of a smaller number of images, never more than 50, with a limited set of interspersed questions. The images used in the internet survey are always taken from the full public survey. The responses from the Internet can be collated with the images and questions in the full survey when a community uses both. The more people who evaluate an image and respond to a question, the better! People responding via the Internet seem to have a shorter interest span, if it is not fluid and engaging. Because of download time, the total time to complete the survey on the Internet is directly dependent on the number of images, the presentation technique, and the speed of the Internet connection. To be safe, **the lower the number of images, the more people will participate in the survey online**. With either format of VSP, digital still images and video clips

are viewed and evaluated individually never in pairs or multiples.

Understanding the Responses

In each type, participants are asked to evaluate images in categories, answering the question "How appropriate is the image you are seeing now and in the future (for the place being evaluated)?" Post-VPS feedback sessions reveal that people think both subconsciously and simultaneously about quality of life, safety, and economics as they evaluate each image. We ask participants to rate every image on a +10 to –10-point scale. This provides a total of 21 possible responses, including a neutral response of 0. The higher the positive responses, the higher the acceptability. The lower the responses, the more unacceptable. Reactions to an image may range from positive ten (+10) to negative ten (–10). If a participant feels strongly that a particular image is appropriate, their score might be a +7 or +8. Very few people give values of +10. If they feel that the image is acceptable but not outstanding, the reaction might be a +2 or +3. Conversely, if they feel that such a development pattern should not be allowed or never again be permitted, the reaction might be a –7 to –9, though seldom a –10.

The range of plus to negative values was selected because every image has a negative or positive response based on values associated with good or evil, positive or negative.

Considerations of heaven and hell, yin and yang, appropriateness and inappropriateness, fear and safety, happiness and sadness, deja vus, etc., are all considered in the Envision Formula. Using a response range from +10 to 0 to–10, a total of 21 potential evaluation responses, provides an appropriate range and mathematical exactness of the positive or negative numerical response to places and spaces. It is possible, with this larger range of positive and negative response numbers, to determine the nuances in the images, leading to a finer-grain understanding and potential implementation of the physical characteristics inherent in the higher value rated image. As an example, two positive images, one with a +4.1, the other with a +4.5 is a very subtle distinction, but there are qualities and characteristics in the higher that are more acceptable. In addition, each image is assigned a standard deviation in order to understand the range of responses. The mean value, with a standard deviation applied to each image, provides a specific quantification to analyze the image for its potential application.

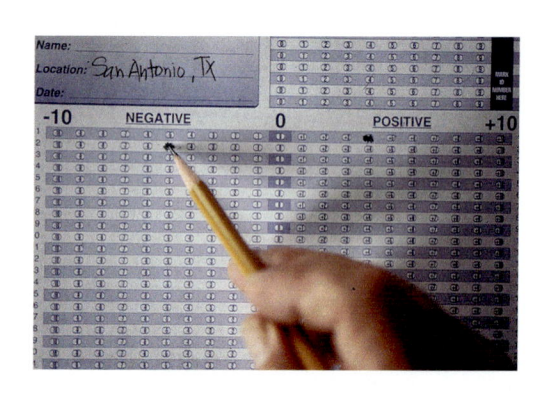

Scantron Response sheet

To record reactions at the public meeting, a specially designed Scantron form sheet was designed and printed with the +10 to 0 to –10

"fill in the dot" format for up to 80 images. As people view an image or video, it only takes nanoseconds for them to determine if it is positive or negative. This immediate response time is extraordinary. Then participants take a split-second pause as participants determine their specific response value, e.g. "Is it a +5 or +6?" People's minds are so fine-grained that some participants want a further breakdown, such as 5.5 to help clarify the subtleties within an image in comparison to other images.

A Scantron reader is used to scan each response form. The algorithm calculates the mean and the standard deviation for each image, along with other data. For the Internet application, the response program uses the +10 to –10 represented by dots at the bottom of the image. Participants use the mouse and click to record their responses. The image on the next page is a typical page used in an Internet application with the image, a brief descriptive heading, and the 21 dots (+10 to 0 to –10) on the bottom of the image.

The Internet based Community Visioning Process was first successfully used by A. Nelessen Associates, Inc (ANA) in 1996 for Blue Print Midtown II, Atlanta. It proved to be well received, but, as stated earlier, only a limited number of images can be used. Nonetheless, it set the standard for subsequent use as more and more people have access to the Internet.

Various handheld clicker devices have been used by planners in community meetings to generate instant feedback. Even though they provide crude immediate feedback (percentage, yes or no), we have found them inferior to activate people's imagination using the intensity of their negative

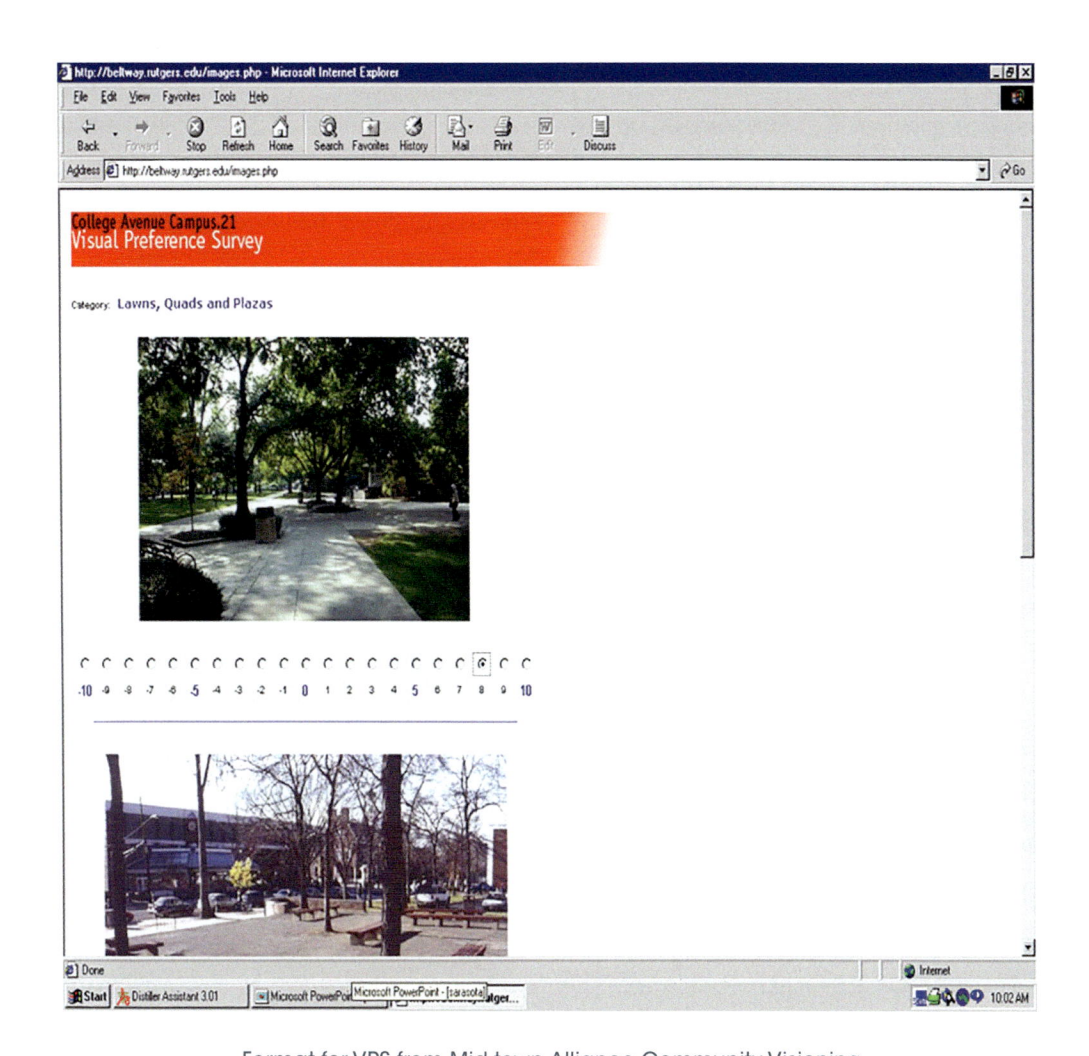

Format for VPS from Mid-town Alliance Community Visioning

Internet VPS screenshot. The first time the Internet was used for a VPS. "Use your mouse to click the dot."

or positive reactions. Understanding these reactions is key to achieving greater public acceptance and therefore adoption and hopefully implementation. Also, in our experience, we don't find the immediate clicker response as effective because it does not allow for appropriate time to analyze the images, and it eliminates the need for additional public meeting(s) for interaction and feedback. Based on a presentation at the follow-up public meetings, the most positive and negative images, and responses to the questionnaire presented at the public meetings "cement" the images in people's minds.

Of all the participation techniques, the large public meeting is clearly favored. It has more energy and interaction that can only come from being with large numbers of people. Other media have been used less successfully, including local public television broadcasting, videotapes, and CDs.

To keep the public meetings interesting and interactive, a selected number of images are shown to the participants for a second time, after they have completed their scoring of all of the images. The values that individuals give an image are determined through a "hand-raising."

For example, they are asked to raise their hands in response to questions like "How many of you give this image a positive rating?", "Between plus one and three?", "Between plus four and seven?", or "Greater than plus 7?" People glance around to see what values others have given an image. The most noticeable verbal response by audience members is generated when there is the consensus to an image of place that is very positive or negative. Targeting specific "before and after" simulations are most instructive. Using morphing programs, or a very slow fade between images, participants can actually experience places and spaces transform. The strongest verbal responses are from images that received very negative ratings as they transformed to positive rated places and spaces before their eyes.

To get the largest number of people to participate in a Community Visioning session, a serious public outreach, public relations effort is required. The most successful use every available media outlet to publicize the visioning sessions. For example, in one community, we used lawn signs which said, "Become the planners and architects of your – block, neighborhood, town!" In other, we used signs which said, "If you do not participate, and this area does change for the worse, don't complain!" On each sign we ask people to attend the Community Visioning sessions with the date, time, location, Internet Website and a telephone number. This can generate a huge turnout. A good public relations media firm who knows the local community, organizations, developers, and politicians is critical. In some cases, language sensitivity and capability must be considered in majority Hispanic or ethnic communities.

The use of newspaper articles and advertisements; handouts; billboards; radio and television interviews; public service announcements added to water, sewer, tax, and electric bills and church newsletters, school newsletters, and lawn signs; and presentations at service organization meetings are all common and now must include social media. Still, the most compelling marketing is the word of mouth that is transmitted after a person attends one or more focus groups or neighborhood and business associations visioning sessions with another scheduled a few days later. The more people that participate, the more successful the visioning process and results because the images that are generated are their visions, not those imposed by officials or consultants.

Using Facebook and an increasing array of social media apps can enhance public participation. With so many things occupying people's minds and time, every available medium is required to ensure that people participate. **As a word of caution**, as people become exposed to more negative media coverage, their confidence in change can become conflicted, particularly when combined with a growing mistrust of government. It may then take extra media leverage to get them out to participate at all. Once they participate, though, they will be hooked.

Participants sometimes tell me, after completing the VPS and questionnaire, "it felt like their brain was squeezed and worked hard," always with a high level of enthusiasm in their voices.

Step Seven

The Vision Translation Workshop (VTW)

The Vision Translation Workshop (VTW) is the most interactive, interesting, and committing next step in the visioning process. The VTW typically follows the completion of the VPS; the Demographic, Market, and Policy Questionnaire; and group feedback on critical images. Before beginning the VTW, schedule a 10- to 15-minute break. Personal interaction will occur during this time. It is a good time for participants to discuss their responses, network, and select team members for the graphic portion of the process. It is important to conduct the VTW immediately after the visioning session because images will be fresh in participants mind, and they are already captured participants. The VTW application opportunity at this phase in the visioning process produces a latent response to an unfulfilled desire. Participants will have just evaluated every image in the survey, with the most positive and negative images fresh in their minds, and have completed the "hand-raising" public feedback to a range of selected images.

The numerical results from the VPS indicate which images are most appropriate and inform the acceptable architectural and site planning visual and spatial character. The **VTW reveals where participants feel the positive images should be located**. VPS images are incorporated and keyed to the specific workshop tasks. Both the negatively and the positively rated images can be used to explain the preferred vision for redevelopment or growth.

A Typical Vision Translation Workshop (VTW)
Teams of people, typically 6 to 12, work together to prepare a concept plan that locates the positive vision.

The VTW generates priorities and specific plans for achieving the consensus vision. When collectively analyzed with the VPS, a two- and three-dimensional plan emerges.

The VTW uses an aerial map of the study area at an appropriate scale, presenting as much detail as possible on a base map. Sets of eight colored markers are used. A typical workshop or "planning and design group" is three to ten participants. Seldom should there be over 12, and never should there be under 3. Each graphic response uses a separate tracing paper overlaid on the aerial base map. Four to six overlays are typically used, based on the specifics and the size of the area being visioned. On the first overlay, each participant is asked to locate their house or business. This orients them to the map and sets a geographic range for their immediate concerns.

Once this first task is completed, on a separate overlay, they are asked to "Locate with a red marker those streets you feel have the most congestion" and asked "Where are the most dangerous intersections?" and "Where are cars speeding?" because they experience such things in their daily lives in the community; it becomes an easy task for them to interact with their design team and draw where this occurs. Each overlay becomes more demanding.

As such, on the third overlay, more intensive responses are required: "With four markers, red orange, yellow and green, outline those areas you and your design group think are the most susceptible to change and should be demolished (red), needs serious improvement (orange), minor improvement needed (yellow), and green (no change required-keep as is)." This map is directly related to those images of places they have evaluated as negative or positive. This map forms the basis of where major and minor interventions into the urban fabric are required and indicates which places require a minimum of intervention or none at all.

The fourth and fifth overlays focus on land uses and building typologies. The negative images, combined with areas designated in red and orange on the Susceptibility to Change overlay, are the

catalyst for recommending places to be changed. The green and yellow represent those places where little change or no change is needed or desired. The positive, "most appropriate now and in the future," images, combined with the Susceptibility to Change map, are used to locate where the positive images should be most appropriately located. What I have experienced over time is that the visual response to the negative images of places are typically one or more of the positive images. The graphic representations of where the participants would locate the places that received positive responses in each of the categories is fundamental to the VTW planning and design process. On the fourth overlay, using the third as an under-layer – the Susceptible To Change map – participants respond to the question: "You rated this (housing commercial, mixed use, streetscape etc.) image very positive, now where would you and your team recommend it be located?"

Following are the typical graphic tasks and coloring codes used during a typical VTW. Most instructions are supplemented with a graphic generated from another VTW. Each of the following is a separate white tracing paper overlay on the base aerial photograph

Overlay 1—Orientation—Location of home and business

> Using a different color for each participant, locate your house or business. Indicate house with an H and business with a B.

Overlay 2—Street Improvements

> **Using a RED** marker, draw a line on streets with excessive noise and speed.

Using a PURPLE marker, draw a line on streets where traffic speed is high and needs slowing.

Using a Black "X," indicate intersections that are dangerous and accident prone.

Using a YELLOW marker, draw a circle where improved pedestrian crossings are needed.

Using a BLUE marker, draw a line where lanes and paths for bicycles should be added or improved.

Using a GREEN marker, draw lines on streets where trees and landscaping should be implemented.

Using an ORANGE marker, draw a circle where gateway features, such as signs, fountains, or special landscaping, should be provided.

Overlay 3—Susceptibility to Change or Areas of Maximum Opportunity

Establish Susceptibility to Change on sites throughout the study area using the required colors. Please evaluate the potential for change for all parcels and buildings based on their condition and susceptibility to redevelopment.

The following color code must be used:

GREEN—NO SUSCEPTIBILITY TO CHANGE

Using a GREEN marker, trace the lots and buildings that are in great condition, will not change, will be there for the future, or are of important historical value. This also includes lands that are considered environmentally sensitive, like stream corridors, wetlands, etc., which can be verified with Geographic Information Systems (GIS) mapping. These lands must be preserved in the future.

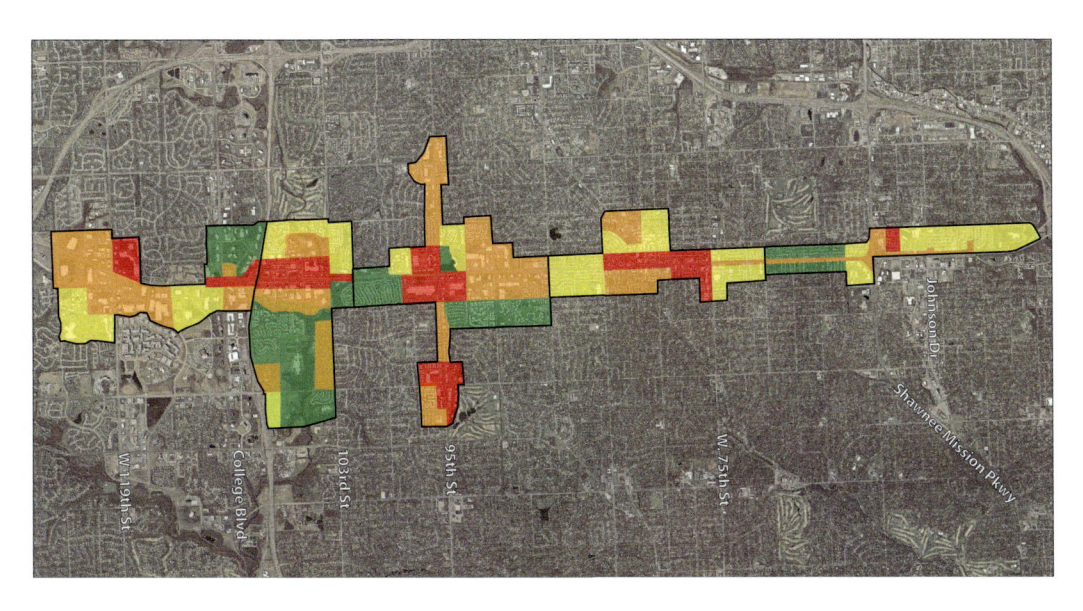

Susceptibility to Change Map

Typical Susceptibility to Change map for a section of a suburban corridor. Green areas are not be touched.

YELLOW—LOW SUSCEPTIBILITY TO CHANGE

Using a YELLOW marker, trace the lots and buildings that are in good condition and could need minor improvements, e.g. painting, repointing, replacement of windows, or enhancements to the landscape. For a regional plan, yellow can be used to designate open lands for hamlets, very low density estates, and farmlands.

ORANGE—MODERATE SUSCEPTIBILITY TO CHANGE

Using an ORANGE marker, trace lots and/or buildings that need major improvements, including possible removal of some existing buildings and rehabilitation of others, with the lots targeted for infill.

RED—HIGH SUSCEPTIBILITY TO CHANGE

Using a RED marker, trace lots and/or buildings that are inappropriate for the location, underutilized, deteriorated, or vacant and thus will most likely be removed for significant new infill and/or redevelopment.

Overlay 4—Short-term Future Growth and Neighborhood Centers

Task 1: Using the BLACK marker and the provided circular plastic template which is at the scale of the base map, locate existing or proposed neighborhoods. The template represents a five-minute walking distance from a possible neighborhood center. Trace around the edges with the center of the template where there is or should be a neighborhood center.

Neighborhood centers should be defined by a shared community place, such as a park, local shops, mixed-use community buildings, local café, or restaurant. This could also be the location for a new village or an agricultural hamlet.

Task 2: Using the one RED dot provided, place and stick the dot where your team feels it is appropriate to concentrate commercial, retail, restaurants, entertainment, etc. in the study area. The size of the dot represents the projected square footage which was determined from market and population projections.

Task 3: Using one BLUE rectangle or a portion of it, indicate where you feel it is appropriate to place offices or light industry. Again, the size of the rectangle represents the projected square footage based on market and population projections.

Task 4: Using three YELLOW stick on rectangles, indicate where you feel it is appropriate to place new residential uses. Please write with a BLACK maker an "S" on the dot for single-family residential and an "M" for multifamily residential.

Task 5: Using two GREEN rectangles, indicate where you feel it is appropriate to place new parks.

The VTW can use multiple overlays with specific or general questions, not necessarily limited to the ones previously described. Every VTW session is unique based on the scale of the focus area and overall vision goals. The VTW is specifically tailored, be it a more regional plan or a specific redevelopment plan for a discrete area. For the large regional study, the projections of growth are used in one overlay where participants use colored plastic chips or colored paper scaled to the map and floor or land area to represent the amount of projected growth that they can distribute. GIS-generated base and aerial photographs at the same scale indicate the locations of environmentally sensitive areas, like lakes, ponds, wetlands, streams, forests, etc., that should not be built on.

An effective and comprehensive vision process uses a specific set of images and questions, and a base map, custom-tailored to that location and policy concerns generated in the initial focus groups. Where the vision is geared to generate a larger regional plan, the VPS, Questionnaire, and VTW questions may focus on places where new streets or roads should be located, etc., while avoiding those areas that participants feel should not be built on.

Participants typically know where different uses and densities can be most appropriately applied. Using a good base map, projected value-rated images on large screens, and understandable instruction sheets, participants can more easily identify appropriate areas for future growth and development. For example, if revitalized community retail or new mixed-use buildings are a highly valued image, participants can easily indicate where they think these should be located. By using multiple teams to provide input to a single planning action, a consensus can be developed not only for the image type but also for the location of that use.

This Community Visioning process (images and maps) used by design teams over many years,

has revealed that **80% of the participants place the positive-rated images in the same locations**, even though they were working in independent teams. Participants' perceptions of appropriate location, size, shape, and configuration of short-term future development becomes manifest.

Near the end of the workshops, each group is asked to present their unique vision for their study area. All participants share ideas, commonalities of their design theme, and redevelopment options which they think are appropriate from the many examples illustrated during the VPS and VTW.

Step Eight

Synthesis of Data

Now, we come to the most interesting and professionally demanding step, requiring a carefully detailed analysis of the VPS and questionnaire results while analyzing each overlay generated by teams in the VTW.

All responses from all Community Visioning session are reviewed and combined, focusing first on the average response value and standard deviation of each image. The collective response value on each image represents the emotional responses of all the surveyed participants, generating the collective visual and spatial consciousness of the participant community. A detailed examination of each image in each category is required based on positive, neutral, or negative responses to assess details and components which contribute to the acceptability and appropriateness or unacceptability and inappropriateness.

What is fascinating and apparent from all VPS results is that **one image always emerges as the most positive and another as the most negative**. First, look at what category it is in. The positive image captures the essence or the "soul" of the community and expresses its greatest pride and desire. The most negative generates the greatest fear, anger, and depression. These single images have extraordinary power as a catalyst for change because they resonate most strongly with people. The category the images are in, should become the first priority for positive intervention.

Next, array all images by score, from highest positive to lowest negative value for each category. Each image is first compared with other images in its specific category. When all images are reviewed, the distinction between the high positive- and low negative-rated images will become clear. The images in the middle that are most problematic have values around 0, with a standard deviation of 5 or 6, which means that half of the participants love it, and half hate it. Positive images are acceptable and represent the visual and spatial character people want, while the negative images are unacceptable represent places and structures that participants want to see rebuilt or eliminated. Desired change becomes evident when their response values to specific images correspond to their notated location on the Susceptibility to Change map.

A detailed examination of the content of the images with the highest preference response value and the lowest standard deviations in each category begins to generate a holistic vision. Visual, spatial, and functional characteristics of these highly rated images are analyzed in general and in detail. The more detailed analysis determines which design elements contribute to the most positive feeling of pride, delight, and love. We can answer, for example,

- "What are acceptable densities and heights?"
- "What types of street are most appropriate?"
- "What are the most acceptable types of residential units in certain areas?"
- "What is their response to open car parking lots?"
- "Do they prefer brick or other types of façade material?"
- "What types and sizes of trees for the streetscapes are necessary to improve a street's appearance?"

In each specific climate region of the country, ANA has teamed with firms of local planners, architects, and landscape architects in many of Community Visioning projects.

These response values also answer the question "What attribute category is most valued by the community?" This image will have the highest positive response value and smallest standard deviation. For instance, are open space and parks, residential development, or pedestrian streets most highly valued? This single image is the essence of the positive desires of the community. When the highest value-rated images in each category are determined, they collectively represent the consensus visions, becoming the master vision for each community.

The highest-rated image in each category, when combined with the positive questionnaire responses, becomes the design goals and objectives for that category. Through the combination of the positive images from each category, planning design goals and objectives emerge to define the most appropriate, as well as inappropriate, land uses and visual and spatial character for use in market feasibility studies, land use plans, and urban design. The positive visual and spatial character are then reviewed for financial feasibility. Only the development strategies deemed the most feasible will be incorporated into the final recommendations.

The neutral images with the highest standard deviations indicate those images that are most controversial from the planning and political perspective. Half of the participants think it is positive, while the other half think it is negative, or everyone gave it a neutral response—neither good nor bad. Through a cross-tabulation process, the specific demographic cohorts with policy and market responses can be isolated, helping to clarify the neutral image response. These images will be the most difficult to address and will require decisive political and economic decisions informing the necessary public policy. These images require intensive discussion and tough policy decisions. This is where the experience of the design team provides guidance for each solution generated from the vision process.

The lowest-rated images provide the vision of those places which people find unacceptable and locations where participants want to see changes, which refer to complete transformation through redevelopment or rehabilitation, not just cleaning and painting. Most visioning sessions include large areas in need of redevelopment. How does a place get redeveloped, and in what form? Look to the positive images and those maps that locate where positive buildings or streets want to be located. By determining which images in each category generate a positive response and then combining all the positive images in all categories,

we begin to see and understand a holistic vision of what people want and desire.

When the positive images are cross- referenced with the Susceptibility To Change maps, those areas needing redevelopment can be easily separated from those needing rehabilitation or minor cleanup and, more importantly, green areas that should not be touched. The negative images and those most unacceptable in their current form provide extraordinary opportunity for future value creation. Change here is highly recommended and would be most accepted by the community. The visioning process has found that the "answer" to improving the negative images is typically embedded in the positive images. Change is further explored in additional simulations as the specific design recommendations are generated.

When all the images in the VPS are evaluated, the demographic profile reveals who took the survey, and how their preferences are categorized and prioritized, and agreed upon by multiple cohorts. Additional synthesis of data compares the market and policy responses to the values of the images. Each question can be cross-tabulated with each image. For example, we know from past work that age plays an instrumental role in determining a person's response values. Therefore, always correlate reactions to each of the images. These are typically presented in pie charts or graphs. The responses to the market-based questions indicate what new uses participants want to see and would support in the area. The policy questionnaire provides specific directions for short-term future action and reinforces in words the character of the images.

The questions of what people want places and spaces to look and feel like, based on their demographic profile, have now been answered.

What is most surprising is that there is always a multi-generational consensus regarding the most positive and negative images. A marketing strategy and policies needed for implementation can now be developed using these positive and negative images.

The range of cross-tabulations is virtually unlimited and provides extraordinary information, custom-tailored to the needs and inquiries of each community. Vision results will provide imagery that can be translated into costs and cost benefit analysis to demonstrate to government agencies, municipalities, and corporations the value of a range of investment opportunities. Conversely, it will demonstrate those investments that would be of limited value.

Once the analysis of the images and questionnaire have been completed, the next step is **the synthesis of all the overlays** generated during the VTW. The composite maps from all the teams participating in

Synthesizing the Mapping Input from Multiple Design Teams

Analysis of multiple overlays generated from the VTW. Tacked on the wall are the individual tracings' paper overlay sheets, generated by each team for each design challenge. Response questions include "Where would you put new housing, parks,?" etc. The synthesis goal is to determine the commonalities and distinctions for all the teams.

the VTW are generated through a process of overlays. The synthesis of all overlays for each task in the VTW requires each to be evaluated and transposed to a composite overlay that graphically portrays a collective understanding. Overlays from each team are reviewed separately, with a single clean sheet of trace laid over it on a light table or large backlit glass surface. The overlays from each team are copied using the same colors used in the workshop. This can also be completed by scanning each trace and overlaying them digitally. As each overlay is copied onto the single overlay, a pattern emerges in the thickness and darkness of the lines or the number of times a line was drawn. Here again, it always amazes me that when participants complete the VPS followed by the VTW; **80% of the teams essentially place their graphic responses to positive or negative images in a similar location**. The 20% of the participants in the VTW that don't provide some extraordinary new ideas. Most telling are the maps that capture susceptibility to change. One of the instructions to the team was to use a RED marker, tracing lots and/or buildings that are inappropriate for the location, underutilized, deteriorated, or vacant and thus will most likely be removed for significant new infill and/or redevelopment. As one overlay after another is traced, a clear pattern of areas emerges for those most in need of redevelopment. A consensus vision will emerge for every overlay set. When all overlays have been analyzed and transposed, composite two- and three-dimensional maps emerge.

In an expanding digital age, this technique might seem old-school, but it works amazingly well because of the personal interactions and discussions that occur. It is highly recommended where possible. It is worth all the time and effort, leading to more nuanced and committed recommendations. The time and the process of redrawing the composite map helps in the analysis process and the preparation of final recommendations. As one is completing the synthesis process, the vast amount of energy and brain power, experience, and information that participants have provided is overwhelming, specifically where they want actions to occur and how they "see" their community in the short-term future.

The final composite overlays are then scanned and digitally redrawn. The combination of the composite graphic response with the visuals and the questionnaire generate a range of plans for land use, urban design, preservation, redevelopment, transit, pedestrianism, parking, parks, and open spaces. The vision plans in the form of plans, images, and graphics can be the basis of the master or redevelopment plans. Using these techniques, comprehensive master plans and urban design plans should take months not years, with a significant reduction in costs.

Finally, the combination of the image evaluations, questionnaire responses, and participant generated maps are reviewed in relation to the existing development regulations and market conditions. Specific questions can then be answered, such as **"Are the existing land use and zoning regulations contributing to negative image values, and will they allow the positive images to be implemented?"** This process provides a frank commentary on the appropriateness of the existing regulations and will demonstrate precisely the range of changes that must be made in order to produce the community that citizen's desire.

To achieve implementable results, there must be a consensus for two-, three-, and four-dimensional visions that understand the present and provide a compelling vision of the desired change that people are asking the political and corporate entities, developers, and bankers to finance and implement. The problem, of course, is that most political decisions are made incrementally within a limited elected time span, influenced by those with the most money, personal contacts and influence—in some cases, outright bribes. Political decisions seldom take into consideration the larger, long-range vision. Imposing personal political desires based on greed unfortunately undercuts the enormous strength of the positive preferences of the community and the desired short-term future that could be achieved if politicians would work with the people and champion the vision. The elected official who champions the consensus vision will always be popular and remain in office.

The approach to working together is not just cost-effective, focusing efforts and grants that holistically meet the objectives of a healthy, safer, more sustainable, and affordable short-term future. When the vision is more clearly focused and has a consensus, people can work more effectively together because there is a common goal, a future vision, and support for one another. Participants will leave the VPS and VTW with an image of solutions to land use and site development issues. They may, as a group, continue to advocate for reforms and investments long after mayors and commissioners leave office. This is the major advantage of committed community betterment advocates.

In order to evolve into that positive future, "this is the way we did it in the past" must be substituted for a more holistic planned approach and a belief in humanity's desire to create better rural and urban environments. The group exercise will reinforce the opinions of individuals when they realize that others have similar feelings about the negative and positive images and places, generating a "we can do it better" attitude which will impact political attitudes.

Through this holistic vision, resources will be used more wisely to create healthier, safer, and more compelling places for people to live, work, and play. When the Community Vision process is incorporated into the production of a comprehensive or redevelopment plan that requires a statement of goals and objectives, the resulting images provide visual clarity on the goals.

By understanding the intensity of the visual reactions and the extraordinary amount of information contained in the overlays produced by the participants, politicians, planners, urban designers, and engineers, we can more properly prepare plans and zoning codes for redevelopment and development. When the final video or animated PowerPoint is presented, illustrating the consensus locations for the highest level of change, it generates reinforcement for decisions to rehabilitate or build on the positive vision. A sense of hope and optimism is established.

During the Obama administration, the Center for Disease Control, Public Health Professionals, New Urbanists, American Planning Association, US Department of Housing and Urban Development, US Department of Transportation, and Environmental Protection Agency saw the economic advantage of coordinating visions rather than developing separate ones.

Step Nine

Presentation of the Consensus Plan and Vision

The next step in the process is the preparation of the consensus vision and plan, which is presented back to the community for their critical review. We call this the "Did We Get It Right?" presentation. This session ends by asking the audience for final feedback. The vast majority of the comments are positive, such as **"I am amazed how much you found out about us and were able to capture what we wanted in this community now and in the future."** There are always a few pointing out potential issues that we should further consider. All comments are taken into consideration when the final presentation and report are prepared.

This public presentation uses PowerPoint or video media with a printed brochure or booklet of the most important images to be given to all participants to use as a reference and a reinforcement of their consensus vision. This is important in the conclusion of a Community Visioning process because participants can take it with them as a "thank you for participating" and to show others who did not participate. These visuals –images, maps and photo of the workshops- helps people realize the actual visual, spatial, and policy content of their input. Seeing the results further reinforces their personal vision and gives them a sense of commitment to the collective vison. The more often they see the images and resulting plans, the stronger it is embedded in their brains and the more they become the prime advocates for the plan **because**

it is their vision, and they become advocates for positive change and commitment to see it done.

At the consensus vision presentation, the number of participants and their demographic data is presented first, starting with who participated and how the profile reflects the overall demographic profile of the community. Following the results of the VPS, the presentation focuses first on the most positive image in the survey and then the most positive images in all the categories. With these images, the responses to the related market and policy questions are presented. Only after the positive images have been presented are the negative ones introduced, starting with the most negative and then the most negative-rated images in each of the categories. The category with the most negative image is an area for serious concentration for changes in the short-term future.

Next, the maps synthesized from the VTW are graphically portrayed using various computer graphic programs and presented as overlays, using a single- or multiple-screen format. Where possible, a multiple-screen format is best. As each composite overlay is projected, images from the survey and responses from the questionnaire are used to enhance understanding. As an example, those places designated in red on the susceptibility to change maps are reinforced with the most negative images. They typically indicate the same place. These places are the most depressing and fear-inducing, requiring change. To present opportunities for each site, many of the positive images can be used. The positive images are always keyed to the overlays. The abstraction of a plan is given form with the images. Here is where the most positive responses from the audience in

the form of body language and verbal responses are experienced. The light goes on; they get it!

Specific recommendations and phasing are then presented. To wrap up the presentation, we ask the audience, "Did we get it right?" and to write any comments on a form, which acts our final feedback in the preparation of the final presentation and report. We close by announcing the final date for the final presentation of the vision plan. The audience is invited back for this presentation, which should be more of a "thank you" celebration and an invitation to continue their involvement.

Step Ten

Presentation of the Final Vision Plan and Recommended Form-Based Code

All comments from the "Did we get it right?" presentation are reviewed and incorporated into the final vision plan, report, and presentation. The final Vision Plan summarizes the process in text and images, and includes all synthesized maps and graphics. Not all images are used in the final report and presentation. Those not used are incorporated into a series of appendices. The final products of the process are a report of findings and recommendations with a CD or video.

Vision Plans have a short- and long-term component. Not all of the vision can be implemented at one time. It will be incremental, always moving toward the final vision, which typically has a 10- to 30-year window of opportunity and depends on the market, financial, and political conditions.

Within each visioning plan, generated at the completion of the ten steps, are more inclusive catalytic projects that can be immediately implemented. The construction of these projects will lead to further long-term implementation. It is critical that smaller, cheaper, doable projects that were generated as part of the vision be implemented as soon as possible, providing assurance to participants that their vision was valuable and, more importantly, beginning the civic healing process. In recent years, planners have begun to refer these initial projects as "tactical Urbanism."

The vision contract might also include a draft of a form-based code that can be used to implement the vision. A form-based code typically includes a Street, Transit, and Pedestrian Regulating Plan; a Building Regulating Plan; a Parking Plan; a Landscape/Tree Planting Plan; Architectural Regulations; and a Materials and Details Design Vocabulary. Using the results of the VPS and VTW makes the preparation of this code significantly easier.

After facilitating 397 visioning processes, what is still fascinating to me are the reactions people have seeing what they really want their visual, spatial, and physical environments to look like and their

Upon submission of the final deliverable, we request that the governing body approve a non-binding resolution which supports the vision plan.

transit systems, buildings, landscaping, and public space to feel like as they go through its phases of implementation. When presented, the reactions are positive and hopeful. When this hope for the future is shared, implementation is possible and probable. Once it is acknowledged that this is their vision, participants become the champions of the vision plan they created, their Genius Loci—"the guardians of place." The politics of implementation become easier. The potential of great places is "born." A "WOW" factor might even be generated.

When the positive preferences are presented, including positive preferences for negative places, a healthy spirit of places and spaces emerges, increasing hope that negative and unacceptable physical places can change.

When positive visions are implemented, with negative visions eliminated, property values increase and new jobs, higher incomes, and tax revenues grow.

Pride, safety, and satisfaction will result as people are experiencing implementation of what they really want their visual and spatial environment to look and feel like.

Rendering of Final Synthesized Vision for Bayside, Jersey City, N.J.

The positive visions residing in the minds and memories of participants will guide future community involvement for the betterment of places and spaces.

A rendering of the composite positive preferences for a new neighborhood park synthesized from a VPS and VTW is critical as an end product because renderings live beyond plans.

A Community Visioning Session

It is imperative to state at the onset of the Community Visioning session that "No one knows this community better than you do" and that "you have the vision power to effect change now and in the future." These statements are projected on the screens as a prelude to the workshop. It is also critical to inform the participants of the following:

"Your mind can imagine and envision. It is a powerful force when given the opportunity. We are going to tap into your collective knowledge, desires, imagination and vision. We will meld your individual visions into a collective consensus Community Vision which will be the foundation of the community planning for this area now and for years to come."

The following is a general description of a typical Community Visioning session. This was one of the many visioning sessions held with the public in Overland Park, Kansas; They were held and in multiple places but with similar presentation format.

About 450 people were gathered in a large ballroom of the Overland Park Convention Center. In the front were two large screens and a podium. The space was filled with anticipation and excitement, with everyone seeming to talk at one time. People were seated six to ten at a table. There was an extraordinary range of ages, hairdos, and clothing, from business apparel to jogging suits, from stylish to grungy. Overall, it was a great cross-section of the city.

On the table were large maps, colored markers, sheets of tracing paper, a multi-page questionnaire, No. 2 pencils, and four curious-looking paper forms: one red and the other three blue. The red form looked familiar, while the three blue ones were unusual. They had rows of numbers across them, ranging from +10 through 0, then to –10. People were anxiously reviewing all the items on the table, with the most curiosity paid to the large aerial photograph and the questionnaire. Some people were starting to answer the 80 questions in the Demographic, Market, and Policy questionnaire.

After a salute to the flag, the mayor presented an eloquent introduction: How the city was changing, how it needed a new vision for the future if it was to remain competitive, and how it needed to become an even greater place to live and work. He informed the audience that the city had hired a consultant after a national search and interview process. The city had hired a firm that could facilitate a public participation process that would produce a consensus-based vision plan and generate an implementable future urban design redevelopment plan while providing direction for policy and future economic development opportunities. The city wanted a comprehensive vision that would promote public health and enhance quality of life. A major goal for the city was a consensus "Vision Plan" that would inform their capital improvement plan and attract new residents, jobs, and investment.

The mayor then briefly described how the study area (a 14-mile arterial strip commercial corridor) would be divided into three focus areas for public participation. He followed these remarks by reminding everyone that the input received would be added to the input received from the three other public participation visioning workshops, one from each focus area, along with an online survey for those who could not attend one of the scheduled public sessions. The mayor closed by reminding participants that the preliminary results would be presented for review in four weeks at the convention center in a presentation titled "What the People Want; Results and Recommendations from the Public Participation Process."

I was then introduced to the crowd. It was great to receive a warm welcome and even more important to feel the anticipation and excitement in the room. I began by saying,

"Tonight, during this public meeting, we will generate a consensus vision for the short-term future of this corridor by tapping the collective knowledge, concern and love or discontent you have for places and spaces along the corridor. No one knows this community better than you do, and tonight we are going to tap into that knowledge.

Visioning is a powerful tool and is perhaps the most important of all the human senses, expressing the psychological and emotional feelings that places represent in your mind. We know that images and videos contain the physical manifestation of places photographed at a specific time. We know that images of places can and do generate powerful physical and emotional feelings. It is your positive and negative responses to these images that provide the key to the present and the short-term future planning and design of this corridor."

The Community Vision Planning Process was then introduced. The excited audience was directed to gather the three blue forms and a No. 2 pencil.

In a few minutes we are going to be showing you a series of images on each of two screens simultaneously. Many of these images were photographed in your community and will allow you to evaluate the existing visual and spatial condition of those places. In addition, we will be presenting for your evaluation, images from other places of similar scale and character, along with simulated images of potential changes in the physical character of place using advanced computer modeling, AutoCAD, Sketch-up and Photoshop.

All the images in this Visual Preference Survey were selected after completing exhaustive focus group sessions and interviews. By preparing "before" and simulated "after" potential conditions along the corridor, recommended by focus groups and individual interviews, an understanding of the community's response to these images determines the acceptability or unacceptability of ideas for changes in the physical character.

"With these 'before and after' images, you are also going to be evaluating images from your community as well as images from other communities you might know. Other images in the Visual Preference Survey (VPS) are taken from our extensive library of places. These images encapsulate physical design options that have been built in communities of similar size and character as yours, and could represent visual and spatial options for your community's short-term future. We want to know, how appropriate or inappropriate are these spaces and places now and in the short-term future for this study area in this community? You will be evaluating 120 images in eight related categories typical of your visual and spatial experience of place. We will start with images in the category of Streets and Roads."

I explained,

"Streets and corridors of movement are a city's most important public spaces, where many of the impressions of your city are formed and reinforced. Because we are such a mobile society, most of these places and spaces are experienced by car, but also by the pedestrian when they typically leave the car. These streets, avenues, boulevards, arterials and highways are the bones of any community, adjacent to which the tissue (buildings) are built and which forms most of the spaces we experience. These spaces are dynamic in that

they are perceived in sequence of time as we move through them. To more carefully analyze the specifics of this experience, we will be showing you a series of stop motion images of various 'street' types."

Visual Preference Survey (VPS) portion of the Community Visioning session

The audience sat attentively and quietly, poised with their pencils above the blue form, ready to respond to the first projected image by infilling a numbered dot on the first line, with response numbers ranging from –10 to 0 to +10. The minus numbers from –10 to –1 provided a range of potential negative responses which indicate the intensity of the negative emotional response and inappropriateness participants feel. The plus numbers from +1 to +10 indicate the intensity of the positive emotional response and appropriateness you feel. A "0" meant there is neither a positive

Visual Preference Survey (VPS) Portion of Community Visioning Sessions

Participants looking intensely at an image and determining their positive or negative preferences in a matter of seconds.

nor a negative response. The first image in the Street and Roads Category is projected onto the two large screens. The careful location of the screens and the tables in the room provided everyone with a good view and ease in recording their responses.

I can feel the energy level increase in this convention center room as the VPS images began to be presented. They look, and then it only takes a few seconds for participants to absorb and analyze each image, determining whether it is positive or negative based on their experience and perception. I watched the pencils move either left or right from 0 in absolute fascination as I have so many times. Then comes the momentary pause. Participants are asking themselves, "How positive or negative is it?" Decisions made, values determined, dot filled in, the image fades from the screen, and the next image appears. The room then falls into a silence of concentration as the 120 visual and spatial images or video clips portraying the present community conditions and options for the short-term future appear and fade away. As more and more images fade in and out of the collective consciousness, the group experiences an empowering sense that their positive and negative opinions and feelings are important, and will be incorporated into their community's plan for the short-term future. Many were able, for the first time, to rate a range of places in and for their community. Thus, the vision and hope for the short-term future begins.

At the end of the VPS image presentation, completed blue forms with their range of dots are collected and electronically scanned. If the survey is administered on the Internet, an internal program automatically calculates the mean, mode, median, and standard deviation for each image. Most understandable by participants is the average or mean value and the standard deviation from the average value. For example, if an image received an average of +5 with a standard deviation of 2, the range of values is between +3 and +7. This means that everyone who took the survey thought the image was positive and acceptable. If an image received a 0 with a standard deviation of 5, the range is –5 to +5. People either loved or disliked it, making it a very controversial image. An image with a mean which has a high standard deviation, e.g. 5 to 6, has a broad range of acceptability. When this happens, it is worthwhile to also review the mode and the median; the mode is the response value number which is given to an image most often. The median is the middle of all the values given to an image.

The participant responses provide a value rating of the present visual and spatial conditions as well as potential short-term future form, character, massing, landscaping, and structure. The numerical value generated for each image provides the opportunity to evaluate existing land use plans and zoning ordinances in order to determine the limitations and opportunities for implementing the vision.

It is always shocking to find the number of images of existing conditions in the community that

received negative ratings and were built in conformance with existing zoning.

All the positive and negative values of places presented in this book are the product of nearly 400 public participation visioning sessions in small and large communities, primarily, but not exclusively, in the United States. Those sessions generated over 200,000 survey responses, which have been synthesized. Some of these images have been used at multiple visioning sessions, conferences, academic settings, and seminars. By presenting and determining a larger collective response value to the same images, in different locations, with other participants, reveals the visual and spatial character accepted by more people and therefore could be more easily accepted and applied. As an important note, these collective images have similar positive or negative response values.

The positive or negative numerical values respond to the question "How appropriate or inappropriate is the image or video you are seeing now and in the short-term future for your community?" The values correspond to the emotional feelings people have to the visual and spatial quality of places. This could be interpreted as a measure of well-being. These feelings and emotions are key to community support, modifica-

tion of Master Plans and zoning codes, and what inevitably gets built. But more important is the embedding sense, the mental positive visions of what could be the new reality. For most people, there is a stirring in their souls, a quickening of the heart rate, an emotional lightness or a burst of energy that comes when seeing or experiencing a place that is "well designed." To be **able to quantify this is a glimpse into the soul of urbanism and to understand its short-term and possibly long-term future potential**.

Determining the positive visions from a broad range of people took many years of work, beginning with photographic and psychological fundamentals, and then a labyrinth of techniques and technologies, testing, and field trials. As with most things in life, generating results was a slow process, revealed through observations, deliberation, reading, and employing every evolving advance in projection and computer technology. Through it, there was always a single driving motivation to identify positive images of place that would "stir their souls" and determine ways of replicating the best parts of the desired positive place. Implementation would generate more positive, healthy, sustainable towns and cities for everyone participating in the VPS process.

A completed visioning process can, at the very least, provide a broad framework for the goals and objectives that can be incorporated into any community's long-range Comprehensive Master Plan, a document required by law in most states. The evaluated images can also be employed to illustrate development codes that control what gets built and where.

Public participation is key to short-term future planning and design, providing that it is broad and inclusive, not just the opinions of a few people with agendas who typically show up at public meetings. Nor should future planning and design be imposed from above by politicians and bureaucratic planners, engineers, and architects. **It is important to involve as many people as possible**, including those with the widest ranges of backgrounds, ages, and incomes. Of particular importance is including our younger generations as they are the ones who will inherit the long-term future.

No one knows their community better than those who live, work, and play there.

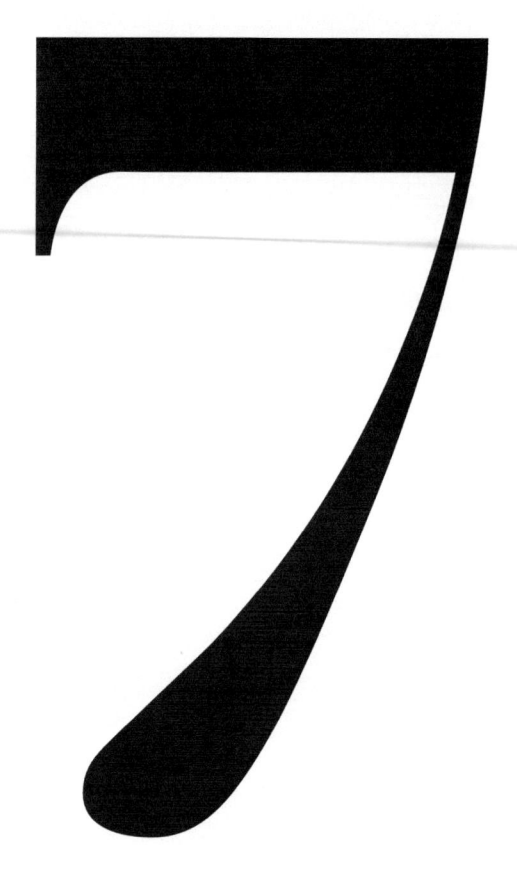

Prologue to the Five Vision Focus Areas

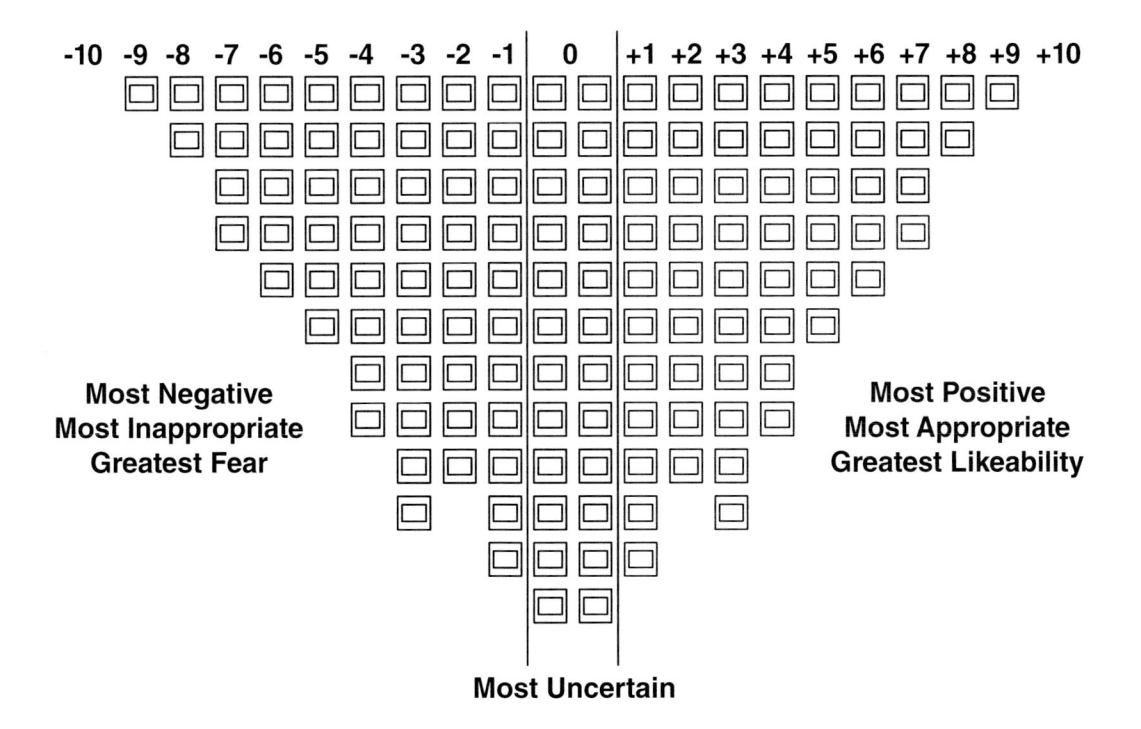

Five areas for future place making were selected for this book. Positive and negative visions for each, with their numerical responses values and recommended policies, are presented. The collective response values determined the visual, spatial, and emotional character of what each participant wanted as well as what they despised. The planning and design recommendations generated from the Vision Translation workshops formulated a conceptual urban design and mobility diagram for future growth and development.

[One area of concern cut from the book was Visions for Cities Susceptible to Flooding.]

Since the advent of the Community Visioning technique in 1973, the most insightful images, policies, and recommendations in this book have been generated from 400 Community Visioning sessions. Value-rated images and policies were generated for natural, rural, and suburban land areas as well as small towns and cores of large cities. An estimated 20,000 images have been preference tested over a broad geography of locations. Representative images have been selected to best portray what people want and feel is the most acceptable and unacceptable for place making and future land use.

Each Visual Preference Survey (VPS) is divided into a minimum of nine vision categories for each of the vision focus areas, including:

- Street, Roads, Thoroughfares
- Housing types
- Non-residential building types
- Pedestrian realms
- Parking
- Parks, Plazas, and Open spaces,
- Mobility and Transit
- Signage
- Civic, Institutional, and Industrial

Each category is further sub-divided. For example, housing can include low-, medium-, and high-rise building types. Non-residential buildings can include ranges of office types as well as mixed-use buildings, etc.

Included in each VPS category are images of places and spaces that have been evaluated in multiple surveys, thereby allowing evaluation of the reactions to these images across a broad cross-section of people at various locations over time. For example, images of ubiquitous arterial commercial sprawl and classic attached multifamily housing types have been value preferenced in most VPSs. Most of these place images elicit similar reactions because the underlying zoning is similar, if not identical.

The most positive and negative images in each vision category were incorporate into future recommendations used to create illustrated codes and site plans. A form-based code is a set of development regulations that can generate predictability in the urban form. The images of positive places and spaces make the code more understandable. Positive images can be incorporated into the goals and objectives of Master Plans, and visions for scenario planning. It is important to note that most zoning ordinances for the five focus areas do

not include images, which would make the ordinances more understandable.

The ups and downs of the financial markets have been and will continue to be challenging to the implementation of the desired preferences for the five focus areas. History has proven that vision preferences can withstand these fluctuations because they have long historical and universal human appeal if nurtured in the public consciousness. Response-evaluated simulations can illustrate how a negative place in any of the categories can be transformed into a positive place.

East. Riverside Suburban Corridor, Austin, Texas

The Community Vision process used the before image above; top to design the desired image of the future on the bottom for this suburban corridor. The visual and spatial character of the buildings and transit were generated from the results of the Community Visioning process.

Harvard economist Edward Glaeser wrote,

> ## "Land use controls have a more widespread impact on the lives of ordinary Americans than any other regulation."

Generating positive preferences in each of the vision categories and for each of the focus areas, with all their interrelated categories, is the ideal basis for new appropriate land use controls.

Most of the positive images have the highest response values and therefore the most demanded visual and spatial characteristics. The visual qualities, densities, and environmental conditions are physical guides for professionals, providing attributes that can be analyzed for their two, three- and four-dimensional context, translated into Land Use and Urban Design Plans, then codified in zoning and/or form-based codes.

Five Vision Focus Areas

The desired visions for these focus areas primarily used the results of Community Visioning sessions in Maryland, Montana, New Jersey, Kansas, Florida, and Connecticut.

Vision Preferences for Natural Areas

There are very high positive response values for natural areas in all surveys. This is one land use where there is little deviation. The primary recommendation is preservation.

Vision Preferences for Rural Areas

This includes positive recommendations for land use, building form morphology, thoroughfares, road edges, rural clusters, rural/agricultural hamlets, and Transfer of Development Rights (TDR). It also includes images of what must not be built in rural areas in the future, including small lot residential single- and multifamily subdivisions and highway strip commercial.

Vision Preferences for Suburbia

The positive and negative visions for this area used locations in Kansas, Florida, Maryland, and New Jersey, and includes positive response images of building form morphology, suburban residential streets, suburban parks and green spaces, and suburban commercial streets and their possible transformation. Two case studies are presented in more detail, including the Robbinsville Town Center in Mercer County, New Jersey, which went from visioning to implementation and Overland Park, Kansas, which used visioning to prepare a redevelopment plan for a long central corridor.

Vision Preferences for Small Towns

This category used the four focus areas of Metuchen and Collingswood, New Jersey; Binghamton, New York; and Oshkosh, Wisconsin. The comprehensive vision for these locations set a standard for small towns in the future and overlap to some extent with recommendations for the cores of larger cities and nodes in suburban areas.

Vision Preferences for Cores of Large Cities

This category is the most extensive, using three focus areas, including the Downtown Plan for Milwaukee, Wisconsin; Midtown, Atlanta (which went through the visioning process twice); and Journal Square, Jersey City, New Jersey.

People's response reactions to places, spaces, and land uses are valuable data sets when beginning to plan, design, and redevelop places and spaces. Participants know their location best and have proven to generate wonderful ideas, plans, and concepts if and when given the opportunity. Your citizens can give you the positive vision to guild future zoning regulations and development for every focus area. When there are negative reactions to places and spaces from the vast majority of participants, take this seriously. Mental and physical health and welfare are at stake, as is future sustainability and economic viability. You, the planning professionals or commission members, should consider incorporating the Community Visioning process into the request for proposals for your next town planning or redevelopment effort. Involve your citizens. Then use the resulting value-rated images and the results of the Vision Translation Workshop to enhance development scenarios. Next, modify and amend your land use, master plans, and building codes. Seriously consider using the conceptual urban design and mobility diagram as an overlay for future growth and development.

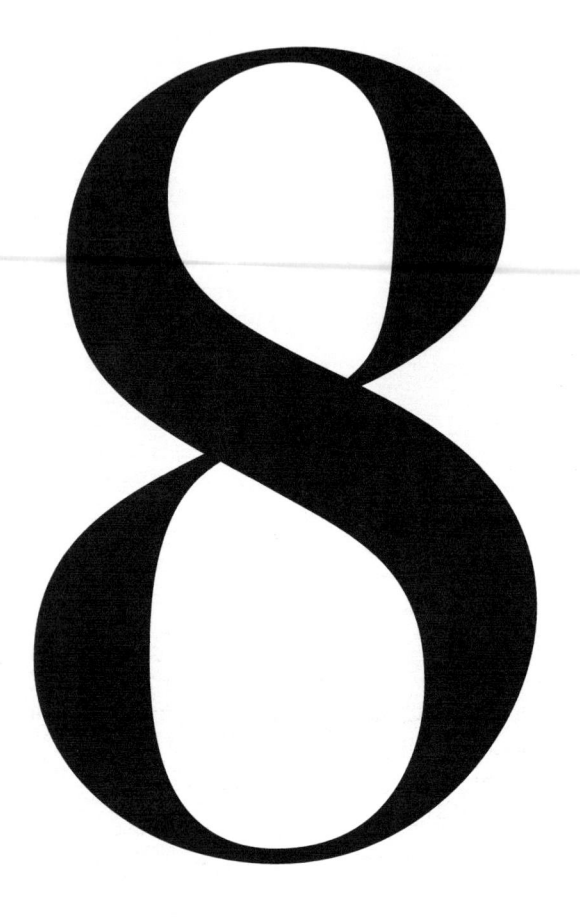

Vision for Natural Landscapes

The Importance of Preserving Natural Places and Spaces

Natural areas have consistently received the highest positive response values in all Visual Preference Surveys (VPSs). These are places important to human and animal species. These areas are now, and have always been, fundamental to our evolution. They are inherent in the DNA and the mind of all species. It is imperative that existing natural areas be protected from development and respected for production of food, water, and oxygen; carbon sequestering; and their calming influence on humans and prorogation of animal, insect, and plant species. These areas include lakes, rivers, ponds, streams, brooks, wetlands, forests, and flood-prone areas, and the adjacent lands currently not considered environmentally sensitive, but which have critical import for human and animal habitation. These need to be protected, meaning that development should be restricted to specific distances from their borders.

and visually and physically appropriate, now and into the future. The intensity of the response tells us that natural areas must be preserved.

Not all VPS locations had natural areas within the focus area, although most contained "green" areas to be preserved, such as parks, wetlands, ponds and a variety of waterways. Nature in all its forms, be this roof gardens or street trees, is highly respected, with high average positive responses and low standard deviations. These urban and rural natural areas are critical to the ecological network and must be protected and enlarged, while new ones are designed, engineered and planted.

The selected images of natural areas represent the essence, characteristics, and qualities that most everyone finds emotionally positive,

The following images are some of the most highly preferred places and spaces in this focus area. For all of the images, the response value

is presented as the average collective value, and the standard deviation is shown with the (). For each image, there are design comments and a summary of the emotional response.

Comment and Design Response

All parks and "green" spaces, like creeks, streams, ponds, and wetlands, within urban and suburban areas, and small towns must be protested and enhanced. Mapping using Geographic Information System (GIS) is the most appropriate graphic technique to determine location and size of all these natural areas.

Some municipalities have a deficit of parks and green spaces. In such cases, new spaces need to be designed as a complement to future development or redevelopment.

Response Value +8(2)

Seashore Beach

View of a long flat beach on the ocean as the tide is coming in.

Comment and Design Response

Clean open seashores with long beaches and rolling waves are cherished places. This is the power of the long horizontal line, experienced along the edges of large bodies of water, no matter where they are located on the planet. A human looking over the water is a one (vertical dimension) to infinity (horizontal dimension) experience, which is one of the most powerful of the

Response Value +9(1)

Green Urban Park

This park is one of the most positive images in all VPSs. This park is available within short walking distance of adjacent residential homes. The large pond and its landscaped edge, mature trees, and lawn areas make it beloved by all! It brings happiness, joy, and pride of place.

spatial senses. Humans have a strong affinity with the sea because it is thought that we, as humans, emerged from salt water, which is now present in our bodies' tears and sweat. With a projected rise in sea level, seashores and beaches must be preserved and protected, keeping development well behind berms and dunes above the high-water lines projected based on future storms and sea level rise. These areas should remain in the public domain, undeveloped. They are an important emotional resource that people need to experience forever.

Emotional response: Beautiful, powerful, and loved. This place type is highly respected. It brings happiness and joy.

but, perhaps more importantly, for the ability of humans today and tomorrow to experience unspoiled nature, which becomes more precious in our growing and developing planet. Incorporating these into green and blue acres, natural parks, and reserves is the right course of action. When combined with both satellite and Lydar data, current Geographic Information Systems (GIS) are now able to accurately map such areas. These are the maximum preservation areas with buffers that are not suitable to be built upon ever!

Emotional response: Beautiful, powerful, and loved. There is hope that it will remain in this condition.

Response Value +8(2)

Response Value +8(2)

River with Marshland Edges

The varying marsh edge is perhaps more important than the lake. It is an ecological imperative for species propagation and water purification.

Wetlands and Marshland

View across existing wetlands and marshes.

Comment and design response: This river, with its marshlands, received high value responses. The area has no visible development, which increases its value. Preservation of these wetlands and restrictions on development are critical not only for ecological reasons

Comment and design response: Marshes and wetlands are the "lungs of the planet," where fish spawn and grow, and where water and air are purified. Maintaining these wetlands is critical for the habitable future of the planet. No development should be allowed in or within specific distances from their borders. They must be protected from encroachment and pollution forever. The values given to these natural landscapes are the highest in all surveys. These places reach the highest emotional response. Might our responses emerge from some deep-seated memory of our evolution?

Emotional response: Beautiful, peaceful, almost a religious experience, nature at its best. The area generates a sense of pride. It is considered a precious resource by all participants. There is a sense of hopefulness that it will remain in its current condition.

Response Value +6(5)

Creek, Stream, or Brook in a Forest setting
View of a natural creek or brook in a forest.

Comment and design response: Streams transport surface and groundwater to large bodies of water and, in certain locations, to the sea. They are interconnected in a hierarchy of waterways. Pollution by any source and in any location along the network of streams and creeks must be restricted. Streams and creeks typically have different types and depths of wetlands on their periphery at various distance from the

border of the river, stream or creek areas for fish, provide habitats and water to wildlife, and act as movement corridors for wildlife. This type of stream is dynamic. In times of heavy rainfall, the width and depth of the waterway increases. In most locations, new development must be restricted to provide a buffer zone from the banks, and places that repeatedly flood must be preserved. All public and private land with streams must be mapped with their wetlands and the appropriate buffer applied. The natural wooded areas through which they flow must also be considered important resources which provide habitats for wildlife and are essential in the food chain, providing oxygen and absorbing carbon dioxide. Pollution by any source and in any location along the network of streams and creeks must be restricted.

Emotional response: Although it is responded to positively by all participants, the emotional value is less, because it is less visually cared for. Raw nature scares some people.

Response Value +8(2)

Lake
View of a small lake with no surrounding development.

Comment and design response: Lakes are so positively regarded that development commonly occupies their edges. In this image, there is no development or septic fields on the lakes' edges. Maintaining these lakes with their green borders is critical. They must be protected from encroachment and pollution forever. Within the hinterlands of urban areas, there are few of these left. Look, but don't develop on the remaining edges.

Emotional response: Beautiful, peaceful, almost a religious experience, nature at its best. Lakes are considered a precious resource by all participants. The values given to these natural landscapes are the highest in all surveys. These places reach the highest emotional response of joy and happiness, with a sense of pride. Does this emerge from some deep-seated memory of our evolution, which, if destroyed or polluted, destroys part of us? In order to use these positive images of natural areas in a Vision Translation Workshop (VTW) for a region or a township, participants are asked to color these areas green, meaning no development. This is readily understood, although the size and depth of the buffer areas surrounding these natural areas are not. Their location and size can now be easily coordinated with GIS mapping.

Summary and Planning Policies for Natural Landscapes

- **In all VPSs, natural landscapes are evaluated as very positive.**
- **People are beginning to understand the importance of these natural systems.**
- **Natural landscapes, including beaches, ponds, lakes and wetlands, rivers, streams, creeks, and brooks, and the buffer areas surrounding them—like forests and areas of intensive tree cover—must be protected from development and treated as an ecological imperative. We must preserve and cherish what we have left.**
- **All natural areas in rural and suburban areas, including parks and green areas in urban locales, must be mapped into a continuous network. Additional natural green areas must be provided as populations grow. The planning, engineering, and design of all future growth must occur outside the buffer zones surrounding natural landscape resources.**

9

Visions for Rural Lands

The Importance of Preservation and Agricultural Production

There will be continuous pressure to build on rural areas. The question is what should be built? In what form? The positive images generated from the Community Visioning sessions indicate the types of development that would be acceptable and that have a positive public perception. Based on the response values to images for rural areas, it is also very clear **what should not be built**.

In most counties in the US, there are vast amounts of undeveloped, vacant, and farmed parcels zoned for building. Land suitable for agricultural production on Class I and II soils, which is found on all US agricultural soil maps from each county, **should not be used for future residential and commercial growth until all vacant urban and leftover suburban lands are utilized**. In urban areas alone, there are large amounts of underutilized and deteriorating buildings, vacant land, surface parking lots, and storage that can and should be infilled at a vertical urban scale and density before valuable agricultural soil and functioning farm lands are built upon. All remaining vacant and underutilized land areas, not environmentally sensitive, located between and among haphazard and leapfrogged suburban sprawl development, with it's incoherent fragmented pattern of land uses, could be infilled, when needed, either to complete a neighborhood or with small organic farms. Active farmland and its rural visual and spatial characteristics are highly valued by all participants.

Local food production is becoming more important in order to feed growing populations worldwide. More local healthy food is produced on small organic farms and in greenhouses. Unfortunately, agribusiness and suburban developments have consumed many of the traditional small farms that were able to produce more natural organic food. Ironically, the small farms and agricultural hamlets which would encourage more local farming have been restricted by current zoning. When long-term cost-benefit analysis is conducted, the costs of sprawl and the loss of existing farmland, food production, and local jobs are enormous.

The small farm has given way to larger, more mechanized, and robotic farming. Agribusiness needs vast amounts of land and extensive amounts of genetically modified seeds, chemicals, and water in order to produce corn, wheat, soybeans, fruits and vegetables, animals, etc.—the staples of most diets. But there are inefficiencies and disparities. The vegetables and fruits we consume travel great distances—thousands of miles, in fact—before they are consumed. In the US, agribusiness means that there is abundant food production and surplus. Supermarkets are typically huge and well stocked. Despite this, there are food deserts, food swamps and malnutrition in too many urban and rural areas as a result of poverty, lack of profitable market, and lack of empathy.

Any development that is built on rural land must complement agricultural production, not diminish it. Quality soils should be planned and designed for food production and for the correct types of habitat for those who live, work and manage the land. The responses from all our vision sessions suggest that large residential and commercial subdivisions must be restricted on such productive parcels and zoned primarily for food production. Zoning must be changed to allow small agricultural hamlets and villages where people can live and devote their land to agricultural production, distribution, and ecomanagement, while enjoying the rural lifestyle.

The following images from the agricultural/ rural focus area were selected from numerous Community Visioning sessions. They represent the essence, character, and qualities that most everyone finds emotionally positive or negative, and visually and physically appropriate or inappropriate, now and in the future.

The Most Negative Images

Generate a depressing feeling, with a sense of hopelessness, as farmland is transformed into suburban sprawl.

Response Value –7(3)

Cul-de-Sac on Farmland

This negative image of a "leap frog" subdivision is typical of sprawl. The layout is considered negative and unacceptable by all except the farmer who sold the land and those who purchased the houses. The new houses are built on 1/2- to 3/4-acre lots on former productive farmland, located in the middle of the countryside on two overly wide cul-de-sac streets attached to a narrow rural road. There is no sense of community, no common space, and no services, with every house on its own septic and completely auto-dependent. There is not a garden plot to be seen. The farmstead with its barns and house can still be seen on the right of the image. All surrounding fields are zoned for more of the same auto-dependent sprawl. The number of homes allowed under this zoning could have been transferred from this area as a "sending zone" to a "receiving zone" using Transfer of Development Rights (TDR) or redesigned as an Agricultural Hamlet.

Comment and design response: Standard suburban sprawl on cul-de-sacs built on farmland zoned for suburban development receives negative ratings in all surveys. The most ubiquitous layout of subdivisions includes curvilinear and cul-de-sac streets. Suburban residential subdivisions focus on the privatization of green areas (lawns) and the layout of as many private lots as possible. Every house is set back with front, side, and rear yards. Everyone has their own lawn. There are no shared public spaces except the access road. Every bit of land is plotted off for lots and built on, except for fenced-off retention areas, when required, and when wetlands are preserved. The layout maximizes the number of houses within the prescribed regulations for lot size but fails to take into account that there is nothing to walk to; it further lacks any sense of community, or public space, and has only privatized yards and lawns. This zoning misses the opportunity for homes to become a rural community in the form of a hamlet or village.

Comment and design response: This suburban "cul-de-sac" morphology arose from the 1928 plan for Radburn—"a community for the motor age"—with its cul-de-sacs off a loop street, its design focusing on and accessible to a large central community park. Every house had direct access to the park. Everyone could walk to the school, shopping, and train station through that park without having to cross a street. Although highly desirable and loved, the Radburn Plan was

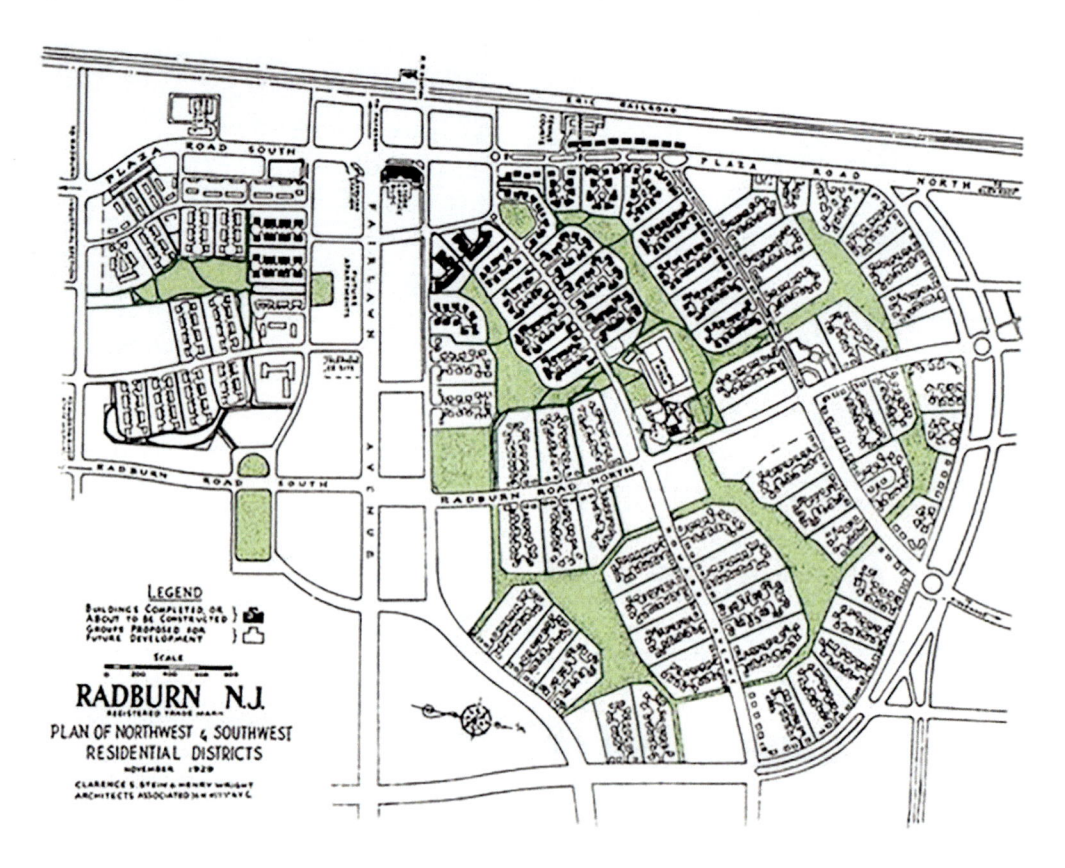

Plan of Radburn

Each house has immediate access via footpaths to a sequential network of open spaces, shown in green. This was the proper use of the cul-de-sac.

seldom emulated beyond its cul-de-sac. All the other excellent design features were eliminated to maximize the number of lots as prescribed by zoning. Instead of public lands that could be used by all residents, the standard subdivision plan privatizes all the lands except for the streets; even some of these are privatized, with many subdivisions being gated.

Programmed suburban living includes a private lot; a large house with a two or more-car garage; and a public local access road, many times surrounded by farmland, that is, until the next subdivision. The location makes these units completely dependent on private cars. It lacks any public open spaces, sidewalks leading to public parks, a center focus, mix of units, or transit services. The location, layout and design portrays the essence of individualism, a "housing product" for people who in earlier generations might have grown up on farms or in housing in more classic suburbia or small towns. Have they been programmed to want a large house, on a large lot, on a cul-de-sac, complying with peer pressure and relentless marketing? Or do they just choose this due to limited availability of alternatives? Or, is it the desire to have a "near castle" to reflect their status of wealth and accomplishment?

Too much rural land is currently zoned for subdivisions of three to five acres. Under this land use policy, lots of this size do not preserve the rural character. Small lots produce more revenues for farmers/landholders and taxes for municipalities, which continue to increase because of more children per acre and maintenance costs. The minimum size lot for farming or gardening is six acres; this would qualify the lot for a tax

break, provided it produces a small revenue from the products grown on it. Three *and four acre* lots are an illusion. Most times, the land is kept in landscaped lawns or flower beds, or a very small portion is left in its natural condition. Typically, food is not produced, and the rural character is destroyed. Maintenance costs and the use of chemicals degrade the environment and pollute surface groundwaters and local creeks and streams. Lawn runoff contributes to stream flooding, and lawn fertilizers contaminate farm, private, and town wells.

Farmland Preservation Zoning, TDR, rural clustering, and encouragements for young farmers are all mechanisms generated through Community Visioning that must be implemented on those lands that have previously been improperly zoned. What makes this land more attractive is the growing demand for more organically grown food close to urban areas: The "farm to table" movement. The increasing in interest in smaller farms is amazing. People go to pick apples and strawberries, and belong to farm co-ops for their vegetables and flowers. Farm stands and markets are now present in many towns, representing an explosion of interest in agricultural pursuits.

We have tested the change in response values when the land is subdivided at multiple Visioning Sessions. The response is always the same: Negative and unacceptable. The farmer's desire to sell the land is understandable as it is his or her retirement income. The land's value is dependent on the underlying zoning which allows the number of lots on the land to be laid out in one or more subdivisions. Division into a typical subdivision housing layout is the worst possible option now and in the future. There are alternatives.

Once streets and structures are built, the town can never again reclaim this valuable farmland. However, when farmland has been zoned, but not yet built, there is still an opportunity to preserve agriculture and satisfy the "ill-gotten gain" for the landowner through TDR.

Comment and design response: To determine participants' response to development on farmland, a series of simulations was prepared in each of the towns where there was excess zoning for sprawled single-family subdivisions on smaller lots. We used the previous image as the base image and tested the responses to it. The value was +6, with a standard deviation of 3, placing it in a range of +9 to +3. Everyone responded positively, despite the deteriorated condition of the farmstead. Vast, open rolling land is a visual and spatial character that everyone responds to positively.

Response Value –5(3)

A Simulation of a Proposed First Phase of a Subdivision on the Farm with Cultivated Fields

This simulation portrays land partially developed into single family lots, based on the underlying suburban zoning.

Response Value +6(3)

Farm with Cultivated Fields

This image portrays the existing farmland and fields with a farmstead and structures evolving into a slow state of deterioration.

Comment and design response: Above is the first phase of the subdivisions with more to come because all the land is zoned for sprawl. The response value drops 11 points from +6 to –5, with a standard deviation of 3, generating a range of –8 to –2, which is an extraordinary drop! Everyone feels that this is unacceptable; it violates something that is considered important by most people. Negative values are generated in every VPS where the early evolution of sprawl is presented for evaluation.

It was stated earlier that the farmland was initially zoned inappropriately, and now the farmer/ landowner has come to rely on it as their retirement income. There are alternatives, including TDR, agricultural clustering/ hamlets, small farms, or a combination of the three. TDR allows the landowner to negotiate with a developer to buy/transfer the number of units zoned for the site to another location (a village or agricultural hamlet) and preserve the land for farming. Downzoning to three- to four-acre lots is not acceptable. Rezoning for small farms of 10 to 20 acres might be acceptable.

Response Value –4(6)

Ground Level View of Standard Subdivision

Pedestrian view of new suburban subdivision with garage frontages used in the National Association of Realtors Random National Visual Preference Survey.

Comment and design response: A national Visual Preference Survey (VPS) was com- missioned to determine Americans' response to a range of images of developing land uses. Surveys were conducted in multiple locations across the country, and the results were published by the National Association of Realtors in their monthly magazine. Many of the same images are used in this book. Others, reflecting similar response values, were generated in the other commissioned vision surveys. As viewed from a car or as a pedestrian, most new subdivisions generate negative responses. The previous image contains features of suburban, low-density, residential sub-divisions that people find inappropriate and negative. This image represents a subdivision of similar single-family homes of consistent building form, color scheme, double-door garage fronts, large and wide concrete aprons, and wide streets with few landscaping features and no trees. The street in this subdivision is excessively wide. There is a minimum of planting on each lot, with sidewalks only on one side. This image received a –4, a large standard deviation with a range of –10 to +1. This indicates that most participants gave it a negative response value, with only a few rating it barely positive. Nonetheless, it is unacceptable in this form and character. In too many places, it is the only permitted lot and street option based on existing zoning and engineering standards. The zoning requires this level of standardization and monotony. But it gets worse!

Emotional response: Depressing sameness in a car-oriented development pattern. It says, "cars live here not people."

Townhouse Development in the Countryside

Townhouses in a rural setting were also tested during the National Association of Realtors Random National Visual Preference Survey and in many other surveys.

Comment and design response: This subdivision of townhouses built on former farmland received one of lowest, most unacceptable responses in all national surveys. The townhouses here are isolated, at best functional and value engineered. There is no charm or visual beauty. They have a consistent building form, color scheme, and on-grade parking in front. The response value of –7, with a range of –10 to –4, is a clear indication of their unacceptability. But they sell. In most cases, there is no alternative design, and unfortunately, too many zoning ordinances and subdivision regulations require and promote this form of development. Or, development approval might have been granted through a waiver of zoning through a Board of Adjustment variance, or, in the worst case, with a substantial political contribution to one or more politicians. Townhouses belong in a town, a town center or a village. It t is inappropriate to build them on rural lands. Housing of this density requires that they be part of a village or town center where services are within walking distance. Being inexpensive is not an excuse for unattractive and dysfunctional land use.

Emotional response: Depressing, hopeless, last-resort housing, ugly, and misplaced.

Images of rolling farmland always receive positive responses, despite the deteriorating condition of an inactive farmstead. The lack of maintenance of the buildings is a sure sign of stagnant economic conditions and changing reality for farms and farmlands. Many have been purchased and agglomerated into larger agribusiness land holdings waiting for the opportunity to subdivide. Existing farmsteads deteriorate because they no longer have a functional use. Their real economic value is the underlying zoning, which allows them to be subdivided into residential or commercial lots.

There is nothing visually or spatially redeeming about a farm being cut up into individual small lots on cu-de-sacs or townhouse developments. Some individuals who purchased their "American dream" next to farmland have temporary views of the open fields. These new home owners will experience discontent in the future as the farmer works the fields around them, or when more adjoining subdivisions are built. If the adjacent land is to remain in agricultural/farming, then it is highly recommended at a municipality adopt the "right to farm act" to prevent new residents from complaining and trying to terminate or eliminate the adjacent small dairy and vegetable farms.

TDR is also recommended.

Comment and design response: If farmland was zoned for subdivision years ago, many farm owners believe that their land will be sold and subdivided. Using the land for food production distributed by local or regional markets is ideal but may not be financially viable until there is a growing demand for fresh fruits and vegetables, and range-grown animals with enough production workers; this will make it more viable and attractive for young farmers. Techniques such as TDR and Agricultural Hamlets could retain much of the food producing farmland and provide a revenue to farmers, while maintaining the well respected rural character. Much of this allure is based on our hunter-gatherer still residing in our memories.

Emotional response: Connects us to our past; sense of wonder, respect, and beauty.

Cluster of Farm Building Surrounded by Fields

Response Value +7(3)

Open Farm Field with Hay Bales

This is a timeless image of the rural character. Here, one experiences a recently hayed field receding to a pond and trees framed by rolling hills. The farm is still viable. No developer houses are present.

Response Value +7(4)

Farm Surrounded by Fields

Working farm. This grouping of farm buildings—house, barn, silos, and outbuildings—forms a perfect cluster within a grove of trees. This image reinforces the early VPS responses.

Comment and design response: This is an ideal form for future agricultural hamlets. The white-painted buildings are in stark contrast to the darker-colored landscape of fields, edged by forests. The land is flat, a powerful, long, horizontal line ideal for farming. Based on response values, preservation of agricultural land on the periphery of urbanization is highly recommended. When these lands are developed into standard subdivisions, more of our positive relationship to the land and our agricultural past is diminished, including our sense of wonder and respect for farming. Because **there are vast amounts of undeveloped and underdeveloped land uses in urban and suburban areas, productive farmland need never be built on for new growth**.

Emotional response: This image responds to our natural and past agricultural programming.

Farmland in Spring and Winter

Do people value farmland differently in the spring and summer or fall and winter? This is one of the questions that the Connecticut Region Organizations of Governments and other rural municipalities wanted answered. The Community Visioning Process wanted to test whether the time of year made any significant difference in response values.

Response Value +7(4)

Spring field
Farmland in the spring and early summer with fresh green.

Response Value +7(4)

Fall and Winter Field
Farmland in the fall with brown and winter colors.

Comment and design response: The above images of farmland during two seasons received identical values, as generated by surveys conducted in multiple municipalities. There is a great visual and emotional appreciation of land that is open with no development present at any time of the year. Operating farms represents a limited cost to local taxpayers in comparison to three- and four-bedroom homes on three-acre lots with several school-aged children, posing additional demands on roadways and municipal services. Every effort must be made to preserve the farmland's character and economic vitality. Zoning for agricultural TDR and land preservation bond issues must be employed to keep farmland viable. Non-developed open land with views of nature and farmlands are always positive, perhaps awakening memories of our past.

Emotional response: Connects us to the seasons; sense of wonder, openness, and beauty. They engender happiness and hopefulness.

RESPONSE VALUE +6(5)

Active Farmland with Livestock

Cows grazing on open pasture land with a new farmhouse in background. Ideally a rural estate. This vision was used in multiple surveys, including the National Association of Realtors Random National Visual Preference Survey.

Comment and design response: When the above image was chosen, participants were asked "how the presence of farm animals, with the assumed associated smells and sounds, would impact the response value." Response values are slightly lower than agricultural images with no animals but are still very high and positive. Animal protein, produced by animals that are allowed to roam on fields of grass (not in feed lots), combined with fruits and vegetables, have been a staple of the human diet for the last 2,000,000 years and must be integrated into the land use pattern

by zoning for a range of agricultural land uses. Quality beef animals require many acres of grass land and a source of water. Land values should reflect this need and be zoned for such uses. The key to future control is to increase the demand for farm products while reducing the market demand for sprawled development. This can only be done by providing land use alternatives and education.

Emotional response: Sense of openness, hopefulness, freedom, healthy food source.

Strip Commercial in Rural Areas

The most defining visual and spatial characteristic of sprawl is what is seen along commercial arterials, edged with low-scale retail, front yard parking lots, and individual large signs for each establishment. Located along multi-lane roadways, images of strip commercial development are universally value rated as negative, unless they are extensively landscaped. People who live in sprawl have to drive on arterials lined with these ubiquitous strip commercial developments (plazas and malls) before they arrive on their local street, cul-de-sac, and their subdivided single-family home or townhome development. This land use form is completely based on access via the private automobile and the dominance of required parking. It seems to be ingrained in the current "American consciousness" due to generations of exposure to it and the seeming plethora of affordable fuel and cars. The view from the windshield driving along these arterials is negative but the response becomes even more negative when one arrives at one's destination's parking lot.

Strip Commercial on an Arterial Highway

This arterial with its ubiquitous strip commercial developments on both sides, was tested in multiple surveys, including the National Association of Realtors Random National Visual Preference Survey. It consistently generates a negative range from –10 to –1. It is unacceptable by everyone's standards. It is a direct result of our increasingly auto-dominant cultural epidemic. Along most highways there are increasing numbers of vacant strip centers and regional malls, all with huge parking lots, slowly deteriorating. A concentrated mixed-use center is the preferred alternative, based on Community Visioning. Suburban retail is currently waning due to the internet and home delivery.

Comment and design response: After leaving the local streets, you turn onto an arterial like the one shown above, which is a major connector to a highway. It is characteristic of all arterials that intersect highways. All are zoned for strip commercial development. The road design has multiple traffic lanes; large signs that can be seen at 65 miles per hour; and one-story buildings fronting onto large, typically un-landscaped surface parking lots. The response value would have been even lower, had such a setting been photographed with traffic backed up during rush hours, which is normal near intersections with highways. This image continues to reinforce the negative emotional responses to this type of development. Currently, these uses continue to be constructed because they are allowed and encouraged by zoning. The land is cheap, infrastructure is provided, there is a flow of passing

cars, and such use yield property and state taxes. Everyone dislikes it but has no choice if they live in suburbia. To the question **"Should your township encourage strip commercial development along its major roadways?"**, the typical "No" response ranges from 82% to 92% of participants.

Emotional response: Depressing. Ugly, chaotic, inhumane and stress-inducing, and environmentally destructive.

Surface Parking Lot

Mostly empty parking lot (field) in front of a strip mall is ubiquitous. The negative responses range from –10 to –4.

Comment and design response: This parking lot is typical of most suburban strip commercial developments that are now only partially occupied and marginally used. Only a small number of cars now use this parking lot. It is empty most of the time. If the view from the car on the highway is not negative enough; response values drop even lower when participants approach or are in the parking lot. Empty parking lots indicate that business in the strip mall is bad, and perhaps many retail spaces are marginal, empty, or for rent. Clearly, the standards for parking space per thousand square foot of commercial property, as required by zoning, is way too high. We know that people dislike searching for a parking space and don't want to walk too far, but this does not justify what is seen and the negative emotional response it generates. Have people become conditioned to this ugliness and inefficiency, accepting it as part of the suburban car-oriented programming? The response suggests not. This parking lot and buildings are likely candidates for redevelopment.

Emotional response: Depressing, ugly, sad, and fear-inducing Ready for a serious makeover. People want another choice.

Four Options for Deteriorating Commercial Strips in Rural Areas

1. Wait and see. "It's paid for, and I can hold it for a while until the market turns." Unfortunately, retail is over-programmed, and new internet shopping is becoming more mainstream. You might have to wait a long time.
2. Search for new marginal tenants to use the space "as is." Possibly dress up the facades and add landscaping, including shade trees and flowering shrubs, which will improve its response value for a better-paying tenant. This will propagate the continued stress of auto-dependent sprawl and prolong its life a few more years.
3. Demolish most if not all existing buildings. Build a new mixed-use neighborhood. Infill with multi-story buildings on a grid of streets over the parking lots with a balance of housing, businesses, civic and social uses, parks, and other natural open spaces.

4. Because these buildings were typically cheaply constructed, designed to last only a generation or two, when deteriorated or vacant, tear it down and let it return to nature until the land is needed or use it as a solar farm or actual food production / processing facility. Some have recommended that the roof may be as or more valuable than the inside of the building for greenhouses, food production or solar installation.

Unfortunately, #1 is the most typical reaction.

Questions Regarding the Character of Roads in Rural Areas

- What road designs would people like to experience in rural areas or land zoned for rural uses?
- What are the appropriate and desired widths and edges?
- Is there a hierarchy of rural thoroughfares from widest to the narrowest (width, edges) that is appropriate?
- What are the primary visual characteristics?

Desired Road Types and Character

Thoroughfares in rural areas are called **ROADS**, which are distinguished from **STREETS** in urban areas. The two should not be confused. Roads are vehicular routes that pass through and service rural areas that have no sidewalks, perhaps with streetlighting at important intersections. Some are narrow, and others are wider because they serve a more regional need. The paved cartway is typically crowned, with surface water running in side ditches. Shoulders are narrow or non-existent, sometimes with a bike lane. There are farms, large lot rural fencing, fields, or forests on the edge, or a combination of all three.

Response Value +7(4)

County Highway through a Rural Area

This rural arterial received high response values from the Community Visioning process in Worcester County, Maryland, and other surveys. It has the capacity to accommodate a large flow of traffic while providing a pleasant, positive driving experience. This is an ideal rural arterial road. This is the widest road people want in rural areas. The edges are tree-lined. All primary rural roads should look like this.

Comment and design response: One of the highest-valued rural roads in the surveys has edges lined by trees, planted at close intervals with a more natural setting on the opposite side. The trees almost form a canopy over the road. The curve in the road with the line of trees define a space resulting in a positive driving experience. Despite the wide lanes, apparent double-yellow no passing zone, and white edge lines, this road received high positive response values. It is important to note that it is the vegetation, color, and rhythmic line of trees that contributed to the high value. Why, then, do all county traffic engineers forbid trees when they provide so much positive visual value?

The precaution against drunk drivers is one of the poorest excuses for removing this level of beauty and spatial character, particularly when most other roadways and arterials are rated negative.

Emotional response: Beautiful, free, natural, safe, enjoyable.

Narrow Rural Roads

Response Value +7(4)

Narrow Rural Road

This is an ideal narrow rural road.

Comment and design response: The next image also received one of the highest response values in the rural streets and roads category. It is the quintessential local rural road, well-maintained and beautiful. It contains every design feature people love and respect in a rural setting. It is narrow. If two vehicles need to pass one another, one of the vehicles pulls over and waves to the other driver. The narrowness keeps speed slow. It has a center crown, grass edges, and side drainage ditches. The low, white "horse" fence is curved, slightly rolling with well-trimmed trees that enhance its character. The white color of the traditional gabled houses enhances the foreground and background through its use of the color for the fence and buildings, which extend into the landscape. This is a classic design technique.

Response Value +6(4)

Narrow Rural Road (Lane) Enclosed by Natural Landscaping

Narrow country lane should be allowed where there are a limited number of units using it.

Comment and design response: The above image is one of the narrowest rural roads to receive such high response values. This is not a driveway; rather, it is a country lane serving a small number of homes or farms. When there is limited traffic, keep rural roads very narrow, but design grassed places for a car to pull over when passing another oncoming car. The surface of this lane is tar and gravel. The edge landscaping is very dense and natural, with a narrow-grassed edge/shoulder.

Ideally, a rural road network would connect the Rural Lanes to narrow Rural Roads and to the County Highways. This network of connected thoroughfares with these design characteristics would be the most positive way to protect and maintain the desired rural visual and spatial character.

Rural Road Edges

Edges of rural roads help define character, proportions, and spatial response. Fences or tree lines, or a combination of both, are an important physical feature in generating a positive response. They define the property lines and communicate the care and concern for the land and the public image it conveys. A concerned property owner can be identified through their maintenance of and care for the public edges. Any roadway that is lined by trees receives more positive responses. If lined with trees and more decorative fences, it is typically valued more positively.

Large Setback with a Tree Row and Fence

Road edges in rural areas are enhanced by fences and landscaping. The design of the fences can be elaborate or simple: post and rail, stone or mud, complemented by a line of planted trees and a grassed edge. The deeper fence setback did not receive a higher value, as would have been expected. Both the trees and the fencing together are a very positive rural landscape combination. The land looks cared for, and the pride of place is high.

Comment and design response: Images of well-designed and maintained edges in the rural road category receive positive values, although they can be very different in their design, landscape, and road section. As an example, a deep building setback with a stately row of equally spaced, mature trees; a wide mowed grass area; and a white, three-rail fence defining the field in the background is always rated as very positive. The image above has the white decorative "horse" fence closer to the road and trees on the field side of the fence. The grassed edge and painted fences require more maintenance but provide a stately elegance and higher response value. These types of rural road landscaped edges are highly recommended for designated rural or preserved natural land areas.

Emotional response: Sense of pride, safety, and beauty reinforced by care and maintenance.

Tree-lined Rural Road with a Parallel Bike Path

This image of a bicycle path through rural landscape was evaluated in multiple vision sessions. The typical range is +10 to +4. It is loved by everyone. We need more of this engineered by municipalities and counties in rural areas.

Comment and design response: This thoroughfare combines the best of rural characteristics, including green farm fields, lines of trees, and narrow country roads with the addition of a bike lane that connects rural communities. The wide bike path for two-way bike traffic is separated from the rural road by a row of trees and edged by an agricultural field with a light fence. It is also a good path for joggers and walkers. It is an ideal road/bicycle section in a rural setting.

If there must be a fence, this metal chain-link fence is visually transparent and allows riders and motorists to view the fields while protecting the farmland. It would be viewed as even more positive without any fence at all.

Desired Building Forms and Site Planning in Rural Areas

Based on Community Visioning responses, more appropriate planning, designing, and engineering of lanes, roads and streets must be required. In addition, four residential development types, with their building and lot, style and character received the highest response values and are highly recommended in rural areas.

FOUR RECOMMENDED RESIDENTIAL DEVELOPMENT TYPES

1. **Rural estate housing**: Houses on very large lots of 12 to 25+ acres each, with farm or garden lands.

2. **Rural clusters** or groupings of 10 to 12 housing units and structures on 1/8 to 1/4 acres, surrounded by 75 to 80% of the site remaining as gardens or farmed lands. This is good for new farmers and farm co-ops.

3. **Rural agricultural hamlets** of 10 to 50 houses surrounded by 50 to 75% of the total lot area used as shared land for food production.

4. **Agricultural villages**: 50 to 500 houses in an assemblage of houses and non-residential structures surrounded by 65% of the total shared land used for food production.

Rural Estates—Large Lot Single Family

Response Value +7(3)

Rural Estate House on a Large Lot Surrounded by Farmland

This contemporary house in the background is sited in the center of a 12- to 25-acre field located on a narrow country road and edged with natural vegetation and a rail fence. The road edge contributes to the overall positive response. Similar results were confirmed in early beta tests.

Comment and response: Images of housing on very large lots in rural settings receive high response values. What is most important is their lot size and design of the buildings and landscaping on the recommended 12 to 25 acre lots. Rural design characteristics that should be emulated, include the smaller size of roads, fencing, and landscaping. The larger the setback, the higher the value of the houses an lots. They must be impeccably maintained with all the land use and landscaping characteristics necessary to achieve this high response value, whether it is a single family or has multiple buildings. If they are well designed and maintained, the positive response would is similar.

The Rural Farm Cluster

A Rural Cluster is a small group of residential buildings surrounded by open space. It is best

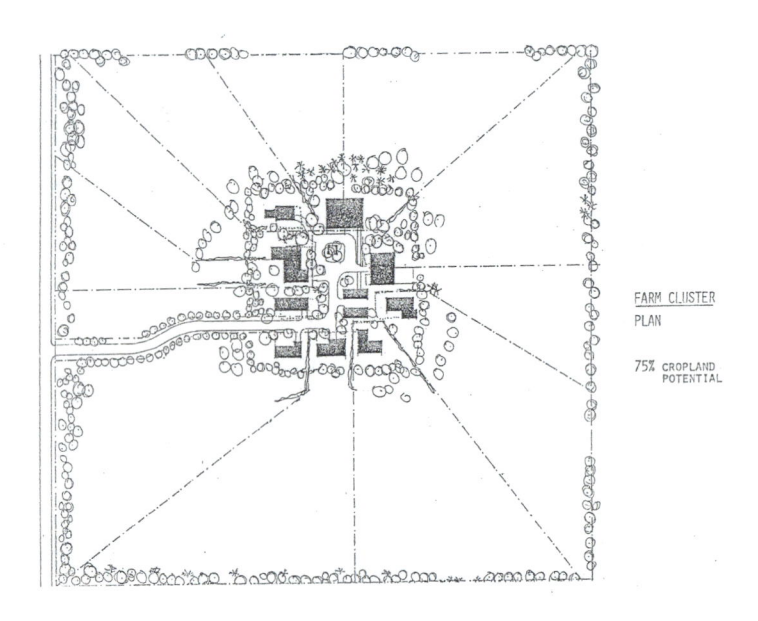

FARM CLUSTER PLAN

75% CROPLAND POTENTIAL

1973 Sketch Designs for a Small Agricultural Hamlet (Farm Cluster)

This is a subdivision of nine homes surrounded by agricultural/food production lands. It was generated after completing early Visual Preference beta tests for rural lands. It has a center focus. It is solar oriented, with a central wind generator. Seventy-five percent of the land is used for farm production, with each lot owning a portion of the farmland. Because of the small number of homes, there is only one community building.

applied on suburban and rural areas zoned for one unit on 1+ acres. Instead of locating every house on a 1+-acre lot, consuming the entire parcel, the housing is laid out on smaller lots of 1/8 to 1/4 acre, and the remaining land is held in common. It is less expensive in terms of road length and infrastructure needed. A percentage of the entire site is preserved as natural open space or dedicated to farming. The remaining land is a highly valued visual amenity when preserved from development. Randal Arendt's books *Rural by Design* is an ideal reference source and underscores the importance, beauty, and responsibility of this type of development. Non-residential uses are typically not present in a Rural Cluster. Individual septic and wells or a shared well and sewer treatment are options. If, instead of a rural cluster, an agricultural hamlet or village is planned, then non-residential uses, like a small community building, office or service, or farm stand, are appropriate.

Response Value +7(3)

Rural Cluster of Houses Surrounded by Farm Fields

Rural grouping of housing with a deep setback. The six to eight housing units shown are grouped together on small lots in the center of the farm field. The smaller the lots and the deeper the setback, the higher the response value.

Comment and design response: The high response value attests to its viability. These units are sited in such a way as to form a rural neighborhood with common central space and a vast surrounding area used for agricultural production. Seventy-five to eighty percent of the land preserved is dedicated to farming. New housing in this development pattern fosters the sense of a small community.

Response Value +6(3)

Rural Cluster of New Homes

This modern grouping of units creates an interesting and appealing sense of spatial enclosure. The building design vocabulary uses traditional vernacular architecture. This grouping of houses has its own spatial sense of enclosure, using the curve enhanced by the picket fences. Many of the existing trees have been preserved, giving it a feeling of having been there for a long time. The corner green acts as a small public space. The picket fences, sidewalks, and streetlights together enhance the character of the place. This is a more modern option for a small hamlet or neighborhood within a rural setting.

Comment and design response: Above is what the interior of a cluster of six housing units could look and feel like. Retain existing mature trees if possible. The traditional design and layout of the houses and yards gives this small community an established feel. Amend zoning to allow Rural Clusters wherever possible.

Center of a Small Rural Villages

A rural village is the preferred development pattern of new subdivisions in a rural area. The response to this image was generated by multiple surveys, including the Connecticut Region Organizations of Governments Community Visioning Process.

Comment: This image of the center of this historic rural village has an organic pattern with a slight curve in the street, creating spatial definition. It has a limited number of units, with the church (tall community building) acting as the central focus. The church steeple, as a vertical element, acts as a legible landmark and the perfect deflector for the curve. The form, scale, and architectural vocabulary is highly rated for rural areas. Even better, this center is surrounded by farmland.

Design response: This could be a prototype for an agricultural hamlet and should be a top priority when new development must occur in a rural landscape. This form should be evaluated and emulated.

Rural Sprawl Model

For the purpose of visually understanding the size and form of an alternative proposed for rural areas and to curtain rural sprawl, the following two models will be helpful. These were used in multiple Community Visioning workshops and are presented **adjacent to** each other to better facilitate understanding. The rural sprawl model typically is four- and five-bedroom houses on three- to four-acre lots, with large landscaped lawns and three- and four-car garages.

Many municipalities have zoned their productive rural lands for expensive houses on large lots (Near Castles, McMansions). Suburban developers believe that the larger the lot and the larger the square footage of the house, the lower the square foot cost, the higher the sales price, and the greater the profit. Some buyers see this as the manifest destiny of their wealth. Many municipalities consider such houses tax ratables, particularly if the occupants' children do not go to public schools or have no children. Many municipal officials think that this will preserve the "rural character." Nothing could be further from the truth. These types of subdivisions destroy it.

Plus, little or no consideration is given to the potential agricultural productivity or the disappearance of high production-quality soil types. Little is produced on the land but could be if a portion of that lot was vegetable gardens. It is primarily used for grasses and landscaping. As long as these types of houses and lots continue to sell, and a municipality promotes this by zoning, the large lot and the large house will continue to appeal to the "nouveau rich." The first alternative to use in preserving the rural character is the Rural Estate, a much-larger lot with a stipulation that a percentage of the surrounding land (lot) be used for food production, like that of fruits and vegetables. One or two outbuilding on the site can be used to temporarily house people who work on this mini-farm and/or for storage of equipment and produce.

There is little concern among people who reside on three- and four-acre lot developments regarding their auto-dependence, the auto trips that must be made because nothing is within walking distance, the additional roads and maintenance required, the traffic and pollution generated, or the social isolation. What buyers have purchased is a massive compromise and an environmental and societal disaster. Three- and four-acre zoning with large houses receive low positive ratings in many VPS, meaning that they are the bottom line that is still acceptable to Community Visioning participants. People buy because there are few alternatives. Due to ignorance, clusters, hamlets, and villages with views of preserved open space and potential agricultural production are not permitted in many ordinances. New housing can be beautifully grouped to form a small community while still retaining houses' size. Unfortunately, this is the exception and not the rule as most municipalities are reluctant to change their existing large lot zoning to allow an agricultural hamlet.

Model Rural Sprawl Housing. The Model Has Six Houses on Five-Acre Lots. The Model Shown Is Approximately 35 Acres

Every large four- to five-bedroom home with a three- or four-car garage is on its own parcel of land, most located off cul-de-sacs. Yards are large grass areas with minimum landscaping.

Rural Hamlet the Second Alternative to Rural Sprawl

A grouping of 10 to 50 houses with a central focus. It could have a

core of non-residential uses in proportion to the number of residential units.

The basic standards for a Rural Hamlet*

Area: 20 to 100+ acres

Dwelling units: 6 to 100

Lot size range must vary: 3 to 6 dwelling units per acre

Non-residential: Up to 60 sq. ft. per dwelling unit

Surrounding farmlands: 50 to 75% of total area

Must have a shared common public space

*For additional information, refer to "Visions for a New American Dream: Process, Principles and an Ordinance to Plan and Design Small Communities" by Anton Nelessen

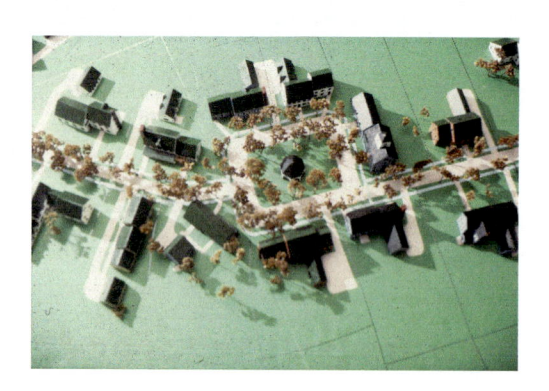

Model of a Rural Hamlet

This model of a Rural Hamlet has 12 homes focused around a common green. Using the same house size shown in the previous rural sprawl model, the rural hamlet consumes approximately nine acres with a center green. The remaining 26 acres could be preserved in farmland, which could be used for gardens, orchards, or hardwood trees for harvesting. Greenhouses for high-quality production would also be appropriate.

Comment and design response: The site plan shown previously is a rural hamlet envisioned in multiple Community Visioning Workshops. It has similar-sized large houses on approximately one-third of the land. It is focused on a shared green or common space, with a gazebo in the center. The cost to builders is significantly less per home considering site prep costs, lengths of streets and sewer lines, landscaping, etc. Then, there is the value of uniqueness, its sense of community, the ecological responsibility, and the profit from the agricultural products. This is an ideal development pattern for rural areas, saving vast amounts of farmland for food production while creating a sense of community. Hamlets can represent a variety of layout designs. Plus, any of these houses could be affordable as multifamily homes for those that work on the farm.

Comment and design response: The value of the land is in its ability to produce food locally which is sold locally, e.g., at farmers' markets, restaurants, etc. There are sufficient available vacant and underutilized lands in urban and existing suburban areas to accommodate most future housing needs. When additional housing is needed in rural areas, this development form, the agricultural hamlet or village, is preferred. This type of development is ideal on lands that are currently zoned for two- to three-acre lots.

The Agricultural Village

A grouping of buildings—residential, civic, and commercial—

with a center green or public space, with limited non-residential / commercial / civic uses, encircled by land that must be farmed to grow and harvest food.

production or other types of agricultural activities.

An Agricultural Village can be implemented on any land zoned for subdivisions, agriculture/farming, or farmland, provided that it has the minimum land area. It can also be a TDR "receiving site" for units located and being transferred from agricultural lands with high quality soils that want to be preserved, but has value for development. Unfortunately, this land was inappropriately zoned in the past for residential or commercial uses and thereby increased in value beyond its use as agricultural lands. To the question **"Are you in favor of new villages and hamlets, in contrast to suburban sprawl, in order to preserve agricultural lands?", the typical "yes" response ranges from 69% to 81%.**

This rural development form can be used as the receiving zone for TDR. The amount of non-residential uses is based on the number of residential units and inhabitants, thereby restricting the over-commercialization of the site. Ideally, this would house a community of people who farm the land. This development type allows households to live and work in a real community.

A Model of an Agricultural Village as a Transfer of Development Rights (TDR) Site.

This model of an agricultural village was used to demonstrate the responses to a Community Visioning process in Chesterfield Township, New Jersey, where the town's vision for the future was to save as many farms from development as possible using TDR. Transferred units would be relocated into this new Agricultural Village.

There are alternatives to the subdivision of one- to three-acre lots in rural areas. An Agricultural Village and/or the smaller Agricultural Hamlet are the most preferred. These two rural development forms mandate a proportional relationship of residential uses to commercial and civic uses. Both also require the agricultural use of land. Up to 60% of the gross lot or development areas must be preserved for food

Response Value +6(4)

Agricultural Village Surrounded by Farm Fields

A simulation of a rural agricultural hamlet/village surrounded by farm fields.

Comment and design response: This photo simulation of an Agricultural Hamlet was used in several regional VPS sessions. It always receives a positive response. It contains between 20 and 100 housing units with a range of unit types and a consistent architectural design vocabulary. It contains retail, civic, and commercial uses in proportion to the number of housing units. It has a central open space or commons, and is surrounded by agricultural lands. It is carefully sited into the landscape, not breaking the ridge line. The tower gives it landmark presence in the landscape and reinforces its mixed-use core.

Design response: The urban form character in this image should guide growth in rural areas adjacent to urban agglomerations. The larger the amount of land devoted to food production and other uses, the larger the number of units and non-residential space that can be built. Many young farmers and people who love rural landscapes would like to live in well-designed small communities surrounded by land that produces food.

Note: *All the standards for three types of small communities can be found in the book* **"Visions for a New American Dream: Process, Principles and an Ordinance to Plan and Design Small Communities"** *by Anton Nelessen*

Mapping Locations for Future Rural Development

The consensus vision for future development and preservation illustrated on the following map was generated in a series of Community Visioning workshops sponsored by the Connecticut Region Organizations of Governments. It is synthesized

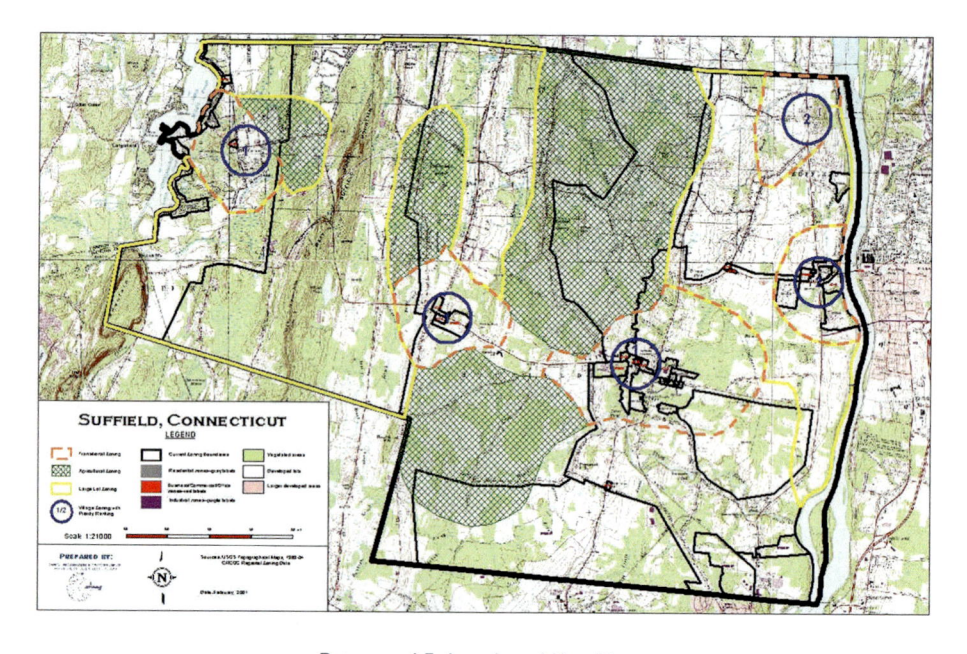

Proposed Future Land Use Map

It was recommended to restrict two-acre zoning and focus new development on the agricultural villages designated by the blue circles. These can be extensions of existing hamlets or a separate village. One is new. The secondary area is defined by the red dotted lines around each village or hamlet for very large-lot, single-family homes and small farms. The darker green areas are specifically zoned for agriculture and applicable for TDR as a sending zone. The remainder of the land is designated agricultural/preservation.

AXONOMETRIC SKETCH OF
ONE OF THE THREE HAMLETS

Sketch of one of the New Agricultural Villages
Providing a three-dimensional model or sketch of what the village could look like is critical for participants to become conscious their positive vision. A map by itself is not enough.

using the positive value-rated images from the VPS to direct a Vision Translation Workshop (VTW) which reinforces the desire to preserve farmlands and to concentrate development in a series of villages, with the result of preserving massive acreage from sprawled subdivisions.

Highest-Rated Image in the Rural Category

The "soul" of the rural/city lifestyle

When the response values of the VPS are determined, always look first at the highest-rated image and then the category in which it was presented. The following image was the highest rated in multiple surveys in rural and small towns. It represents the visual and emotional "soul" of the rural community.

Response Value + 8(2)

Line 79   Farmer's Market

8 (3)

Farmers Market

This in-town farmers' market is selling local fresh produce, ideally grown and raised within a short truck drive of the market.
This image was used in multiple Community Visioning sessions and always received very positive responses. It resonates with so many people, not only for the interactions it generates but because the produce is local and fresh and the sellers are knowledgeable and friendly.
Every town must have one or more. If your town does not have a farmers market ystart planning for one butalking to the local farmers, advertise, and then temporarily close off a street or parking lot on Saturday and watch what happens.

Comment: The highest positive response to this farmers' market reinforces the recommended rural land use pattern and indicates the importance of the rural way of life, human interaction, walking, and local healthy foods. Farmers' markets are great facilities to bring people together while providing a valuable, healthy community service and supporting local farmers. Combining farmers markets with Agricultural Hamlets and Villages is ideal. Farmers' markets and street fairs enhance a town's vitality by drawing more residents and visitors, who walk and interact. Food is a primary draw. Such markets also bring crafters to sell their creations, along with fruits, vegetables, flowers, baked goods, etc. Add in entertainment and local bands to enhance the experience.

Emotional response: Appeals to our basic human desire for interaction and seasonal local food and flowers. Farmers' markets generated the positive emotional values of joy, happiness, safety, and pride. Perhaps the most important was hopefulness for the future.

Recommendations for Land Use and Preservation of Rural Areas

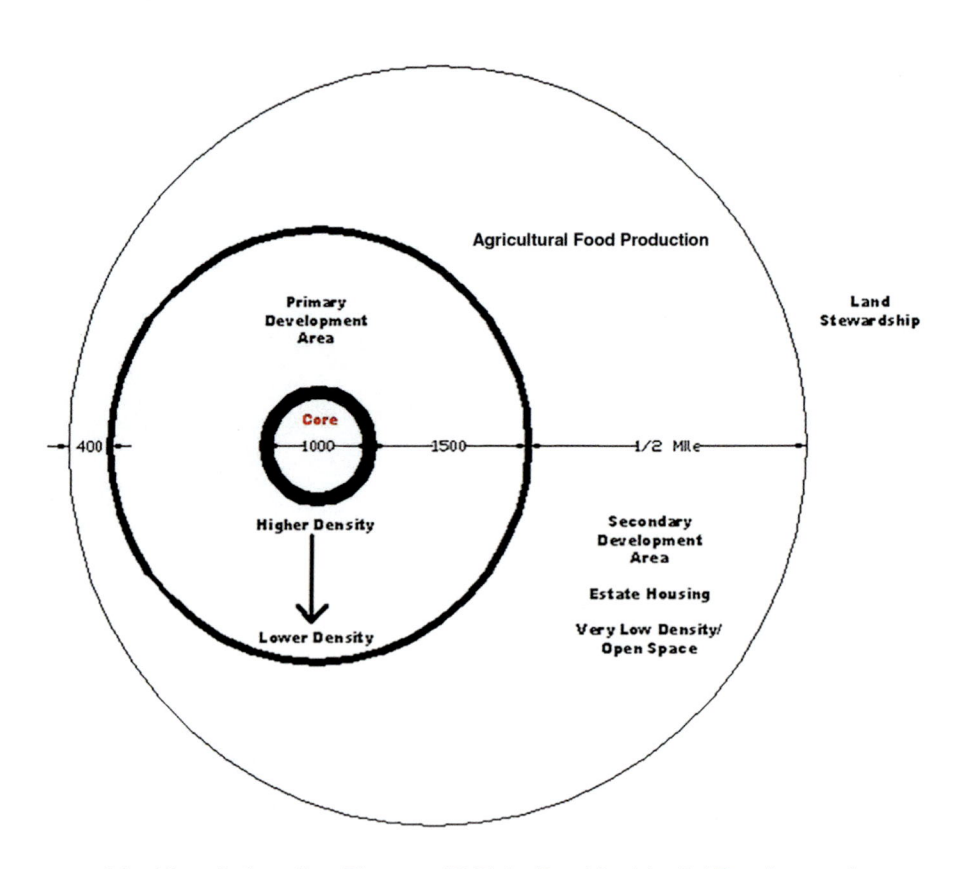

Ideal Density Location Diagram (DLD) for Rural Residential Development

The core of an agricultural hamlet or village is the heart of a rural community. It extends no more than a five-minute walk 1,500 feet to the edge of the farmland or areas of very large lots. The secondary and food production area can extend from 400' to 1/2 mile from the edge of the urbanization.

Summary Recommendations for Rural Areas

1. *General*

Rural lands must be maintained and possibly enhanced in its natural condition, retaining their overwhelming beauty, views, and character. Standard subdivisions and strip commercial development would not only destroy and diminish their natural ecological and psychological beauty but also would rob future generations of the capability to experience these high-value places and the food they produce. Building more subdivisions and strip commercial developments would also curtail nature's ability to heal itself after gross generational transgressions. If we continue to plan and build subdivisions and strip commercial development in rural agricultural areas, the emotional, physical, economic, and environmental prices will be extraordinary, leaving an everlasting debt. Rural land areas must be designated on Comprehensive Plan and controlled by new Zoning Ordinances.

2. *Future development*

Remaining rural lands must be reserved and zoned for agricultural production and properly zoned for small and large farms, agribusiness, mixed-use Agricultural Hamlets, and Villages, and very large estates of 10 to 20 acres, following the Density Location Diagram. All the recommended uses are viable alternatives to the standard subdivision, strip commercial development, and wider arterials. Comprehensive planning using GIS land and soil characteristics are recommended to determine primary and secondary development areas for new Agricultural Hamlets and Villages or infilling existing smaller villages. Use the Density Locational Diagram to scale as an overlay on the GIS maps to plan the future of these areas.

3. *Food production*

Utilization of productive rural lands close to urban centers will become even more important and valuable as populations increase; considering climate change and decrease or increase in rainfall, drought, or the frequency of flood conditions, along with the depletion of underground water reserves, will increase demand for remaining productive land near urban areas. Future energy costs may also limit the distance and cost of the transportation of food, although these costs may be reduced using driverless trucks. Heretofore, too much good farmland has been zoned for commercial or sprawled residential uses because it was more profitable to "grow" houses than to grow food. Much of this land is still not built upon.

Promote farms, farmers, farmers' helpers, organic food, canning, seasonal eating, and harvest festivals. **Promote farmers' markets and co-ops** in all urban areas within walking distance of most residents.

4. *Thoroughfares*

A network of three primary rural thoroughfares (country lanes, narrow rural roads, and rural highways) are recommended. These must located and graphically displayed in the Master Plan (Comprehensive Plan), specifically illustrated in the Thoroughfare Regulating Plan of a From-based Zoning Code. These thoroughfares must have appropriate widths (lanes) and edge conditions complementing the appropriate building typologies. Public expenditures should be limited for road maintenance and infrastructure, particularly public water and sewer expansion, except to service new villages and possible agricultural hamlets in designated rural areas, which could alternatively use community wells and wastewater treatment. These measures will reduce the cost to taxpayers and maintain the rural character and value.

5. *TDR*

Adopt and fund TDR for Clusters, Agricultural Hamlets, and/or Villages to concentrate new development into a receiving district while preserving farming on the remaining lands. TDR allows a farmer or rural landowner to sell some or all of the units that have been allocated on his or her land through improper zoning to another more suitable location in a land use form other than large-lot zoning, thereby allowing farming to continue on the original parcel while the owner/farmer is compensated for his or her "loss." In this way, the farmer receives just compensation for not selling and subdividing his or her land while retaining use and ownership of the land. Transferring units to an agricultural hamlet or village is ideal. The builder buys units from towns that pay the farmer for the number of units zoned on his/her land. If TDR is used to transfer housing from existing zoned areas to a hamlet or village, provide a bonus of additional lots in the receiving district. Hamlets and villages must have a specific plan and a sufficient number of units to make this feasible.

6. *Zoning amendments*

Eliminate the one, two- and three-acre Euclidian zoning in all rural areas. Rezone single-family lots to a minimum lot size of 10 to 20 acres. Allow the preferred visions for areas including rural estates, clusters, Agricultural Hamlets, and Villages as of right. Locate potential sites, and use the Density Location Diagram to determine zoning.

Amend zoning to eliminate any new strip commercial development. Encourage growth and redevelopment where existing commercial development is in the deterioration cycle.

Note: Refer to Preferred Visions for Suburbia for specific recommendations.

10

Visions for Suburbia

Suburban sprawl: Vast areas of land planned since the late 1940s for single use mono-type development including: residential subdivisions fronting on a cul-de sac and/or loop street with isolated locations for multifamily apartments, offices, parks, with strip commercial development fronting onto arterials. All land uses are entirely auto-dependent, using a network of wide local streets, collectors, arterials, and freeways, and do not require walking or transit.

Mono pods of sprawl housing and strip commercial are ubiquitous and still being built. Many developers want to build with the cheapest construction and land development techniques, and do not want to challenge the existing zoning which not only permits sprawl but mandates it. Aerial views of communities zoned for sprawl confirm that there exist vacant, underdeveloped land and underutilized buildings within a fragmented "leap frogging" discontinuous and disconnected development pattern. Existing zoning and the lack of proper planning promotes this random pattern of development. The availability of open land in suburban areas, combined now with deteriorating commercial areas, suggests that **no additional rural lands should be built upon until this vacant land is developed** in a dense mixed- and multiple-land use, positive urban design pattern. Until there is expansive population growth, and even then, an alternative development pattern within the areas currently zoned for sprawl must be considered. It is unsustainable to develop land in three-quarter-, one-, and two-acre lots for "estate" housing with more traffic, pollution, and surface parking dominant strip commercial uses.

Planning and designing an alternative land use pattern in suburbia will be a challenge because it is instilled into the consciousness of the current generations both negatively and positively. Many people now in power grew up in suburban sprawl, dependent on the car for all trips. That is what they are comfortable with and consider to be normative behavior. To be like everyone else, or the motivation to comply, "what sold yesterday will also sell today," is the house on a lot on a cul-de-sac with a front yard accessed garage.

There are alternatives that are more efficient, sustainable, beautiful, healthy and community-based, and that reduce negative environmental impacts and use remaining land resources more efficiently. Only bold new urbanists have been successful in challenging and overcoming much of this old stereotype zoning. The results have been glorious and financially successful. More of it can happen with a commitment to a positive vision, adopting a responsible land use plan, memorialized in a written and illustrate Form-based Zoning Code.

Of the multitude of small suburban places where Community Visioning sessions have been conducted, Spring Hill, Kansas; Burlington County, New Jersey; Washington Township (now renamed Robbinsville), New Jersey; Vision Delaware; Worcester County, Maryland; and Overland Park, Kansas have been selected.

Value Responses to Suburban Residential Land Uses

The value-rated images that follow inform us how people feel about suburban places and spaces, what should be built, and how to retrofit places evolving from optimization into deterioration. New suburban single-family housing scores mostly neutral to low positive, with high standard deviations. Neutral numbers (–1, 0, and +1) with high standard deviation illustrates a love/hate relationship with this form of development. Many people find standard single-family developments minimally acceptable. There are few other choices. Houses on large lots are still considered a symbol of prosperity and status. The same house in a Traditional Neighborhood Development (TND) with an alley or "residential lane" that fronts onto a green park receives higher response values, has a more positive quality of life, and is more sustainable.

The general response to suburban housing is more positive where it is single family, leafier, and greener, and where streets are narrower and front yards are smaller and better-defined. New housing on wide streets with a front yard driveway and garage are typically scored more negatively. The following images set the physical and emotional tone for the suburban areas.

Reactions to Negative Responses

Places and spaces with poor visual and spatial quality, responses "–0" or below, should not be allowed. When conducting post evaluations of the responses with participants, sociologists, social workers, religious leaders, and psychiatrists, the agreement was that negative reactions fundamentally generate stress, depression, anxiety,

hopelessness, anger, and fear, as was stated earlier. The greater the negative reaction, the more these conscious mental states prevail. Inevitably, people and society must pay the high price of dysfunctionality, discontent, stress, drug abuse, and loss of tax revenues as the result of poor planning, deteriorating buildings, streetscapes, and parks. The negative responses to so many images conclude that the lower the negative response to places and spaces, the more people want change. Change is possible when using positive images from a Community Visioning process.

Response value –2(6)

New Subdivision of Garage-front Houses
This is a typical, recently constructed subdivision in growing town. The negative characteristics are the 36-foot-wide local street, the garage frontages, similar color pallet, lack of street trees, and lack of sidewalks on both sides. Although negative, the minimum positive design features include its spatial enclosure based on the location of the houses on the curved street, setbacks, and sidewalk with a four-foot parkway. The high standard deviation suggests a range of –8 to +4. Most disapprove, but there are those who find this minimally acceptable.

Comment and design response: It doesn't matter where one travels in the country; 1/2- to 1/3-acre subdivisions are quite similar with their engineered site plan with a garage front layout, similar roof pitches, building scale, building form, and color. From a distance, it is difficult to distinguish one from another, particularly when there is repetition of the unit types. Most subdivision regulations require, at most, three facade types. This is generic, at best, as well as boring and environmentally unconscious. What is unfortunate here is the total lack of knowing or acknowledging alternatives. It is unconscionable that so many planners and civil engineers continue to propagate this land use, despite its generally negative response and its fragmented randomness of pattern, leapfrogging over existing subdivisions.

Responses to New Subdivisions

These are presented starting from the most negative. Each time, the negative value drops because some features have improved.

Response Value –4(5)

Suburban Garages

Garages fronting onto the street command most of the front elevation. The front doors can't be seen.

Comment and design response: The form and character of the buildings say, "cars live here,

not people." The lack of a parkway (the area between the curb and the sidewalk) and street trees, combined with the wide driveways, contributes to the negative response values. There is a large response range, from 0 to –9. Few give this a neutral response. House designs must be modified to prevent the garage from extending beyond the front façade. They must be recessed or located behind the front façade. The best response is to design the garages in the rear of the lot off a residential lane.

Response Value –3(4)

Suburban Houses on Wide Roadway

Super wide roadway (wide enough to be a small airport runway) of this cul-de-sac edged by a strip of concrete with masonry mailboxes.

Comment and design response: There is no parkway, trees, or street landscaping. Houses have a similar design, materials, and color. This is viewed as less negative because of the visual termination; hills in the background; and some street landscaping, like lower-scaled decorative streetlights. There is no reason for a street cartway of this width. This street could be cut in half by expanding the parkway and adding street trees.

Positive Alternatives to the Standard Subdivision Housing Types and Land Uses

Traditional pre-1930s neighborhoods with their traditional housing forms generate the most positive responses. These lot configurations and building forms should be zoned/allowed in every suburban municipality, particularly in areas where there is unbuilt suburban land between fragmented disconnected subdivisions. The housing types that follow were generated from multiple Community Visioning sessions. Some of these images are from traditional older subdivisions built in the 1930s; others are new, having site plan and building design characteristics that emulate the older traditional classic suburban neighborhood homes. These images express the desired design vocabulary for new residential construction.

Response Value +7(3)

Classic "American Four-Square" House

An older classic "American four square" home in an in-town neighborhood. Notice that the garage is located in the rear with a narrow driveway. There is semi-public, well-landscaped setback and front porch.

Response Value + 5(4)

Neo-traditional House with Large Porch

Above is a new home in a new Traditional Neighborhood Development (TND). The front porch and rear yard garage contribute to its positive response. The lack of a parkway and street trees lower its positive response value.

Comment and design responses: The previous image and the one above, are variations on the traditional American Four-Suare house. They are sited on relatively narrow, well-landscaped lots with a small front yard. They are two story plus attic, with pitched roofs and front porches. All are raised above grade. Garages are in the rear, off a residential lane or a narrow side yard driveway. There are many site plan and design techniques that can be extracted from these images and which can be included in any subdivision ordinance. Of particular importance is

Response Value +6(3)

Traditional Houses Fronting onto a Public Park

Housing in a new traditional neighborhood development with front porches. This image has been used in multiple VPSs and every time receives high positive response values.

the location of the garage. Many of these new units have garage access from a rear lane, maintaining a more dignified front yard.

Comment and design response: The housing shown on the previous page located in a traditional neighborhood development (TND) is the alternative to the negative suburban subdivision. These units have narrow lot widths sited along a narrow street. They are raised above grade, with a front porch overlooking a small, defined front yard. Porches are used as outdoor spaces and encourage neighbors to interact. There are front sidewalks connecting to each unit and a larger neighborhood center. The large lawn of the typical sprawled subdivision lot is concentrated in a large common green onto which houses front. There are no garages or driveways in the front yards of the homes. Rather, they are located in the back yard, with vehicular access, garbage pickup, and utility service from a residential lane.

Response Value +6(4)

Townhouses Fronting onto a Public Park

Brick townhouses fronting onto a narrow street and a public park. The parking and garage are in the rear yard off a lane which gives these homes their traditional positive look and feel. This image has been used in multiple VPS sessions and always receives positive responses.

Comment and design response: Classic brick townhouses, two and one-half stories, with pitched roofs and dormers. Each townhouse has one or

more unique features on its facade, providing individuality. These front onto a narrow street and a common park. They are located logically near the center of a neighborhood and the retail and mixed-use core. The adjacent park increases the response value of the building types, which will become more positive as the trees grow. Garages and parking are located in the rear, accessed from a residential lane.

Suburban Residential Streets

Positive engineering and urban design standards for suburban streets and blocks are basic requirements if a high-quality character of community and high market value is desired.

Suburban residential streets are typically value rated positive if they are lined with trees, have sidewalks on both sides, and are relatively narrow. Most of the more positive images are of older suburban streets built on or before the 1930s, or located in new urbanists' communities or eco-subdivisions. The images of streets in a low density residential eco-subdivision consistently receive the highest response values in the suburban street category. They have flat curbs at the edge of the asphalt pavement without storm sewers. Instead, there is a bioswale in the parkway between the edge of the pavement and the sidewalk. This has been engineered to control surface drainage.

Response Value +7(3)

An Ecologically Responsive Suburban Residential Street

A narrow residential street with a bioswale appropriate for low-density residential buildings. Storm water flows in the "fold" (ditch) from right to left.

Comment and design response: This street has a narrow cartway of 24 feet with a center crown to facilitate water drainage to the sides. The flat curbs allow storm water to flow into the side bioswales. The bioswale is the substitute for curb storm water collection. Bioswales delay runoff, reduce local street flooding, and increase percolation into the ground water. Underground storm drain pipes are located only at intersections, where they flow into large collector system. The grassed bioswale acts as a water filtering device as well. Notice that the trees are planted in the center of the bioswale, facilitating new, rapid, and healthy growth. The bioswale is six feet or more wide to allow tree roots to spread and absorb storm water. The trees are rapidly forming a canopy over the street. Driveways are contoured to match the swale. The street has sidewalks on both sides. This is an ideal

street section for any new suburban development. Trees in a narrow three-foot or less parkway strip will be slow to grow and may not survive to maturity due to the limited area for root growth.

Response Value +5(3)

Tree-Lined Canopied Residential Street

A narrow residential street with tree-lined parkway is most appropriate in suburban neighborhoods of 1/4- to 1/3-acre lots. The rolled curb, parkway, and sidewalk on both sides enhances its value. This image has been used in numerous VPS, including the National Association of Realtors national random survey, and it always receives positive responses. This street character increases property sale values; also, residents tend to live here longer. This is an ideal street engineering standard.

Comment and design response: Despite the low density, the wide lots and large setbacks, the narrowness of the cartway (approximately 20 feet wide), the rolled curbs, and particularly the form and character of the trees give this street its high response value. The trees are planted in a six- to eight-foot parkway at approximately 30 foot intervals. Notice that where one tree is missing, a new tree has been planted to maintain the rhythm of the street. This is a classic "leafy" street form that could be considered a **suburban greenway**. If it were designed with a bioswale, the response value would have been higher. If there must be curbing for storm water catchment, use low height or roll curbs.

Residential Lanes

A third type of desired suburban residential street is the residential 12- to 18-foot-wide lane. Located in the rear of a narrow residential lot, it provides access to the garage. All the infrastructure (sewer, water, cable, gas) is located below grade. The garbage is collected here, not in the front. Each house with a residential lane has a proper frontage, with no garage or drive apron or curb breaks in the front yard of the lot. The rear lot garage is located 15 to 20 feet from the edge of the lane. The lane is planted and has a green character. It is approximately18 feet wide. Eliminating curbs reduces construction costs for builders and future town expenses. If curbing is used, it is important to create openings in curbing to permit runoff into the bioswales.

Response Value +3(5)

Landscaped Residential Lane

Residential lanes in new TND, located in the middle of the block, provide access to garages, garbage, and recycling. Infrastructure, including sewer, water, electric, and cable, are all located here. It has a center storm drain. The cartway is 12 to 18 feet wide. It must be well landscaped. Garages are preferred off residential lanes as opposed to off the front of each house. The garages are set back from the edge of the pavement with an apron providing the opportunity to park a car and give sufficient space to back out of the garage. It must be well lit at night.

Typical Block and Lot Layout with a Residential Lane

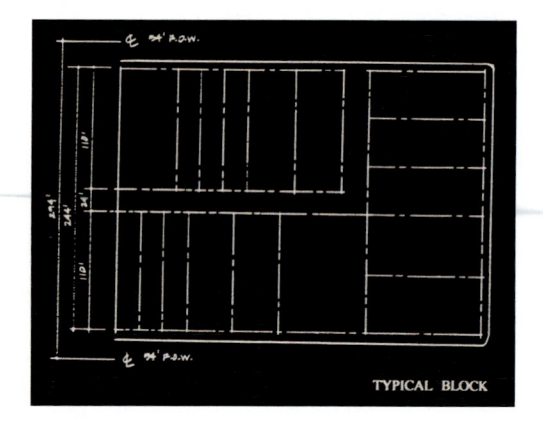

Lot Layout with Residential Lane

A typical block plan with an "L"-shaped residential lane.

A Model of a Block with Houses, Garages, and Residential Lane

A model illustrating typical blocks with houses and garages off a lane and adjacent adjoining streets, with sidewalks, crosswalks, and street trees. Notice the traffic calming pattern at the intersection.

Comment and design response: Blocks, streets, residential lanes, and structures using this pattern or some variation of it always receive high positive response values. The recommended planning and design standards call for residential streets with narrow cartways, from 24 to 28 feet, and a 4- to 8-foot parkway or bioswale planted with trees in rhythmic intervals; sidewalks on both sides of the street; and possible bike ways to create "complete streets." They are pleasant and interesting to walk and drive. Additional positive visual standards include: Shallow front yards and first floors raised above sidewalk grade, with stoops and/or porches that are close to the sidewalks as well as a semi-public divider and picket fence or hedges. Lots should vary in width to create a more organic look. Locate the infrastructure and garages to the rear of the lot with access off a residential lane—this assures the positive response value to the frontage street.

Suburban Parks and Green Spaces

Response Value +9(1)

A Beloved Neighborhood Park with Pond

The extraordinary response to this park is reinforced by the high value of the homes that are adjacent and within walking distance.

Parks are a requirement in all neighborhoods and must be appropriately located, planned, designed, and equipped. They should be planned and built, and available within a three-minute walk from most residents' homes. Local parks should not be a secondary consideration. They

should be part of the everyday experience and be connected to every home by bicycle paths and sidewalks. Plan, design, preserve, and incorporate all environmentally sensitive lands in suburban areas into a network of green spaces, linked parks, and greenways and belts. Use native, mature plant materials with intensive and effective landscaping. Also, set aside a parcel for productive community garden plots.

The images and response values that follow portray the desired suburban parks and open spaces. Probably the most important feature of suburban development is immediate accessibility to parks, playgrounds, and other green areas. When these areas are more natural and contain water features, like a lake or pond, the response is highest. Notice on the following positive image that fencing is not needed for safety purposes because of the shallow side slope. Kids and pets can wade in safety. The image below is one of the highest-rated images from every survey in which it was included.

Response Value +7(3)

Local Neighborhood Parks

Small, well-designed, and equipped neighborhood parks. These parks and playgrounds are highly valued, particularly when they are within walking distance.

Comment and design response: Small parks and playgrounds must be located within a two- to five-minute walk of every residential unit and designed to achieve the most positive response and satisfaction by residents, particularly households with children and older adults. They should contain, at a minimum, safe play equipment, grassed areas, shade trees, places for parents or caregivers to sit, and places to eat and share.

Response Value +7(3)

Housing on Narrow Street Surrounding a Neighborhood Green

This linear green park enriches the sense of community and neighborhood for all the units fronting on this open space called a community green. It is enhanced by trees, play equipment, and lighting. The narrow street with little traffic allows easy and safe crossings. Other features contributing to the positive response are the sidewalk, picket fence, defining the semi-public realm, street lights, flowers, and variation of housing types shallow building setback, period-pedestrian lighting with porches. This image has been used in multiple surveys and always receives very positive responses.

Comment and design response: In new TND, the common green framed by units fronting onto this green contributes to the increased value of the homes and improved quality of life. This green defines the neighborhood identity and location. The surrounding streets have parking on one side. Houses are laid out on narrow lots of varying widths, close to the right of way, with small semi-public front yards, defined by picket fences, hedges, or a low wall. Street trees, sidewalks, and decorative lighting are located on both sides, enhancing the character. Driveways do not connect to this frontage street, eliminating garages facing the street and the disruption of the pedestrian sidewalk with a driveway. The garages and parking are located in the rear of the lot accessed via a residential lane.

Response Value +5(3)

Mixed-use Retail in a Small Neighborhood Center

To enhance a neighborhood, a center focus, gathering place of mixed-use buildings is ideal.

Comment and design response: This neighborhood core includes retail and services in a two-story, mixed-use building where retail is located on the ground floor, with offices or housing on the upper floors. It is located on a street corner with parking on-street and/or in the backyard of the building. It has a classic facade, pitched roof, and interesting architectural details, giving it a unique character. To render these feasible, there has to be enough housing units within easy walking distance while accommodating driving customers. The changing nature of retail suggests that restaurants with outdoor seating, health and beauty services, wine and liquor, and green grocers are most desirable.

Response Value +5(5)

Live-Work Units

These new three-story live/work units have retail, offices, or services at the sidewalk level with residential units above; typically, these have the same owner.

Comment and design response: The ground floor offices can be converted into commercial/retail units or the reverse. It is a good investment to live and work in the same building. This is a high-valued building type. Each live-work unit is separate and individually defined by color, brick texture, or window details. This should be allowed in suburban town centers or villages and codified in zoning ordinances.

Response Value +7(4)

Green Grocer with Outdoor Covered Display

Fresh fruits and vegetables available in convenient locations within the pedestrian realm are highly desired in both suburban and urban settings. Selling fresh food that comes from local farmers is even more desirable.

Comment and design response: The good health benefits of fresh fruits, meats, and vegetables are becoming understood by more people, and therefore their convenient availability in town and community centers is well appreciated. Consuming healthy food, a positive relationship between farms on the periphery of urban areas, while promoting the farmers' markets and pedestrianism. Green grocers, farmers' markets, and street displays enliven any sidewalk pedestrian experience and encourage personal interaction.

Suburban Town or Village Center

A well-designed suburban downtown or village center results in a more viable, walkable, and healthy community.

style. These structures are two and three stories high, with individually designed buildings adjacent to each other. They create a continuous retail frontage along the sidewalk. This image of a small town uptown has been shown in many surveys and always receives high positive responses. A Main Street form as opposed to strip malls with the field of parking in front is most desired and has proven to be a success.

Response Value −1(5)

Existing Condition
BEFORE
The "before" images portrays the existing condition of the downtown streetscape and store facades.

Response Value +6(3)

Mixed-use Town Center
This mixed- and multiple-use town center is about 1,000 linear feet, making it very walkable. It has wide sidewalks and continuous shopfronts. The diagonal parking makes it convenient for drivers to park once and walk to all their destinations.

Comment and design response: This positive community center shopping street has a cartway wide enough to accommodate diagonal parking on one or both sides, wide sidewalks, and well-designed landscaping. Retail and commercial buildings are more traditional in scale, character, and

Comment and design response: Most disturbing is the −1 value with a high standard deviation, giving it a range of −6 to +4. This indicates that the majority think it is negative and unacceptable in its current condition. However, many participants find it acceptable and positive. Perhaps some people have become conditioned to seeing this type of street in this condition for so many years that they just accept it as is or don't think it could get any better.

Response Value +6(4)

Façade and Streetscape Improvements
AFTER

A simulation of what it could become, using features and recommended improvements generated from the Community Visioning.

Positive Public Spaces Are the Heart of Any Community

Response Value +6(4)

Public Space in the Center of a Suburban Town

Every community center wants and needs a public gathering space.

Comment and design response: The increase in response value is due to the application of quality urban design features. The value increase from a –1 (BEFORE) to a +6 (AFTER) is based on those features that people perceive, primarily when walking. Changing the texture and character of the sidewalk, adding decorative lighting, street trees, and well-designed shopfronts with awnings and flower pots must be incorporated into the street and landscape portion of any negative street if the downtown is to become more desirable. To enhance this downtown, a streetscape and landscape plan must be generated, followed by specific engineering plans which incorporates these features. The investment will be worth it, with improved business and community pride.

Comment and design response: This public space feels comfortable and inviting. Towns need more of these. They can be easily planned and designed with movable chairs, tables, umbrellas, and a few ledges and edges, supported by a local restaurant. This public space is formed by a large setback on a corner. The size, location, and character are ideal for people to meet and greet others. This space has a café, with movable chairs and tables, and additional edges and ledges to sit and watch people. Pedestrian circulation is maximized due to the corner location and connections to other blocks, with mixed-use frontage and sidewalks. Many of the criteria for a good public space are met, including sun, light, shade from trees, places to sit and see other people, activities, and food. The addition of a small fountain or water feature would further enhance this space.

When community leaders are open to implementing a collective consensus vision, great things can happen.

The Robbinsville Town Center and Four Surrounding Neighborhoods

Background

The plan for the Robbinsville Town Center emerged from many comprehensive visioning sessions with township officials and residents to plan, design, zone, and implement a mixed-use town center with a Main Street that is walkable from most residential units. A primary goal was to locate the highest-density residential and mixed-use buildings closest to the center, redesign the existing New Jersey State Highway 33 into a Main Street, and enhance the existing wetlands. The design and engineering of a small wetlands into an attractive water body for surface water detention and retention that was edged with parks and recreation enhanced the

aesthetic, functional and market value of the community. TDR was used to achieve the goals of preservation of peripheral farmland, encouragement of higher walkable density and affordable housing in the Town Center.

The resulting plan included a major Town Center core with four neighborhoods, each with their own public space focus. The two small "lakes" emerged from the need for storm water detention and retention, and to create a natural focused large park. These community goals correspond almost exactly with positive response values expressed in the VPS.

TDR was used to preserve farmlands in the township. Potential future lots were purchased from farmers under New Jersey Farmland Preservation rules, and the units were transferred to the town center to increase the density, specifically within walking distance to the Main Street. In this respect, both the vision of a denser town center and the preservation of farmland was achieved. The transferred units increased the viability and marketability of the town center, gave older farmers a retirement income, and made it more likely for young people to farm while retaining the rural character surrounding the town center that people rate so very positively.

In retrospect, this plan emerged because the mayor, the council, and the planning board members at that time collectively realized that their Township was becoming just another sprawled municipality that had no center or traditional village character. The township's three small rural hamlets had been swollen by scattered residential sprawl and random strip commercial structures and were losing their rural character, which they loved and wanted to preserve. In the future, they wanted a real town center, like the many small successful walkable villages in other parts of New Jersey. Most importantly, they realized that the existing zoning was promoting sprawl which they did not want but could not control unless the zoning was changed.

They were searching for a method through which to implement their collective desires. What was required was a new master/comprehensive plan and a zoning ordinance to implement the preferences in their minds. To give substance to those desires, one of the first Township-wide VPS and VTWs were commissioned which would present a visual consensus of what the people, businesses, and farmers wanted the township to function, look, and feel like in the future. From these positive visions, a new Master Plan and zoning ordinance emerged which allowed the town center and its neighborhood to be built. Despite some initial developer/builder objections, like "buyers want garages in front not off alleys," "they want larger lots," "it will be more expensive," the mayor and council held fast to the vision, and today, that vision is a reality. The developers wanted the status quo, what they knew and had built. It was the vision that prevailed.

When community leaders are open to generating a collective consensus vision, great things can happen. When there is division and conflicting personal preferences, little gets done, and the spaces and spaces are neutral or nega-

tive. Armed with their community consensus, positive preferences were incorporated into a revised Master Plan and then the first Form-Based Code in the State of New Jersey. The Planning Board and members of the Council stayed in office long enough to see the resulting plan through implementation. The town-appointed landscape architect-planner was instrumental in the final implementation of the Form-Based Code.

The first concept plan for the Town Center, completed in 1994, has housing wrapped around the mixed-use retail/residential/office core, with connected adjacent neighborhoods. The plan responded to one of the very first Community Visioning contracts awarded to the new office of Hintz Nelessen Associates. This plan became the urban design of the final adopted plan.

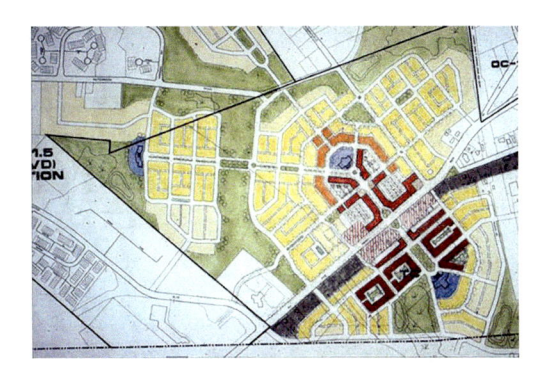

Concept Vision for the Town Center

The mixed-use retail housing is red and pink, townhouses are in orange, narrow lot single-family homes are in yellow, civic uses are in blue, and parks and public recreation spaces are in green. Residential lanes are located in the center of all blocks. Greenspaces surround the town center and are incorporated into the plan in small parks and neighborhood squares. Farmland was saved, and additional housing units were allowed using TDR.

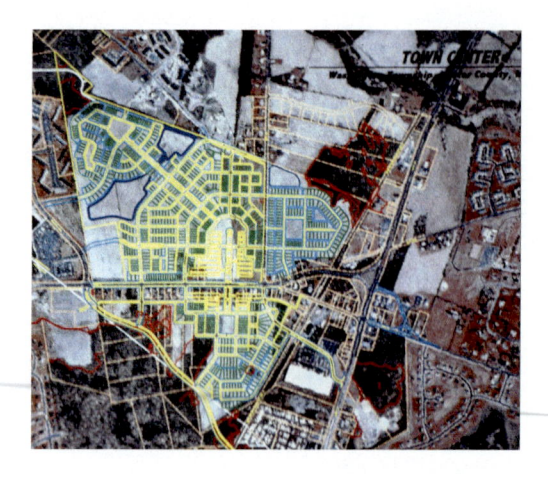

Final Adopted Plan for Town Center for Robbinsville, New Jersey

The adopted Street, Block, and Lot Plan is illustrated in yellow. The wider street near the bottom left of the plan is the proposed State Route 33 bypass required to convert the original highway into a Main Street. The adopted Street Regulating Plan from the Form-Based Code refined the first draft plan, adding more streets, reconfiguring others, and adding more parks and green spaces.

A Form-Based Code was the first to be adopted by a Township and implemented in the State of New Jersey. The code included a Street Regulating Plan, Building Regulating Plan, Open Space Plan, and Architectural Vocabulary.

Today, the Robbinsville Town Center is a multi-awarded, financially successful community including a Charter Award from the Congress for the New Urbanism.

Images in four categories portray the built character of the

Robbinsville Town Center, reflecting the positive responses from the Community Visioning Process.

- Boulevards, Streets, and Residential Lanes
- Housing Types—Single Family and Townhouses
- Public Parks, Greenways, and Natural Area
- Town Core

Streets, Boulevards, and Residential Lanes

"Streets are a community's most important public spaces. It is here where the first and major impression of place and spaces are formed."

Nelessen

Typical residential street with parkway, street trees at regular intervals, and a semi-public edge. The streets are wide enough for guest parking and bicycles.

A boulevard with a center green of trees; a wide parkway with more street trees; and a larger front yard, semi-public space defined by hedges. This boulevard connects one of the neighborhoods to the mixed-use core of the town center. Note the lack of curb cuts, garages, and paved driveways in the front yard.

Housing Types—Single Family and Townhouses

All blocks have rear access lanes to provide for garage, infrastructure lines, and garbage collection. Keeping these operations out of the public domain allows a proper positive front street image. No garages or driveways exist along the pedestrian realm. Typically, two-car garages are located off the residential lane. When a one-car garage is provided, an additional uncovered parking space is provided.

Narrow lot, village-type, single-family housing based on the adopted street, lot form, building-regulating plan, and design vocabulary. These units front onto a small neighborhood park. Each has a shallow front yard (semi-public space), front porch, first floor raised above grade, with a garage located in the rear of the lot accessed from a residential lane. All features conform to the Form-Based Code.

Typical residential street edge. The regulations require a defined semi-public edge setback from the sidewalks with a low fence or hedge. Each home raised above grade is accessed by steps to a stoop or a porch, enhancing privacy and security.

Townhouses are located near the center of the mixed-use town core or surrounding the large public green spaces in the center of a neighborhood. Townhouses were designed close to the sidewalk's edge, with a smaller defined semi-public space, stairs, and a stoop.

The individuality of the townhouses was expressed in the facade and entrance treatment. The streetscape of a narrow parkway with trees at regular intervals, sidewalk, and planting in front of the low metal fence and pillars give it an urban intimacy.

Apartments are located in the center core area of the town center. Four-story, double-loaded apartments have well-defined unique entrances and semi-public space. Facades are stepped back, with articulated upper and lower cornices and planters to reduce the institutional look of a long unarticulated facade. The step back reinforces a more individual look by using an Individual Building Module (IBM) technique.

Although a consistent window was used, multiple unique looks were generated through the header and lintel treatments. The use of the bolted-on semi balconies on most windows adds visual interest to the facade.

Public Parks, Greenways, and Natural Areas

As a walker or driver, you are exposed to green everywhere.

The parkway: *Def.* The planting area between the curb and sidewalk into which trees are planted, which extends the parks and other green areas into the community, and is considered a major component of the open space landscape network plan.

The parkway is planted with trees at close, regular intervals. It is the continuation of and the beginning of the green experience, connecting everyone with the many park and greenways throughout the town center and its neighborhoods.

A green way through the town center.

The community park and series of small ponds/lakes that also function as detention and retention ponds.

Wide sidewalk on Main Street with parallel parking and street furniture.

Small children's playground in the center of the neighborhood adjacent to the residential lane.

A mixed-use loft building in the town core with retail or offices on the ground floor and residential units above. Each building has a varied and unique facade architectural treatment, adding to the visual complexity, interest, and delight.

Town Core

Mixed-use with retail, offices, and residential buildings.

The town center was built in phases in proportion to the number of new units that were occupied. In the old phrase that "retail follows rooftops." The first phases were built along one edge and perpendicular to NJ State Highway 33. This is the first time the State of New Jersey and Mercer County have converted a highway into a Main

One of the mixed-use apartment buildings in the town core.

Street, incorporating wide sidewalks, parallel parking, decorative lighting, street trees benches, and flower pots. The shop width dimensions are narrow and well-articulated, creating a more intimate and traditional feeling. The upper floors are residential and/or offices. Parking is on-street and in large surface parking lots in the interior of the blocks.

In time, as the Main Street grows, and the next phase of the town center is built, a bypass roadway will be engineered and constructed, allowing a full two-sided Main Street to emerge.

Suburban Commercial Development

The negative visual and spatial responses to suburban commercial sprawl are ubiquitous everywhere from almost everyone.

Most commercial development in suburban areas along arterials were rated as negative and unacceptable well before the retail downturn around 2010's. Much land is still zoned for more of the same, and many of these strips are boarded up or in marginal uses which could provide positive opportunity to redevelop in a form and character that people find positive if and when the market changes.

Suburban Strip Commercial with Large Parking "Field"

This strip commercial zone with its large parking lot is typical. Notice that there is only one tree. Soon, this commercial strip and many others will be vacant and become prime sites for redevelopment.

Comment and design response: Always located adjacent to wide multi-lane arterials, with surface parking laid out to maximize the number of spaces. Outdated commercial zoning called for five to eight cars per 1,000 square feet of retail. These ratios provided the maximum opportunity of finding an empty parking space at any time. A car and an over supply of parking spaces were required for shopping by those living in adjacent suburban subdivisions. The nature of the design, and the layout of the stores and parking, destroys any possible sense of community, pleasure, or beauty. It was all about access and parking convenience.

The zoning that created this building type with this parking layout must be amended. In every location where it is in the state of deterioration and hits the bottom of the urban evolutionary spiral, new zoning or a Form-Based Code should be approved—but not before a preliminary concept has been developed, and there is a proven market. So much of what exists might have been appropriate in the 1950s, but that time has passed.

With the nature of retail changing, most of these centers are doomed to extinction. Complete redevelopment of this site is a potential alternative, as is some variation of commercial TDR for more mixed-use, higher-density town or regional centers with parks and greens. The last options are to use it as storage, warehousing, or a solar field, or let it return to nature.

Response to the Transformation of Rural, Emerging Suburban Land to Strip Commercial

The following sequence of images illustrates the transformation of an arterial that could be located anywhere suburban land is zoned for commercial sprawl. In this sequence, values decrease from positive to negative. The final simulated negative condition is quintessential to the many strip commercial conditions along arterials worldwide. The negative values of the image set are a clear indication of the desire for the preservation of the green corridor or an alternative layout.

Response Value +2(5)

Before Current Condition of Arterial Highway
This existing green edge of this suburban arterial is zoned for strip commercial development.

Comment and design response: This "before" image is characteristic of many rural four-lane highways with wide paved shoulders. In this form and condition, it receives both negative and positive responses, with a range of +7 to –2 with the mode (most often given) of 1, which can be interpreted as barely acceptable. The free flow of traffic and the green-edged fields are positives. The abandoned and deteriorated buildings in the background reduce the positive value. Abandoned and deteriorated buildings that have been vacant for a while without maintenance should be removed as soon as possible.

Response Value –4(4)

SIMULATION ONE: Strip Commercial on One Side

A negative response of –4 is generated when commercial sprawl is simulated only on one side of the arterial. The range from –8 to –0 indicates that everyone dislikes the visual and spatial character of function of this land use. The wide shoulder allows for multiple curb cuts. Major users are car dealers, which communities like because of the sales taxes generated. Typical of rural suburban commercial sprawl is the cacophony of allowed signs.

Comment and design response: Existing zoning encourages, allows, and mandates that this negative physical form be built. Everyone finds this unacceptable and inappropriate. It is clear from the responses that policy and zoning can and must be amended before this is proposed, approved, and built again. Zoning should not allow negative physical development places and spaces to be built.

SIMULATION TWO: Strip Commercial on Both Sides

A more negative response value is generated when development is built on both sides, with a response range of −9 to −3. Everyone finds this unacceptable, depressing, and environmentally degrading. Notice that with more traffic, a concrete reinforced barrier is placed in the centerline for traffic safety.

Retrofitting Suburban Commercial Areas

Plans and conceptual models for new or retrofitting existing suburban commercial area developments were the results of multiple Community Visioning sessions and responses to specific images of unacceptable strip commercial areas, balanced with acceptable images and solutions from VTW.

The development of new mixed and multiple-use retail, and the retrofitting the edge of an older suburban arterial are challenging, particularly with existing zoning promoting more strip commercial developments. There is an overwhelming desire for a walkable retail/commercial streets, which can be combined with one or more big boxes. The following street

design and building layouts suggest a positive alternative.

A design strategy for infilling or redeveloping along an arterial suggests a frontage street separated from and parallel to the arterial. In strip commercial locations, this is underutilized surface parking. The plan lays out a network of blocks of various sizes, with buildings fronting onto streets. The model illustrates a network of small and larger blocks, with larger and smaller building footprints along the street frontages. The location of the smaller shops is along the new frontage street that parallels the arterial. The model is divided into a series of buildable and walkable 400-foot blocks in the front and larger 800-foot blocks further into the site. Smaller mixed-use retail buildings are located along the frontage and parallel streets to the arterial. Multiple building variations are possible on this grid of streets. The parking for the smaller blocks are on-street and the interior of the block in the rear of the buildings, accessed from perpendicular access streets.

Directly behind the smaller block are larger 800-foot square blocks that would allow for big-box stores, other shops, or mixed-use commercial buildings with their on-grade parking. This diagram contains the fundamental street structure and layout for future commercial areas along arterials while hiding most of the surface parking. The next evolution of this street network could be the addition of more streets to further divide the larger blocks incorporating mixed-use structured parking or embedded parking if and when a mix-use residential devel-

Plan for Suburban Commercial

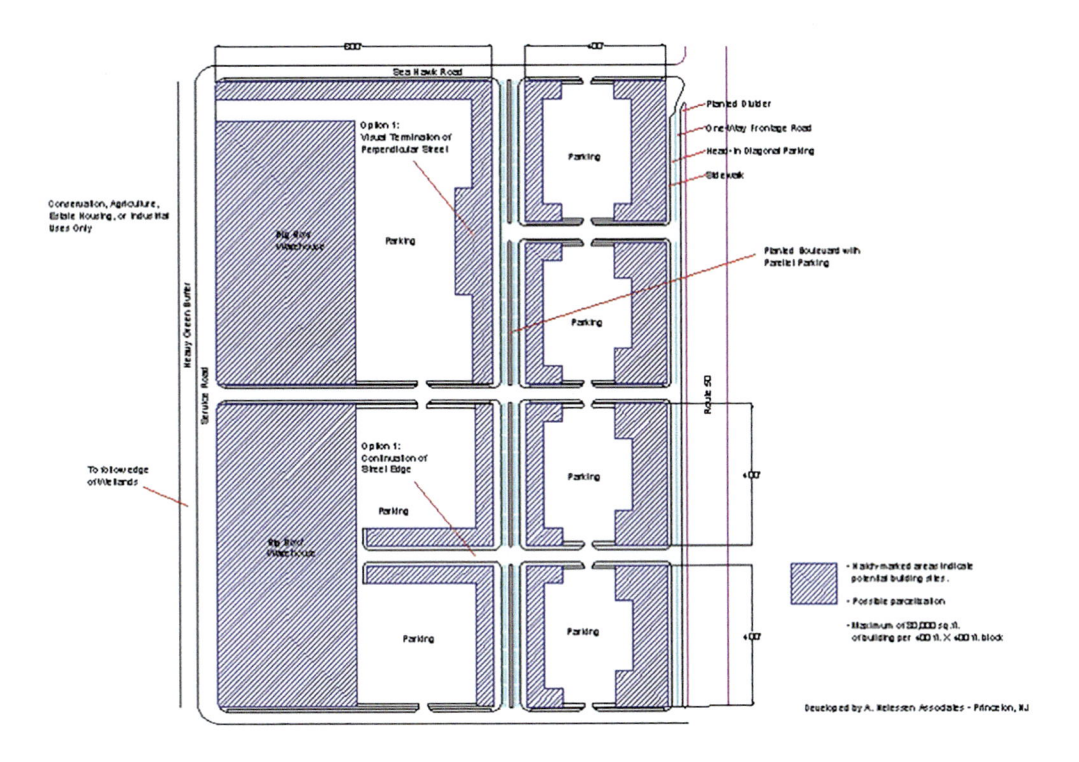

Alternative Development

This plan illustrates 400- and 800-foot blocks with a potential figure ground plan that could be infilled by a range of building types and sizes. The recommendation was made to develop a new commercial node in lieu of the typical one-story strip commercial layout with the large front parking lot.

Response Value +6(4)

opment was proposed. Elements of this alternative received positive responses in various Community Visioning sessions.

A New Frontage Street with New Mixed-use Retail

This simulated view from a car of the new frontage "slip" street illustrates a new retail façade of smaller shops with diagonal parking.

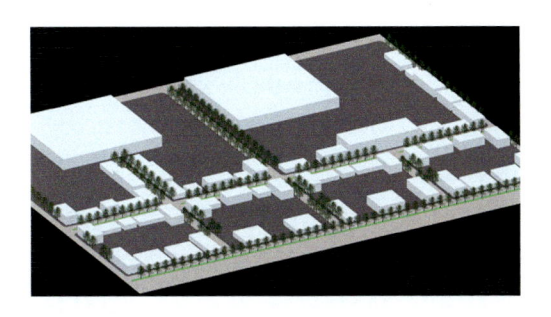

Aerial Model

Axiometric massing model of the concept plan shown above. The dark areas are parking lots shown without trees or other landscape features which would be required.

Comment and design response: Most buildings are two and three stories. The frontage street is separated from the arterial by a landscaped island. Based on its response value range of +10 to

+2, this form is highly valued and recommended. To implement it would require a modification of the circulation element of the Master Plan for the town, county, or perhaps the state. It would require a revision to the zoning code and an enlightened planning board and town engineer. It would be instrumental in the positive redevelopment of most strip commercial land uses.

Response Value +3(4)

Frontage Street

This simulation tested a frontage street parallel to the arterial.

Comment and design response: It has a bicycle path and diagonal parking, separated from the arterial by a planted island which could be a bioswale. Two- to five-story buildings are recommended. It has response value range of +7 to +0. This provides a model of possible redevelopment.

Response Value –5(4)

Existing Condition—BEFORE

Typical strip commercial development that everyone evaluated as negative.

Response Value +4(3)

Redevelopment—AFTER

A simulated "after" image of possible redevelopment. The response value increased from –5 to +4.

Comment and design response: A major intervention is required for strip commercial areas that have fallen into the deterioration phase of the cycle shown in the "Before" image. The redevelopment "After" image of this strip includes planning and designing a grid of streets with new and enhanced facades and landscaped streets. Surface parking lots are infilled with mixed-use retail/housing/offices. It has an enhanced pedestrian realm, including new sidewalks, street trees, and appropriate scaled lighting. Connections across the major arterial have been added, along with the elimination of blank facades facing the existing arterial. Parking is on-street, behind the buildings, and/or in a possible mixed-use adjacent parking structure. Any remaining buildings fronting onto the grid can be re-purposed with new facades.

Sometimes, it only takes minor landscape interventions to improve the

preferences from negative to positive.

Response Value –2(4)

Existing Condition   BEFORE

A sidewalk in a new redevelopment area with its open surface parking in the side yard. It received a negative response, even with good street landscaping. The range was –6 to +1.

Response Value +3(5)

Additional Landscaping   AFTER

Due to the addition of a low hedge and tree to screen a parking lot, the response value increased from –2 to +3.

Comment and design response: Whereas the municipality planned, designed, and constructed the new pedestrian realm, the private landowner did not do his or her part to complete the vision. Perhaps it was not required by zoning. It is important that zoning standards be amended to obscure the view of open parking lots, which always receive a negative response.

Retrofitting—Suburban Commercial Corridor

Multiple Vision Plans have been prepared for suburban corridors as strip commercial development age and become more obsolete. Response-valued images will be shown from selected contracts, but the one used most often is the nine-mile Metcalf Avenue corridor in Overland Park, Kansas. It best represents the vision and recommendations prepared for the other corridors.

The consensus preferences for this corridor were generated from an extensive public participation process called **"Vision Metcalf."** Over 4,000 people participated in generating the consensus preferences. It was the belief of the municipality that a project of this **scale would never be implemented without the input of the community**. The multi-mile corridor was the focus avenue for the city as it grew. Certain portions of the avenue were approaching the deterioration phase of the urban evolutionary spiral, while others were in the growth and optimization phase. The community was looking for its positive transformation and reinvigoration along the entire length of the corridor.

The recommended vision was a transformation of this typical auto-oriented retail strip into a series

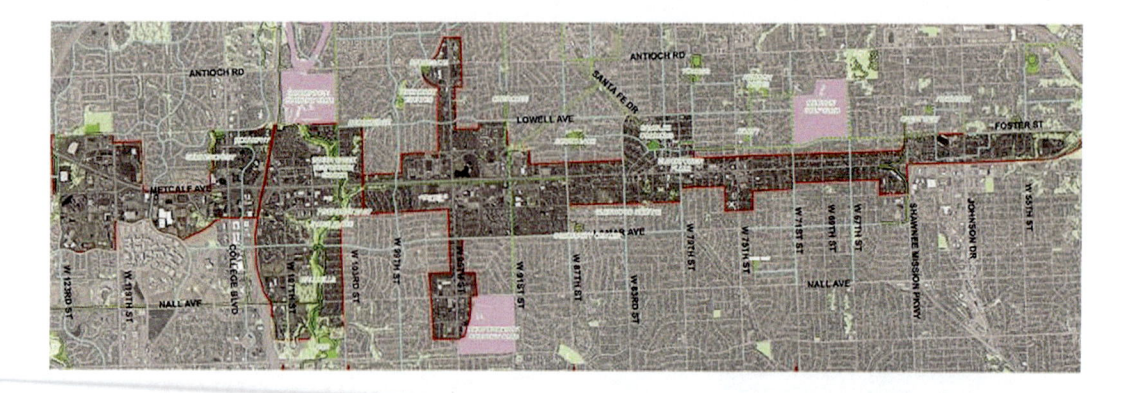

GIS Map of the Corridor

The GIS map of the entire nine-mile corridor. The area outlined in red with the darker color defines the vision area. It has various widths, with two linked sub-nodes on adjacent parallel streets.

of walkable, concentrated, mixed-use nodes connected by Bus Rapid Transit, walking, and biking. The increase in floor area ratios (FAR), mixed-use buildings, parks, landscaping, and green architecture make up some of the visual and spatial enhancements that will significantly improve the image of the corridor while increasing its economic and tax values, competitive edge, and quality of life.

Overview

Overland Park, Kansas Metcalf Avenue Study Area

- 9 miles long
- 6 square miles or 3,833 acres
- 5 unique sub-areas
- 4,960 building structures
- 4,609 parcels
- 22 acres wetlands
- 1,711 acres of impervious surface, 45% of study area

Criteria for the Vision/ Redevelopment Area

The true vision of what the Metcalf Avenue participants wanted it to become was generated from the hearts, minds, and preferences of the people of Overland Park. Reimagining the Metcalf Corridor presented the City of Overland Park with the opportunity to revitalize one of its most recognizable thoroughfares and establish a new identity for Metcalf Avenue and the entire city. The goal of the contract was to create an area that is appealing to both current and future residents, workers, businesses, and investors, and to create a more vibrant, active, and exciting place to live, work, learn, play, and invest.

Criteria that had to be met were generated through focus groups with the Steering Committee, Council members, Chamber of Commerce, bankers, major developers, and predominant merchants.

- Must generate a competitive advantage.
- Must generate wealth, tax ratables, and economic vitality.

- Must improve the quality of life and future demand for the area.
- Must be sustainable for generations with quality construction and landscaping.
- Must have positive identity
- Must promote mixed-use development.
- Must provide new mobility options

Response Value –8(2)

Older Strip Commercial

Much of this type of development is in the deterioration phase of urban evolution.

Comment and design response: Understanding negativity begins with understanding the era in which it was built; the change in uses and population that occurred; the advanced age of the structures; the low rent, vacancies, lack of maintenance, and continued disinvestment. The structures that are strong candidates for redevelopment have value responses from –3 to –7+. For them to be redeveloped, there needs to be a perceived market and zoning that will allow increased density and use. One of the keys to success is **increasing the intensity of use from three to five times the current square footage**.

Simulations of Positive Transformation

On the following pages are a series of simulations used in Community Visioning of corridors in various locations across the country. The positive transformation of these negative places clearly suggests that people want a humanism of place. The transformation of older strip commercial areas into walkable, livable, and transit-oriented areas is illustrated in the following "before" and "after" pairs. When a place improves in response value, those features that increased the values can be analyzed and incorporated in new zoning and design standards.

Response Value –5(3)

Existing Condition   BEFORE

The existing (BEFORE) condition photographed on Metcalf Avenue is characteristic of the zoning for this area, with its low floor area ratio, high parking requirements, single story box building, parking in the front yard, and multiple curb cuts.

Comment and design response: Despite the low signs and presence of sidewalks, it received a value of –5, with a standard deviation of 3, which translates into a range of –2 to –8 that is unacceptable to everyone. No one wants to shop here. Clearly, the area is in need of transformation as it is near the bottom of the urban evolutionary spiral.

Response Value +6(3)

Desired Vision   AFTER

The visioned character (AFTER) portrays a complete transformation from a deteriorating negative strip commercial development into a vibrant pedestrian based mixed-use node served by Bus Rapid Transit (BRT).

Comment and design response: The most desired transformation includes three- and four-story mixed-use buildings, lining a new wide, paved sidewalk and new street trees, along with street furniture, small signs, and outdoor café, and, in the center of the street, BRT. The response value indicates that everyone felt that this place was very positive and desirable with a change in response value from –5 to +6. The urban design features of this image were incorporated into the final recommendations and Form-Based Code.

Response Value –6(4)

Existing Condition   BEFORE

The sub-area in the historic "downtown" of Overland Park currently has scattered small single-story buildings, an overly wide street, front yard surface parking, and discontinuous narrow sidewalks without landscaping. It is a "sea of asphalt" and deserves its –6 response value.

Response Value +4(4)

Desired Vision   AFTER

This simulation portrays a classis streetscape evaluated in many VPSs. It contains all the urban design features participants find positive and desirable.

Comment and design response: A new Urban Design Vocabulary as a section of a new Form-Based Code which uses these positive streetscapes and building wall features will generate the type of pedestrian and retail experiences that participants want in other areas. Features that have to be designed are the width and texture of the sidewalk; the location and types of trees; the pedestrian and street lighting; the modulation of the store fronts; the height of the buildings; the facade design and material; signing; night lighting; parking; and deliveries.

Vision for Sub-Nodes

These smaller shopping and service areas are not on the corridor. They are located some distance away at the intersections of secondary parallel streets. They typically have one-story buildings, localized retail areas, and commercial units on scattered sites with large surface parking lots. These can complement or detract from the corridor.

Response Value –3(4)

Existing Condition BEFORE

The sub-node or secondary retail/commercial area is located on this wide intersection with a one-story building on the corner. It is valued negatively by most participants.

Response Value +4(3)

Desired Vision AFTER

Proposed redevelopment of the corner envisioned a landscape treatment for the intersection and infill and rehabilitation of this sub-area node.

Comment and design response: The street/intersection was improved by paving, crosswalks, street trees, center safe islands, and pedestrian-scaled lighting. The corner area was enhanced with a three-story mixed-use retail building on wide, textured, and landscaped sidewalks. The three-story building on the corner and the clock tower gives greater legibility and landmark identity to the sub-node. Parking is on-street and the interior of the block. The transit servicing this node is an electric bus which connects to the BRT stops on Metcalf Avenue.

Prototype Block and Infill Model The Redevelopment Diagram to Create New Nodes along a Corridor

There are many larger one- and two-story buildings, and even larger underutilized parking lots that provide opportunities for infill and redevelopment. Designing a series of new blocks creates a framework for infill and a potential

new node of mixed-use activity. The following set of three axonometric drawings were generated from VPSs and the VTWs.

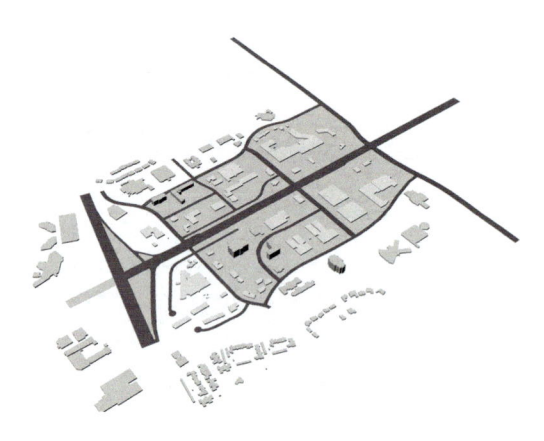

Aerial View Model of Buildings Surrounded by Large Surface Parking Lots

This three-dimensional model/diagram illustrates an existing location along the corridor at the intersection of a major freeway. Existing buildings, mostly one story, are shown in the lighter gray with shadows. The remaining gray areas are surface parking lots. The entire area is divided into only seven large "super blocks" by streets and driveways providing access to the surface parking lots.

Proposed Area Divided into Buildable Blocks

This diagram illustrates a proposed street network (in red), creating 35 smaller potential development blocks. This new street network creates a street and blocks network that promote effective redevelopment and infill, with an active pedestrian realm.

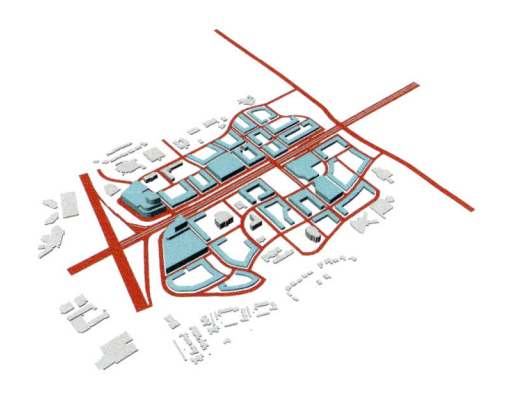

Proposed Area Divided into Buildable Blocks

An extraordinary number of new buildings with street frontages are possible with the new street and block configuration. Potential new buildings are shown in blue. The existing buildings to remain are in gray. The parking is on-street and on grade in well-landscaped parking lots or embedded in mixed-use parking structures located in the white areas in the model.

Comment and design response: The urban design starts by locating the existing buildings, access street and driveways, property lines, and current surface parking lots. The new streets are carefully laid out using the existing circulation pattern in the parking lots and paying close attention to adding streets along the shared property lines in order to interconnect multiple parcels. The number of blocks could be more or fewer than shown. The new streets have to be carefully phased as parcels change ownership. Now, many developers can participate in the redevelopment effort on the smaller blocks, while the existing owners reap the benefits. Specific street sections were included in the Form-based zoning code in order to assure a positive pedestrian realm and vehicular circulation. It is an opportunity to build complete streets.

Response Value +6(3)

Vision of the Buildings and Streetscapes within the Proposed New Block and Infill Model

This simulation of one of the infill buildings in the model. Every participant thought it very appropriate. Major features include mixed-use buildings with retail on the ground floor and residential or office units above.

Comment and design response: The simulation shows very wide sidewalks and quality street landscaping with room for large cafés, mid-sidewalk planting, and singing. The widest sidewalk should be located along the most intensive pedestrian flow. The height of the building can vary but should not be less than five stories.

The Block and Street Plan for the Entire Corridor

The Vision Plan established a coherent and positive identity for the corridor by creating a series of unique destinations (nodes of activity) using the block and infill model. The resulting plan enhanced the economic vitality of the corridor and the city by expanding the level of residential and commercial activity and promoting a pattern of mixed-use development. New buildings combine residential and commercial areas, entertainment, recreation, and parks, creating an environment where living, shopping, and working are all possible within a five-minute walk to one another and transit.

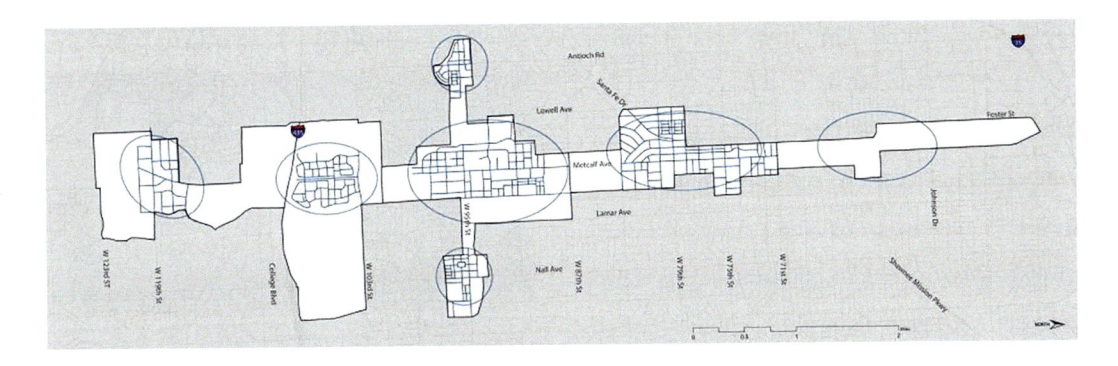

Street and Block Plan for the Corridor

Seven nodes of development were recommended after completing the Community Visioning Process, including the Translation Workshops. Each node was redesigned into a series of blocks with a combination of new streets and existing lanes in surface parking lots. The recommended street and block configurations are shown in blue lines. The areas between the nodes would be heavily landscaped, and existing buildings would be enhanced where possible. New street grids, with smaller blocks, were designed. When streets were laid out over existing parking lots, they created irregular blocks where existing buildings could be accommodated and into which new buildings could be infilled.

Parking for Suburbia

Commercial corridors that are 100% auto-dependent require enormous numbers of parking spaces with a large percentage unused except for certain days. Forty-five percent of the Metcalf corridor area was made up of impervious surfaces, with the vast majority of that in open, un-landscaped surface parking lots. Parking lots prove an extraordinary development opportunity.

> ## "Surface parking lots are the land banks for future development."
>
> *Tony Nelessen*

Additional parking will be required with the projected number of mixed-use and residential buildings, even with the implementation of the BRT. Alternatives to surface parking must be provided. Multiple alternatives exist, including mixed-use parking buildings, embedded parking, automated parking, and now the possibility of an automated car that does not park but is just used for drop-off or pick-up. All of these must be considered as a requirement for future growth.

Until redevelopment occurs, open "seas" of parking lots will be located adjacent to every building. All these parking lots are negatively rated, with a low standard deviation with a range of responses from –7 to –2. Many drivers take large parking lots that are not landscaped, with an excess of empty parking spaces, for granted. To test a landscaped surface parking lot alternative, this simulation was prepared. The results revealed that, to be perceived as positive by all, existing surface parking lots must be landscaped and screened with hedges, trees, low bushes in planting areas, and pedestrian accessways. Screening to hide cars but not signs is particularly important along the highway or street edge. The interior of lots must be planted with trees suitable to provide shade.

Landscaped Surface Parking Lot   AFTER

It is important that the view of surface parking, particularly the edge, be heavily landscaped to partially obscure the negative view. The cars do not have to be completely hidden, just screened.

Response Value –2(5)

Existing Surface Parking Lot   BEFORE

The before image of a typical surface parking lot. This one has a few trees at its edge.

Comment and design response: Hedges at 2.5 to 3 feet high allow a view of the lot and the facades. Planting in this form can make a positive difference. The plant types will vary according to location, but a good landscape architect can specify the right plants for any location. Drip irrigation is recommended. To ensure plant survival, towns should require plant replacement for two growing seasons.

Location and Recommended Design of Parking Structures

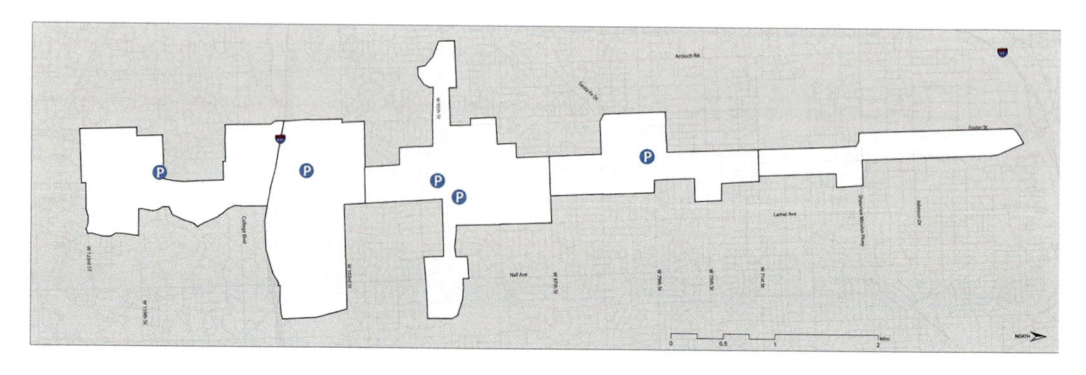

Location of Proposed Parking Structures

Locations are recommended for mixed-use parking buildings along this corridor. Five are recommended, with one or more located in each of the major nodes. They must be contextually designed to complement the adjoining urban fabric. They should also be within a short walk of all uses within that node and located close to the BRT stations.

Comment and design response: A map showing potential locations for mixed-use parking buildings needs to be prepared for every redevelopment area.

Response Value +5(4)

Mixed-use Parking Buildings

This mixed-use parking building has a facade design that looks more like office or residential units on the top floors. It received high response values and was acceptable to everyone.

Comment and design response: It is important that these structures not look like the typical value-engineered parking structure. Buildings must be mixed use, with well-designed lower-level retail or services, awnings, appropriate small signage, textured sidewalks, good lighting, and articulated upper facades with openings that look like windows, complemented by high-quality street furniture. The very contextual design using similar materials, colors, and scale to make it compatible and visually complementary to the adjacent and adjoining building facades.

Nature and Urbanism for Suburbia

Green areas, parks, and natural areas are highly rated. They are best when integrated into a green network of parks, plazas, bioswales, natural amenities, and streetscape treatments. To meet expectations generated by the Community Visioning sessions, it was critical to design interesting, beautiful, and functional public green spaces and plazas in all

redevelopment areas's and new town centers. The highest-rated images were public parks of different sizes, both with water features. This high response suggests the hyper-importance of these parks within walking distance of commercial and residential buildings.

Comment and design response: It became manifest in the 1990's that many who lived in suburbia wanted to experience a small town "main street" character of place and not just another typical strip mall. The "life quality" center was born. To meet market demand, developers received variances in suburban areas to build a walkable and interesting regional center or, in some cases, a town center on a grid of streets with a green town square. More of this character is needed when retrofitting suburbia.

Response Value –3(4)

Open Concrete Drainage Ditch   BEFORE

Above, a typical engineering solution used a concrete paved drainage ditch and culvert.

Response Value +8(2)

Small Public Square in a New Town Center

A highly rated vision of place with a center fountain surrounded by grass and to- to three-story, mixed-use commercial buildings.

Response Value +6(4)

Bio Swale—Water Garden   AFTER

This simulation removes the concrete and re-designs it as a well-landscaped water garden/bioswale, and a retention pond with additional vegetation.

Comments and design response: The "after" images reveal an extraordinary increase in response value. It will be a real pleasure to walk here. It will enhance the value and marketability of the adjacent buildings. It will improve water and air quality. This design should be used as often as possible where grades and flow volumes permit.

Mobility for a Suburban Corridor

Provide for balanced multi-modal mobility. Community Vision consensus recommended the provision of a balanced mobility system that would provide multiple travel options within the corridor, including walking; normal and e-scooters and bicycles; BRT; regional buses; on-demand cars, like Uber and Lyft; as well as vertical and horizontal elevators, stairs, and escalators in multi-story structures. Private cars, standard or autonomous, will still dominate for many more years, but when they are parked, the "park once" concept is recommended. Walking and other

transit modes should enhance the experience of place and interconnect nodes of mixed and multiple-use activities. Mobility starts with a positive walking experience.

Response Value +7(4)

Infilled and Enhanced Streetscape   AFTER

This simulation provoked a very high positive response with a change from –6 to +7. The increased vitality of the sidewalk's pedestrian realm is enhanced by setbacks; textured paving; parallel parking; trees; new lighting standards; and mixed-use, two-story infill buildings. The building wall is set back at a diagonal, creating a simple defined public space. The wide sidewalks, public space, and parallel parking create a buffer to the moving traffic.

Response Value –6(4)

Existing Condition   BEFORE

The existing condition in one area of this corridor had completed its useful lifespan and was in the lowest quadrant of deterioration ready for rehabilitation. The existing condition is typical of many pockets along older suburban corridors. No one wants to walk here.

Comment and design response: Focus on designing a positive walking experience and visual sequence. Study and apply all these urban design attributes anywhere that a positive pedestrian walking experience is desired. These planning and urban design features must be included in any final recommended urban design/redevelopment plan.

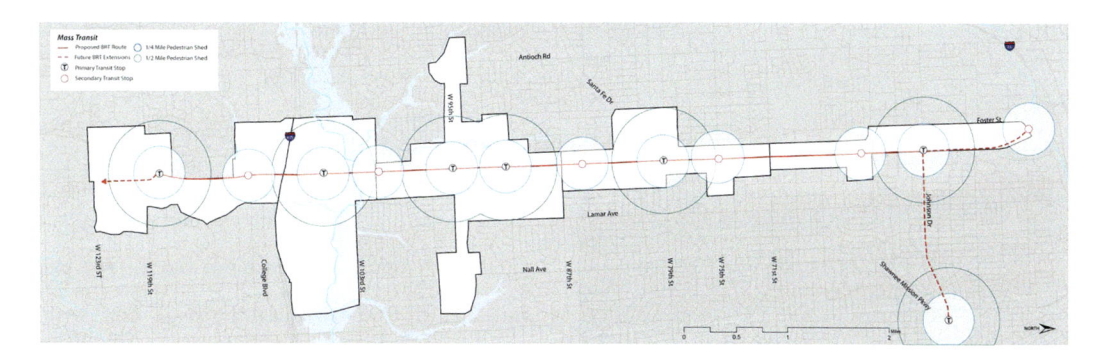

The Bus Rapid Transit (BRT)
Map of Proposed BRT Stops and Their Walking Distances

The proposed bus rapid transit line is shown in red. The important five- and ten-minute walking distances are shown by blue circles.

Comment and design response: The location of the transit line and stops were generated from the Community Visioning process and the VTWs. The map locates the stops in each designated node along this corridor. The primary stops are indicated with the double circles, the approximate center of the recommended primary node, which are planned for the highest-intensity redevelopment. The secondary stop has a single circle. The stops must be as close as possible to the center of the node.

Response Value +7(3)

Bus Rapid Transit Line and Vehicle

A BRT is highly desired for the corridor, given its high response value, with a range from +10 to +4.

Comment and design response: The BRT has its own right-of-way and could be located in a wide, center median or in the side lane. It has movement priority at intersections with priority signaling. Stops and stations, if located in the center lane, must have designated crosswalks.

Existing Boulevard   BEFORE

This before image illustrates the grassed center median forming an immensely wide and ill-defined and landscaped boulevard.

Response Value +5(4)

**Center Boulevard with BRT and Stop
Street Landscaping   AFTER**

This simulates the BRT arriving at a station/stop in the center median at one of the designated future nodes.

Comment and design response: The early phases of the BRT would be a catalyst for infill and redevelopment, significantly improving the viability for redevelopment within the designated nodes. The addition of a new wide crosswalk, sidewalks, street lighting, and some additional tree plantings and landscape infrastructure would start the redevelopment cycle. Engineering and construction would require public and private funding. A district tax per square foot for lots and building areas above a certain Floor Area Ratio (FAR) has been implemented elsewhere to find district improvements and is recommended here. This corridor transit plan for Metcalf Avenue in Overland Park was one of the first to be awarded one of the first TIGER (Transportation Investments Generating Economic Recovery) Discretionary grants from the Federal Department of Transportation.

Bicycles in Suburban Linear Corridors

Enhance Bicycle Access and Use. Plan and design an interconnected network of bike lanes and trails that connect adjacent

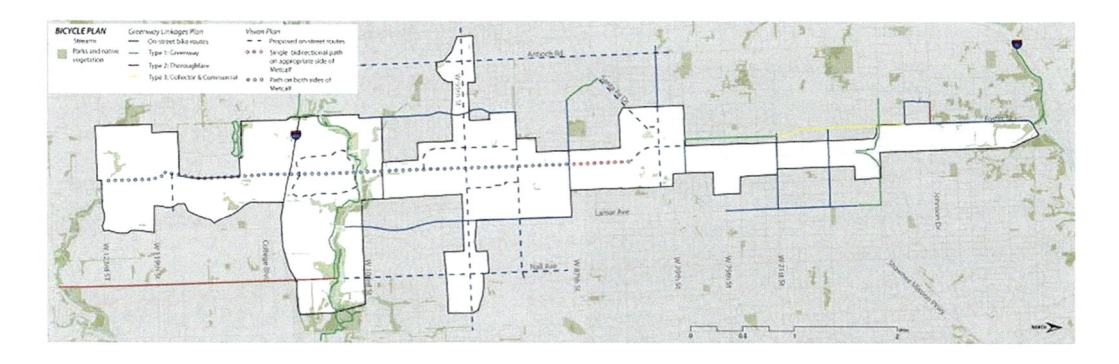

Map of Recommended Bike Routes

The map shows the recommended major and minor bike routes. The dashed lines are locations for on-street bike lanes on shoulders; the dotted circles are the separated bike paths. The proposed routes connect the nodes of redevelopment along the corridor and all the adjacent greenways.

neighborhoods, transit stops, commercial centers, existing bike trails, and greenways. Prepare a bicycle route map.

The following images decrease in response values as they are exposed to traffic.

Bikes lanes can extend access up to 2½ miles from origin to destination on well-designed paths and lanes. Travel by bike to work, transit, recreation, and shopping should be encouraged. Because so many streets are over-engineered with excessive widths, which increase speeds, these streets can be narrowed or put on a "street diet" by adding bike lanes.

Response Value +7(3)

Landscaped Bicycle Lane

This is an ideal setting for a bicycle path as part of a larger bicycle network. It is wide, with a well-land-scaped edge on one side and a park on the other. It provides a wonderful, safe riding experience.

Response Value+4(4)

Painted One-way Bike Lane

This bicycle lane is painted on the street adjacent and outside of the parallel parking area. It received a low positive. There is implied danger from driver-side car doors opening onto an oncoming bicyclist. This is the default condition in many locations where parallel parking is not removed.

Response Value +2(4)

Bike Lane Defined by a Landscaped Planter

This on-street bike lane has a high response value. With no parallel parking and a low landscaped barrier between moving vehicles, this bicycle path is an ideal road edge condition. It means that parallel parking has been removed.

Comment and design response: Bike and pedestrian planning are becoming more common in many cities because of the desire for greater sustainability, ecological responsibility, and understanding of the negative impacts of the use of the private automobile. Every Master Circulation Plan must have a bicycle element, including a primary network up to 2½ miles from the center. This includes designated place to park and a bike share program.

Summary Recommendations for Retrofitting Suburbia

Retrofitting sprawl Is A Great Challenge. So much of it exists and is deteriorating therefore having significant potential for new place making. Revise suburban zoning, site planning, design and engineering standards to limit, if not prevent more standard "cookie cutter" subdivisions and strip commercial developments. More appropriate and

> positively acceptable visions for suburbia are communities of interconnected real neighborhoods, villages, and town centers. Plan on infilling vacant areas already zoned for residential and retrofit those that are falling into the phase of deterioration. Promote mixed use walking, transit, bicycles, and integration with nature.

Residential Subdivisions

Require appropriate design standards that include:

- Applying waking distance templates which locate a center, the five- and ten-minute walking distances, and the 2½-mile bike ride.
- Planning and designing for real neighborhoods, not standard subdivisions of cul-de-sacs and loop streets. Plan and design a range of housing types, not just one with variation. Include live-work units.
- Locating an on-demand transit stop, ideally in the center.
- Ensuring that residential streets are narrow and form blocks with semi-public spaces, sidewalks, and parkways, with street trees at regular intervals.
- Promoting the use of the residential lane with garages and infrastructure in the rear of lots, not in the front. Or, as an alternative, making sure garages are set back from the front facade.
- Ensuring that all residential units are walkable or a short bike ride to commercial and recreation areas, particularly parks and green spaces
- Providing gathering spaces for social interaction
- Providing for some form of public transit within three or a maximum of ten minutes walking distance from any home or job.
- Promoting a jobs-to-housing balance within the 2½-mile radius of the center.

Commercial/Retail Areas

Retrofit older suburban, commercial arterials and office parks into mixed-use centers with an emphasis on residential, multimodal access and integration of green amenities. Use a grid of walkable streets and blocks, not to exceed 400 feet.

- Larger areas consisting primarily of surface parking lots must be subdivided into small blocks with streets to access parking lots or mixed-use parking buildings.
- Three- to five-story, mixed-use buildings with services and/or retail on the ground floor with housing or offices above are the most desired building types. Mixed-use buildings must be located on both sides of the street with wide sidewalks.

- Detailed design of the pedestrian realm must include wide textured sidewalks with street trees at regular intervals; awnings; small signs and sidewalk cafés; and decorative lighting with planters, banners, and flags that attract pedestrians and encourage walkability.
- Locate taller mixed-use buildings at gateways to serve as landmarks in redevelopment nodal areas.
- Promote multi-modes of transit, including but not limited to walking as the primary mode, bicycles, scooters, BRT, light-rail, jitneys, etc. Locate public transit stops within five-minute walks, ten minutes maximum, to serve all uses. Design stops with extended safe crosswalks connected to a network of sidewalks.
- Plan and lay out parking in the rear of the buildings, in mixed-use parking buildings, or embedded into the buildings. If surface parking is allowed, require it to be extensively landscaped on the peripheral and interior.
- Implement a comprehensive bike network with appropriate lane design and configurations connecting all residential uses to major nodes of activity, recreation, and schools. The bike network must extend 2½ miles out from the center or a 15-minute optimum bike ride.
- Relocate overhead wiring to the rear yards or place it underground

Preferred Visions

Final renderings summarize people's

vision and are critical to implementation.

public to grasp than plans or maps. They are critical for promotion and public relations, and should be included in all printed materials and videos, particularly for extended dissolve simulations.

Composite renderings are generated from the most positive images and plans generated from VTW. They visually summarize the desired spatial and visual character for infill and redevelopment efforts for the short- and long-term future. To capture many of our visions, we commissioned Dan Harmond, who was one of the nations' best architectural renderers.

Redeveloped Mixed-use Area with BRT Station Stop

Rendering of the frontage along Metcalf in one of the primary nodes. The rendering is a synthesis of the consensus vision located adjacent to the intersection of a major circumferential freeway. The rendering portrays a BRT area station; frontage streets on both sides; and green-roofed, five-story, mixed-use buildings with separate pedestrian frontages. The high-rise mixed-use buildings were designed and located as gateways adjacent to the highway. Major pedestrian paths, crosswalks, and separated bicycle paths form new cross sections of the retrofitted corridor. New landscaping includes trees, bioswales, and flower beds. Lighting is focused on the BRT stops and crosswalks. The BRT, sidewalks, and bike paths intersect with a regional bus stop located on the bridge edge of the circumferential highway in the background.

Town Square with Farmers' Market and Community Center

This rendering portrays the recommended new infill development and public park in the downtown. Shown in the center of the space is a community pavilion with the existing linear farmers' market building surrounded by mixed-use retail and residential buildings, many with green roofs. The brick tower on the right is a currently recognizable landmark.

What lives on after the Community Visioning/ public participation are the composite consensus visons: The renderings and video simulations. They portray the physical and spatial preferences at the specific known locations. These images are incredibly important since they are much easier for the general

Renderings embedded into the mind, have political power, when people see the vision.

11

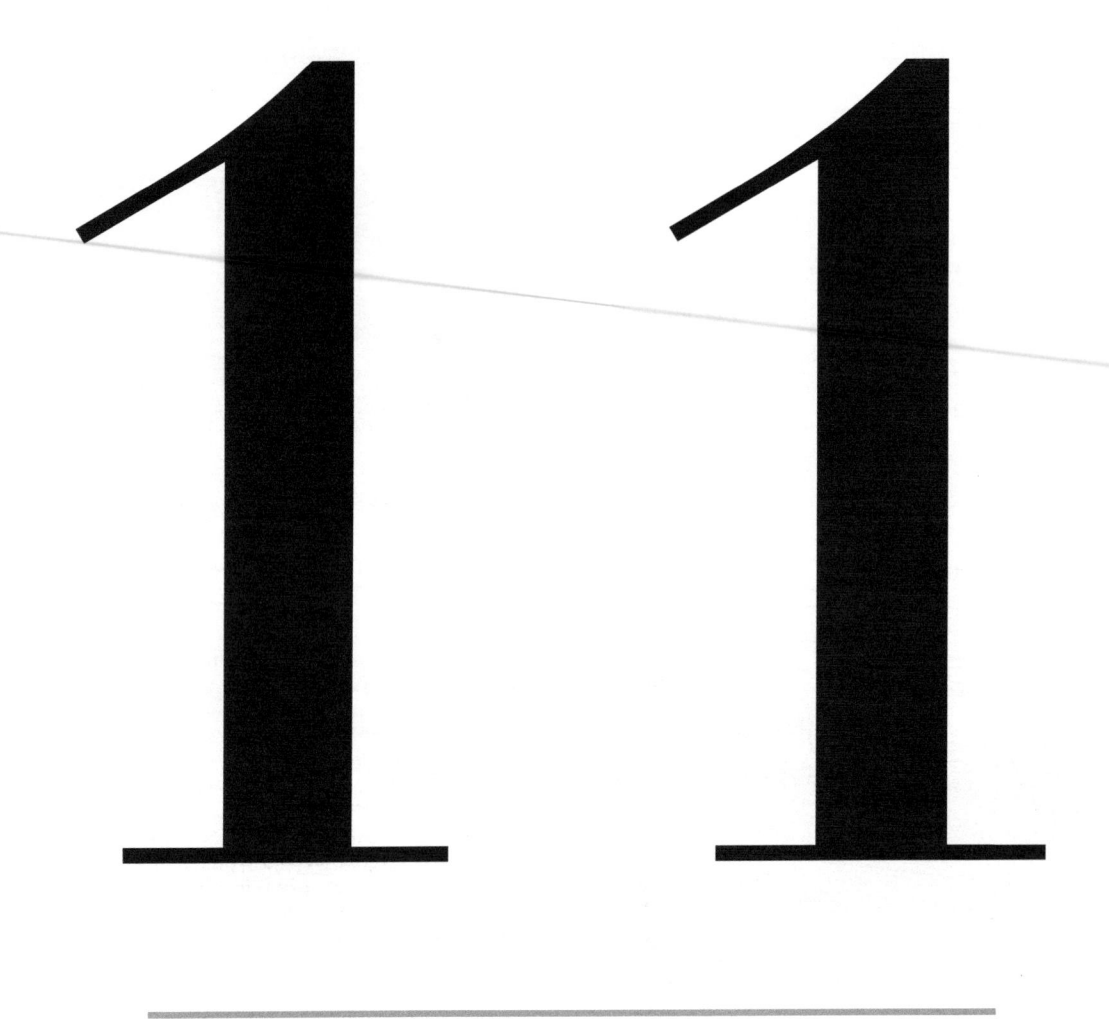

Visions for Small Towns

Well-maintained and dynamic small towns are beloved urban habitations. However, many are endangered, evolving into states of deterioration as the character of retail has changed. Too many structures have been removed to make room for surface parking. Many small towns are now being infilled, redeveloped, and revitalized.

Of the multitude of small towns that conducted Community Visioning, the towns of Metuchen and Collingswood, New Jersey; Oshkosh, Wisconsin; Spring Hill, Kansas; and Binghamton, New York were selected to represent positive and negative visons for small towns.

Most cities in the world were at some point in history a small town. They provided a sense of community, neighborliness, shared activity, values, and beliefs. Up until the 1950s, most small towns had a core of retail, services, and residences, with a center accessible from surrounding neighborhoods by walking, bicycle, or streetcar. Some had a train station. Usually, the primary and high schools were located in or adjacent to the downtown, along with municipal functions. All of this began to evolve and change as sprawl became dominant. Many of these towns lost some, if not all, of their retail, service core functions, and rail stations. Many were subject to disuse, lack of parking, and lack of maintenance. Conditions reached a sense of desperation when multi-story buildings in the core were demolished so their land could be used as parking. Surface parking lots in their downtowns were probably the worst thing that could have happened to the fabric of these small towns as they tried, understandably, to compete with suburban retail strips with unlimited parking. Still, some small towns survived the phases of deterioration to emerge again into the growth and optimization phase.

Small Town Main Street
This small town implemented its vision for renewal with great positive results for merchants and residents.

Saving the Small Town

After years of decline, some of these small towns are searching for new vitality. They want desperately to evolve into the next phase of redevelopment and optimization. Many will continue to shrink unless a more positive functional form and character is envisioned and implemented. Many towns require a serious makeover, increase in local population, and higher density within the five- to ten-minute walking distance of their cores. People from the community can provide a vision of what is feasible and practical. As these communities implement their specific vision, they will become more livable, valuable, and sustainable.

Strip commercial developments and big-box stores on the periphery injured the small towns. New commercial areas were built after adopting new zoning that allowed big-box retail and strip development, with large front parking lots and no pedestrian amenities. Strip commercial development was frequently built close to the small-town core but in a different jurisdiction that cared little for the town's character or viability. It is also unfortunately true that some, perhaps many, traditional small towns adopted this zoning on their periphery, with similar zoning for their downtown, which was a tragic mistake. This type of action stripped small towns of their character and function. All strip developments close to a small town resulted in its downward spiral towards deterioration.

The difficulty and sometimes the opportunity for many small towns is the local politicians' interests, which are more focused on personal preferences and favoritism. These preferences are approved by planning boards appointed by the elected leaders. This prevents a true community visioning process because of the "I know best" attitude and the fear that most public meetings are more negative than positive. Some municipalities conduct town hall sessions with ideas summarily "taken into consideration." This is code for filed away and never used.

Other leaders see the benefit of involving their community. Where there is a collective vision and leadership that believes in the preferences of the people, the town will change for the better. With no vision, the status quo will be maintained. This inevitably leads to desperation among citizens, deterioration of infrastructures, and loss of ratables.

A strong and enduring community-supported vision is required to facilitate positive change over time, particularly when leadership changes due to local elections and the potential replacement of vision supporters every few years. This can be good or bad depending on who is elected and their specific visions. **To implement a consensus vision for a small town has proven to take many years and requires consistent, informed, committed leadership**. It also requires public-private partnerships. When many developers participate in the Community Visioning process, implementation is almost assured.

Most small towns have limited resources, and therefore, the vision process must be efficient, cost effective, and combined with the revision to the master plan or the municipal building and development codes. The amendment to the zoning is critical for the implementation of citizens' visions.

The Preferences and Visions

The following were selected from only five of the multiple small towns that contracted Community Vision sessions. These images best represent the consensus, taken into consideration by all the other towns that participated.

Most Negative Visual and Spatial Characteristics of Small Towns

The negative responses are greater than the positives in many of the small towns.

The most negative images of small towns were in the Pedestrian Realm category. These are unacceptable and disliked, generating negative emotional reactions. The longer the negative condition exists, the more they influence the mental and physical health of those that experience it.

Response Value –8(2)

Rear View of Building along Main Street

Many buildings in small towns were demolished for surface parking in order to compete with the free parking in strip commercial developments. Stores and shops are accessed from the parking lots through the rear entrances.

Comment and design response: Every image portraying this character of place received negative responses. At the same time, small towns are reluctant to give up any parking. It's a classic dilemma. Important is to locate and design parking in a way that makes the front of the stores the most visible and used.

Response Value –7(4)

Sidewalk by School Gate

This is the pedestrian realm in front of the entrance to an elementary school in a small town. Not only is it dirty; it also lacks maintenance and has a prison-like chain-link fence. It lacks any landscaping or proper streetscape features, like trees and curbing. It looks and feels dangerous. The dirty asphalt from the street extends into the playground. This has profound short- and long-term implications as it is experienced each day by many young children and parents, who also experience a sense of extreme negativity.

Comment and design response: Collective negative responses below (–1) demonstrates a lack of concern and the presence of ugliness. In this case, that is experienced by schoolchildren and their parents, teachers, and neighbors, and everyone else that passes by. It's an extraordinary negative value that demands change. Clear violations of a positive pedestrian realm are unacceptable. Is it any wonder that there is, in this town, a sense of negativism, disbelief in the possible, and high drug use?

After a few years, the small town will enter a stage of deterioration. If this happens, the new planning vision must include maintenance, upkeep, safety and shrinkage, and focused revitalization, or the town will continue to fall into a deeper phase of deterioration. It must capitalize on its remaining historical, physical, and social resources. Other small towns equipped with a vision and leadership evolve into the phase of redevelopment.

Response Value –7(4)

Vacant Lot in the Downtown
Lot was previously a lumber yard.

Response Value –7(5)

Access Street to the Downtown Core
The character of this street, just outside of the downtown, reveals lack of maintenance, gaps in the fabric, continuous blacktop, and inconsistent setbacks.

Comment and design response: The older buildings are covered with new aluminum siding, the street has overhead wires, and sprawl development in the background, with no streetscaping. When small towns lose their major employers, their tax base is typically encumbered by increased social and physical obligations. The cost of maintenance is the first to be sacrificed.

Comment and design response: The buildings were torn down after the business could no longer compete with the big-box home improvement stores. The site provides an opportunity for redevelopment. In its current condition, it is very negatively perceived. Fortunately, in this case, the town commissioned a Community Visioning process and moved quickly into approval for infill, possibly due to the leadership of the mayor, who is a redevelopment attorney, and the planning director who championed the community vision.

Empty Stores in Too Many Small-Town Downtowns Response Values –5(2) to –7(3)

After businesses moved to the new strip malls along the highway, images of empty storefronts and upper stories generated negative responses. These were viewed as a manifestation of depression and hopelessness. The "Prevent Suicide" sign on one prime corner building reinforced this negative sense.

Comment and design response: The potential character of downtown buildings and street walls provide a great opportunity for innovation, transformation, and investment. Downtown users want positive, pleasant, comfortable places to walk. With Internet shopping devastating local sales, merchants, today more than ever, require a positive pedestrian experience in order to be competitive.

Response Value –5(4)

"Re-muddled" Storefront

In a desperate attempt to improve the visual and spatial character of the downtown, some store fronts were rehabbed. On this building the quintessential mansard roof was used along the front and part of the facade on the perpendicular street. Badly done.

Comment and design response: The form, character, and current condition of this building were rated as negative. Empty buildings with inappropriate "remuddled" facades were common while the vision plan was in progress. This building and front facade demonstrates a complete lack of sensitivity to the architectural context. The value-engineered solution is unacceptable if the town wishes to attract new residents and businesses.

Response Value –3(5)

Mostly Empty Main Street

The Main Street of this small town is barely viable. Its important visual features are the remaining collection of extraordinary Victorian multi-story buildings with cream-colored brick facades.

Comment and design response: As is typical of most of these older cities, the street was widened, and sidewalks were narrowed to accommodate car traffic. The traffic engineers believed that, to compete with strip malls, every place had to have maximum accessibility and traffic flow. Thanks to the building of a "highway" through the center of town, the Main Street could no longer compete as a walkable, viable downtown, and it is now nearly empty. Merchants want slow traffic, so customers linger, look, and then buy. Most traffic engineers couldn't care less about the pedestrian. Car flow and "safety" are their primary concerns.

Response Value –2(4)

An Unacceptable Pedestrian Realm
"Not good enough."

Comment and design response: The negative response to this image is mostly due to its narrow concrete sidewalks; non-interactive, discontinuous facade; lack of street landscaping; and an uninviting concrete bench. It is functional but not a pleasant place to walk.

Infill and Development Diagram (IDD)

It sets the optimum location, intensity, and use for infill and development in and around a small town. This diagram was synthesized in 1998 after hundreds of Community Visioning sessions. Superimposing this Infill and Development Diagram (IDD) in scale over the existing land use map of a municipality can help future redevelopment and master planning efforts. The form

and shape of the resulting plan will vary by geography and existing land use, but the relationships and metrics should be held. Some municipalities will generate a poly centric plan based on this diagram.

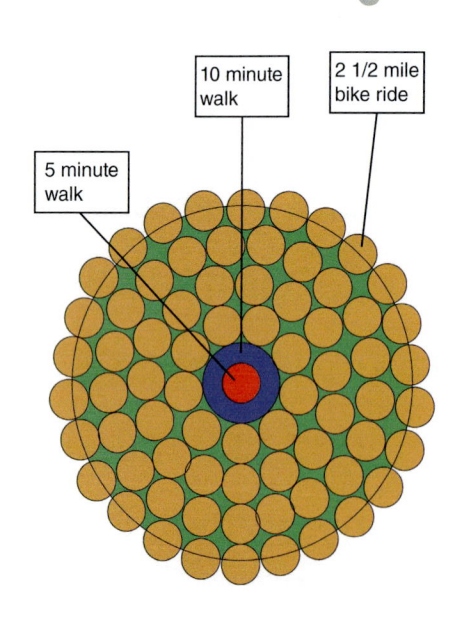

The Intill and Development Diagram is a Conceptual Planning model for Small Town Urbanism

The ideal Infill and Development Diagram sets forth relationships and metrics against which communities can plan and design to become more sustainable, livable, and efficient.

Comment and design response: This planning diagram contains metrics and relationships that are fundamental but flexible. The key is to see how your community conforms now or can conform more to this diagram in the future. The core of the small town (shown in red) located in the geographic center should have the highest intensity, height, and Floor Area Ratios (FAR). Buildings in the core should be a mix of retail, offices, services, and housing. The core must have the most positive and extensive pedestrian realms. The area of the core is delineated as a five-minute walk, or 1,500 feet, from the geographic center: An optimum ten-minute walking distance from one edge to the other. Most civic facilities and public gathering areas should be located here. This area should be the first priority for redevelopment of mixed-use infill at the highest possible intensity and height. The center core is 3,000 feet across and can accommodate a range of Main Street Central Business Districts (CBD). The area is 64 acres, larger than most small-town downtowns.

The development area surrounding the core (in blue) should have the highest intensity of residential uses. The buildings surrounding the core will not be as close together as those in the core.

The development area surrounding the core is a ten-minute walk from the center of the core and should be designed primarily for housing with limited mixed uses. Townhouses and apartment buildings are appropriate.

Extending 2½ miles out are multiple neighborhoods (shown in the orange circles) at even lower densities. The smaller orange circles represent the classic Traditional Neighborhood Development (TND) with a maximum five-minute walk from each of their neighborhood centers and their on-demand transit stop. These neighborhoods will be primarily single-family detached units on smaller lots. Each will have a public space and/or building as their center focus. Smaller towns will have fewer neighborhoods surrounding their core than shown on the IDD. The 2½-mile distance is the optimum bicycle ride to the center. It will be necessary to design, engineer and construct bicycle lanes within this radius to maximize their use for many people within these neighborhoods with connections to other neighborhoods, schools work places and the core.

When superimposing this IDD diagram in scale over the existing land use of an existing small town, **the form and shape of the resulting overlay will be unique**. The time/distance relationships and defined neighborhoods should be determined. If, for instance, a small town has multiple "cores," e.g., a downtown and an outlying shopping center that has or could have housing around it, the resulting overlay becomes polycentric and unique to this small town. Relationships overlap, and the town evolves to greater complexity.

Determining the size and center of the downtown is typically easy. Determining the dimensions of neighborhoods might be difficult. Most communities grew not according to any logical plan with a public center but more or less as the market and other forces demanded. The result has contributed to the current dysfunc-

tional and negative character. To determine the size and center of the downtown and neighborhoods, use Google Earth and walking observations. GIS is a great planning and design tool to graphically perform this locational analysis. Overlaying the diagram on the existing land use contributes to a better understanding of the dimensions of what exists and what needs to be done to plan for greater conformity, community harmony, and land sustainability. Or, at the minimum, it provides the hypothetical demarking lines or isobars of the ideal land use sizes. Many traditional towns continue to do well where their pattern more or less conforms to this IDD, particularly the viable length of the core. The walking and area relationships are fundamental.

The blue areas of residential buildings supporting the core may not conform to the exact geometry of the IDD. Nonetheless, defining the area of the core, the immediate surrounding residential neighborhoods and the 2½-mile bike ride is important to future sustainability, which is key, no matter what the geography. The green areas in the diagram represent the opportunity for green parks, parkways, community gardens, and natural areas in and between neighborhoods. Each neighborhood should have a separate focus for social engagement and on-demand transit pickup and drop off. Beyond the 2 ½-mile bicycle line can be low density residential land uses, including larger-lot single-family houses, rural estates, small farms, orchards, greenhouses, forests, or other types of low density uses.

Positive Visions for Small Town Downtown Cores

The images with the highest response values portray the *"soul"* desires of the community. The category this image is in, e.g., opens spaces or streets, becomes one of the most important urban design attributes. The image below was seen earlier in the rural category and now repeats itself in the pedestrian realm category for small towns. The high response in multiple vision locations testifies to the importance of and desire for farmers' markets. There is a powerful connection between local grow food, the agricultural community, and distribution via farmers' markets. Traditional communities surrounded by farms typically had markets one or more times per week. Farmers' markets are making a big resurgence.

Response Value +8(2)

Downtown Farmers' Markets

This is one of the highest-rated images in the VPS for small towns and rural areas. It indicates the importance of human interaction, walking, and local healthy foods.

Ideally, start with a farmers' market by closing one or more streets in the downtown on the weekends, then extend it as more people rediscover downtown and other community events. After initial success, make the market more permanent.

Comment and design response: Farmers' markets are great facilities to bring people together while providing a valuable, healthy community service and supporting local farmers. If other merchandise and music are added, the experience is enhanced. Weekly or daily farmers' markets have been held continuously for over 4,000 years in the center plazas of towns and neighborhoods worldwide. They are popular and well used. This testifies to the continued importance of farmers' market for nutritional and social value.

Provisions must be made to institutionalize these in smaller towns.

Small Downtown—Pedestrian Realm

Deemed highly desirable streetscape for smaller towns. It has a comfortable scale and character.

Comment and design response: The building form and heights, street furniture, signs, shop fronts, and proportions of the street are excellent for small towns. The most positive physical components are the wide brick sidewalks, staggered street trees, outdoor displays, small signs, parallel parking, street furniture, banners, and inviting and interactive street level. The urban design is simple and elegant.

Response Value +7(3)

Active Downtown

Another high positive image in the Pedestrian Realm Category portrays the desired character of a more compact, active, and viable downtown.

Comment and design response: Wide active sidewalks prove to be the most necessary. Many of these smaller towns would like to have the vitality of larger towns, which means that there must be a greater concentration of residential/commercial/business places within walking distance. Much of the traditional building street wall can be preserved in many small towns, which could be enhanced by wider sidewalks, cafes, active engaging storefronts, signing, and streetscapes. High density in the background suggests more people living and working in the downtown.

New higher-density residential buildings in the downtown should be encouraged. The more people who live and work in the downtown within the 2½-mile bike ride distance, the better. The core of these small towns, the buildings and streets within five- and ten-minute walking distance, should be the first priority of mixed-use, residential infill.

Response Value +5(3)

Busy Intersection for a Small Downtown

In most small-town Community Visioning sessions, this image receives positive responses, with the range of +8 to +3. It is busy and active with many pedestrians, narrow streets, and adequately wide textured sidewalks. It has mixed-use, three- to four-story buildings of distinctive facade design and character, and a continuous ground floor with retail extending to the second floor in some buildings.

Comment and design response: It has an intensive and interactive ground-floor level, with defined crosswalks; basic street furniture; and, perhaps most importantly, the safe shared use of the street by cars, cabs, and buses. Most small towns would love to have this intensity of activity character. To achieve this, the downtown needs to be compact, with many people living, working, and playing within easy walking or short transit distance.

Visual Preferences for Small Towns—What Could Be

The overwhelming response from the community visioning sessions was to restore and revitalize the CBD and surrounding neighborhoods. The vision recommendations focused on the center and surrounding neighborhoods within walking or transit distance of the core. The recommendations included saving and enhancing the structurally sound buildings; occupying the upper floors; widening sidewalks; adding new street furniture and landscaping; creating events that will draw people to the downtown; and encouraging young entrepreneurs, businesses, services, and educational uses. The following "before" and "simulated after"

images with their response values, portray places that are in or approaching the deterioration phase with vision opportunities for positive change.

Response Value +5(3)

What Is Desired   AFTER

The positive image is a transformation of the streetscape, street edge and building wall.

Comment and design response: Remove the existing deteriorated, under utilized, vacant and one story buildings, and replace them with multistory mixed-use buildings that are within five- to ten-minute walking distance of downtown. The planning goal is to create a more walkable, sustainable community, focusing on the downtown. This assumes that there is balance between the number of residents, jobs, and retail/commercial uses within a reasonable, walking, bicycle and transit ride. **A minimum of jobs to housing, and retail/service per the number of residents must be planned.** Ideally, this should range from a minimum of one job per housing unit and higher, if possible. This is not at all easy. It assumes new types of planning and financing strategies that negative places do not attract. The image simulation on the right may provide some of the urban design qualities to increase the viability of the downtown, which is critical for its survival.

Response Value –7(3)

Existing Condition   BEFORE

This before image is typical of the deterioration of the urban fabric on the edge of a shrinking downtown.

Comment and design response: The lack of maintenance is manifest. The market has disappeared, along with jobs and residential populations. The buildings no longer have a valued function, having outlived their useful life. The negative value is extreme, with a range of –4 to –10. It seldom gets lower. The asphalt sidewalk, lack of street trees, and poor drainage further contribute to its negative preference value.

Enhance the Downtown First!

Response Value –0(4)

Existing Condition   BEFORE

The existing downtown of this small town has a value of 0, with a range of –4 to +4. A zero or neutral response is the most difficult because half like it, and the other half dislike it.

Comment and design response: This downtown is still the focus of this region, and the building fabric is still intact and well maintained. To keep it from further deterioration, the simulation which follows made several minor improvements based on discussions in the early focus groups which were reinforced at the community visioning sessions. The response value was more positive.

Response Value +3(4)

What Is Desired   AFTER

The simulation portrays infilling and revitalizing with mixed-use green buildings complemented by street landscaping. The goal was to compact the downtown as much as possible and make it more of a walkable destination. Ideally, the university would occupy more buildings in the core.

Comment and design response: Given the overly wide street, institute diagonal parking to increase street parking. Add streetscape elements, like lighting and crosswalks, to balance the car with the pedestrian experience. Add as many "green" elements as possible, including roofs, terraces, etc. Convert empty upper office floors to loft apartments. Encourage innovations and start-ups, and use rent and tax incentives to attract the economic base. Promote the new image/vision of place in all marketing material and videos. Focusing on the university moving downtown will instill new and lasting vibrancy.

Response Value –3(5)

Existing Condition   BEFORE

This photograph portrays the condition of the Main Street in this small town at the commencement of the Community Vision process. This was once a very vibrant downtown.

Comment and design response: Most of the original facades are still present. Many of the stores are empty and for rent. Most of the upper stories are vacant. In the past, the street was widened, and the sidewalk width was reduced to accommodate more vehicular traffic flow, typical of so many small towns. The response ranges from –8 to +1 suggested that there is still some positive response to this historic street.

Response Value +5(5)

What Is Desired   AFTER

This "after" simulation takes the existing Main Street and incorporates all the features recommended in the focus group and the results of the visioning sessions.

Comment and design response: Design interventions include widened sidewalks, narrowed traffic lanes, active storefronts, new street lighting and street trees with lower branches removed, selected parallel parking, blue-painted bicycle paths on both sides, and textured street surface on which drivers lower their speed. The reduced traffic speed permits safer pedestrian crossings. The change in response value went from –3 to +5. With this high positive response, this range makes it clear that participants want these physical features for their Main Street.

Start Small!

Once you determine what visions the community really wants, the positive images are the catalyst for the Vision Translation Workshop (VTW,) which will determine a consensus of where the positive images should be located. From this, a more specific urban design plan with street sections and a design vocabulary can be prepared. This can then be translated into ordinances or form-based zoning codes, provided there is political agreement. In the interim, **tactical interventions** may be employed to encourage more people to come downtown, including Saturday farmers' markets, using empty stores as "pop-up" shops or parking spaces as mini parks, etc. Grants and downtown development district tax incentives must be explored.

Some additional tactical interventions include:

- **Widened and enhanced sidewalks, with cafes, and displays created by removing some parking for mini parks or more pedestrian spaces**
- **Public gathering places, made by closing portion of streets or using empty lots**
- **Painted-on crosswalks or "Barn Walks"**
- **Narrow traffic lanes, achieved by repainting edge lines**
- **Painted-on bicycle paths**
- **Temporarily closed-off street for farmers' markets**
- **Programmed cultural activities and events on weekdays and weekends**
- **Displays of the ultimate positive vision in various display mediums**

Response Value +6(4)

Downtown Plazas and Active Public Spaces

This image appears twice in the book. It has been used in multiple VPSs for suburban and small towns. Every time, the response is very positive, testifying to its importance and desired implementation.

Comment and design response: Every small town center needs a public gathering space. This image reflects the size, location, and character desired for people to meet and greet others. The space has a café, with tables and places to sit that are both movable and fixed. It is located at the 100% corner with the most pedestrian flow. This meets many of the criteria for good public spaces, including trees creating shade, places to sit and watch other people, and food activities, and is only missing a water feature. This image is applicable in multiple locations in town centers and small-town downtowns which are quite similar in desired form and character.

Note: *All the recommendations generated from the many public VPSs were similar to those recommended in the seminal book **Social Life of Small Urban Spaces** by William Whyte.*

Response Value –3(4)

Existing Condition   BEFORE

When there is no opportunity to create an adequately accessible ,centrally located and sized public space, the possibility of closing an underutilized secondary or tertiary street is an option.

Comment and design response: This short street in downtown received a negative evaluation in the VPS. The simulation of an "after" condition was used to determine the responses to possibly converting it to a full- or part-time pedestrian plaza.

Response Value +3(5)

Proposed Vision   AFTER

The redesign of the existing negative condition is portrayed in this simulation. It converts the street to a paved plaza with tables, chairs, umbrellas, trees and planters, and a possible café. The paving continuing across the intersection gives it greater spatial presence and makes crossing safer.

Comment and design response: This is the perfect design and location of a public plaza and center focus for this small town. It received a positive response but with a high standard deviation, with a range of +9 to –2. The high standard deviation initially led to some hesitation in the implementation of this vision.

Response Value +8(2)

Waterfront Walkways

Whenever there is the opportunity to include a waterfront walkway park, the enhancement to the value and livability of the small town is significantly increased. It is worth the price.

Comment and design response: People love the opportunity to walk, sit, interact, or ride a bicycle along a waterfront. Important design components are the paving texture, benches, transparent railings, and separated wide walkways and bicycle path; the spacing and location of the trees are also important urban design inclusions. In the highly rated image above, two linear spaces are created. A wonderful, well-used urban design plan.

Surface Parking Lots in a Downtown

They Provide an Extraordinary Opportunity for Infill, and Should be the First Priority for Infill.

Comment and design response: The elevated train line and station with its surface parking lot received a negative neutral response value with a range of +6 to –6. This value range is the most difficult of all responses because half of the participants find it positive/acceptable, and half rate it as negative/unacceptable. It provides a functional use for the commuters, mostly out-of-towners who use this station to park their cars. The mixed response values reinforce that it provides a functional use. The question "where else would we park?" was raised. Parking would be incorporated in the development plan into mixed-use structures or embedded into blocks, thereby permitting more new buildings, parks, and other uses on this heretofore surface parking land resource.

Response Value +6(3)

Redeveloped   AFTER
The envisioned very positive design and character of this redevelopment area.

Response Value –0(6)

Existing Condition   BEFORE
This surface parking lot in the core of this small town is located adjacent to a regional transit stop connecting this small town to other towns and a major city center.

Comment and design response: The surface parking lot provides an ideal opportunity for redevelopment into a vibrant district of the downtown. The "after" simulation has a high response value, with a range of +9 to +3. It contains mixed-use buildings on both sides of an active vibrant pedestrian realm with a plaza, wide sidewalks, and retail on the ground floors with housing or offices above. Parking for the station and other uses is embedded in a structure behind and beneath the buildings. The high response value signals that all surface parking lots in a downtown are more valuable as mixed- and multiple-use buildings and spaces.

MIXED-USE INFILL in the Downtown Core

Response Value –7(4)

Existing   BEFORE

This lot was previously occupied by a lumberyard. It is unacceptable in its current vacant condition in the downtown. It is prime for redevelopment.

Response Value +6(3)

Vision of Potential Infill Character   AFTER

The simulation infilled the lot with mixed-use buildings with retail on the ground floor and residential above, combined with a vibrant streetscape.

Comment and design response: The "missing tooth" on Main Street was filled to allow the building fabric to be continuous. The value response changes from –7 (empty lot) to +6 (infilled). All participants responded positively to the character and design of this infill. This image is more small town in scale, with its pitched roofs, dormers, etc. Mixed-use residential buildings are typically 64 feet deep, with retail and/or offices on the ground floor and multiple floors of housing above. The building heights range from three to six stories. A step back can be incorporated based on the form and detail context of the adjacent buildings.

Computer Generated Model of Recommended Mixed-use Building with Parking in the Basement

Comment and design response: This mixed-use building has retail, with higher ceiling heights on the ground floor and housing or offices on the upper floor. This design has a two-story cornice before a setback with terrace. The building fronts onto a wide tree lined sidewalk with parallel parking. Parking, primarily for residential uses, is located under the building, with parking for the retail and offices in an off-site shared parking facility or on the street. There should be 16 to 18 feet of sidewalk between the building wall and the curb, with quality street furniture, lighting, trees, and canopy/awning for shade or rain protection.

Comment and design response: The elevation and street edge plan of the infill building that was constructed is a mixed-use building of three stories with pitched roofs, and small balconies facing the street; it is as reflected in the image generated during the Community Visioning and can also be seen in the previous image "Vision of Potential Infill Character -AFTER Response Value +6(3)." The new design very much reflects the character of this recommended mixed-use building.

Signs for Small Town Downtowns

No big garish signs.

OLIVIERI, SHOUSKY & KISS, P.A.
KANALSTEIN DANTON ASSOCIATES, P.A.

LumberYard Condominiums
Borough of Collingswood   Camden County   New Jersey

Façade/Elevation Actually Constructed

Response Values +6(2) to +8(2)

Signs Appropriate for Small Downtowns

Range of sign types and sizes that have received positive responses.

Comment and design response: The highest response values for signs are smaller, custom-designed, hand-painted, attached and/or projected, and typically externally lit. They should be pedestrian-scaled, not scaled to be perceived by a car moving at a high speed.

Residential Buildings

Neighborhoods Surrounding the Downtown Core

The following residential building types are most appropriate and desired in a small town. The visual and spatial character, lot size and form, dimensions, and details are all highly appropriate. The greater the number of residential units within a five- to ten-minute walk of the downtown core or CBD, the more successful the CBD and the more engaging, safe, and interesting the pedestrian realm. The highest-density housing—typically attached—is most appropriate surrounding the core. As one walks further away from the core of a small town into adjacent neighborhoods, single-family housing on a range of lot sizes is recommended. The lot widths should increase in size as one walks further out from the core.

Illustrative Model of Residential Building Immediately Adjacent to the small towns Core

This computer model illustrates a three-story residential building, with its first floor raised three to four feet above grade. It has a front stoop and stair.

Comment and design response: It has a depth of 60 to 64 feet, with apartments on both sides of a central hallway. Parking is under the building and on the street. It has a semi-public front yard, wide sidewalk, street trees, and parallel on-street guest parking.

Response Value +5(4)

New Townhouses and Flats Adjacent to the Core

Classically designed, three-story modern townhouses and flats, with varied facades of stone and brick. The entrances are designed to give the appearance of attached individual buildings.

Comment and design response: They are complemented by a curvilinear streetscape and semi-public, well-landscaped front yards. Parking is at the rear and under the building. This is a highly desirable building type.

response given to this image. **Before approval of any large development, require a set-aside for parks and plazas**. They are the most highly prized public spaces by residents of the new housing and surrounding neighborhood.

Response Value +6(3)

New Multifamily Fronting onto a Park

One of the highest-rated multifamily images in the housing category for small towns is a multi-story apartment building overlooking a park.

Response Value +6(3)

New Townhouses

These contemporary townhouses are two and one-half stories with a pitched roof; well landscaped, semi-public, green front yard; wide sidewalk; parkway; decorative street lighting; and a bus stop. They are highly rated by everyone.

Comment and design response: The building is four stories, with a more traditional articulated facade, vertical windows, and a heavy upper cornice including a central architectural feature that defines the entrance. Parking is located under the building. As a condition of approval by the city, a new park was designed and constructed by the developer, as required by the city. The combination of the new parks, immediately adjacent housing, or mixed-use is highly desirable and contributes to market success. Landscaping treatments play an important role in the high visual

Comment and design response: The scale and streetscape are perfect for the second tier (blue area shown on the Infill and Development Diagram— IDD). Analyze the scale, character, dimensions, and details. All are worth careful study and inclusion in the architecture form-based code for this area of this small town.

Any infill must respect the architectural context. Semi-public front yards, sidewalks, parkways, and decorative pedestrian-scaled lighting are required. Bike paths should line the streets.

Desired Character as one Moves Further Away from the Core

Response Value +6(4)

Bungalow with Rear Yard Garage

This smaller bungalow-type home received an equal response value to larger homes. It too is well maintained. The garage is located in the rear yard with a side-yard driveway. It has sidewalks and parkway. It would be well located in one of the peripheral neighborhoods within the 2½-mile bike ride zone.

Comment and design response: These homes are well received and are compatible in the same neighborhood or appropriate in any of the adjoining neighborhoods. The site design and architectural standards should appear in the Design/Architectural Vocabulary of the Form-based code.

Parking Options for Small Downtowns

Providing parking for the small downtown is always a challenge. Even with the emphasis on walking, bicycling, and limited public transit, there will always be a need for parking. The design and location will impact the visual, spatial, and functional character of all small town downtowns.

- Prioritize on-street parallel or diagonal parking with bicycle paths.
- Hide parking from public view, behind buildings.
- Eliminate all open surface parking lots. They always receive negative responses.

- **Build mixed-use shared parking buildings as part of downtown redevelopments.**
- **If surface parking must be used, ensure that it is well landscaped on the edges and on the interior.**

Response Value +6(3)

Parking Behind Buildings—Access Under/ through Building

This parking lot is accessed by an arcade opening under the building.

Comment and design response: The buildings frame the parking lot and hide it from direct view. The street wall is more continuous, and the wide view of an open parking lot is avoided. Use this as a parking design as many times as possible.

Response Value +5(3)

Mixed-use Parking Building

This mixed-use parking building is the ideal solution for downtown parking.

Comment and design response: It must not look like a functional, value-engineered, T-slab structure. It must have retail or services on the ground level along the street frontage, with a facade that has a higher ceiling height along the pedestrian realm. The most positive facade design uses a contextual architectural form with standard window openings, upper and lower cornices, articulated corner treatment, defined building modules, and changes in height.

Response Value +5(3)

Landscaped Surface Parking Lots

If there must be surface parking, then it must be extensively landscaped, starting with low shrubs along the edges.

Comment and design response: The interior of the parking lot must be landscaped, with trees and planted islands. In colder climates, using the excuse the "it has to be snow plowed" is no excuse for not investing in interior landscaping and walkways. Parking lanes and planted areas should be designed to allow easy conversion to standard blocks and streets that can be infilled with buildings at a future date. Trees should be aligned to provide shade in the summer.

Bicycles, buses, and on-demand transit; and personal devices, such as scooter, are the most desired modes after walking. There is an overwhelming desire to have a complete network of bicycle paths and lanes in these small towns. Bicycle lanes should extend an optimum distance of 2½ miles from the center of the core to be most effective. Regional and local buses should serve the core and have stops in the higher-density neighborhood surrounding the core. On-demand transit provides the opportunity to have door-to-door service; even more highly recommended is pick-up and drop-off in center locations within a three- to five-minute walk of all residential

and commercial spaces, specifically at the center of neighborhoods.

Designing a multi-modal town with an emphasis on walking and bicycling, in addition to car and bus/transit, would mean a positive improved character for any small town. A complete network of bike paths would move the town toward the goal of sustainability while providing a new marketing /publicity opportunity. Many cities and towns have begun to implement bike and pedestrian plans, which have contributed to their growing success.

Comment and design response: The recommended bike path width is four feet in each direction. Where streets are not wide enough, provide share-road graphics at close intervals with reduced speed limits (15 mph).

Response Value +4(4)

Bus with Front Bike Rack at Transit Stop

Public transit must be provided to and from all small towns and cities with stops provided within easy walking distances to all retail and commercial uses and ideally in the center of every neighborhood.

Response Value +7(4)

Bicycle Paths Connecting to Downtowns

Multiple safe bicycle paths to and from the downtown are fundamental to a sustainable mobility network.

Comment and design response: Buses are a rational and available public transit alternative to connect to outer neighborhoods, jobs/shopping locations, and other towns and cities. A bike rack on the front of the bus improves its response value. The downside is that buses must flow with normal traffic and cannot serve all neighborhoods; therefore, on-demand transit from a single collective point in the center of each neighborhood along with other alternative modes are required.

Response Value +5(4)

On-demand Transit Stop

On-demand transit, like Uber and Lyft, are additional alternative mobility modes which must be available not only at your front door but also at a collective stop within short walking distances of all homes, making it less expensive.

Comment and design response: Well-designed bus/multi-modal stops must be provided in downtowns and in the center of each neighborhood. Each pick-up and drop-off should be no more than a five-minute walk away from any home. A two-minute walk would be even better.

Advanced communication now allows a pick-up time to be specified, with fares that are cashless. This mobility option was first described in the book *Visions for a New American Dream* by Anton Nelessen.

Implementing Small Town Preferences

Buildings, parks, and streets of the character shown in this chapter with positive response values must be encouraged and incorporated into the form-based Street Regulating Plan, Building Regulating Plan, and Architectural Design Vocabulary sections of the code in order to achieve the maximum livability and market value for small towns. Implementation is facilitated when there is a Comprehensive Community Vision Plan enhanced by multiple positive real and simulated images which portray the preferences of the community. The location of these preference is the result of the VTW. The combined results, in two and three dimensions, with positive images, can be used to create a form-based zoning code. This must be coordinated with staff, builders, and developers to assure implementation.

Community Visioning Sessions—VPS

Participants during the Community Visioning Sessions form Planning and Design teams. Here, they are evaluating images to determine the most positive in each category.

Community Visioning Sessions—VTW

During the VTW, participants form planning and design teams to translate their visions onto an overlay base map. In this image, there are 26 community design teams. The overlays generated were then synthesized into the recommended Vision Plan.

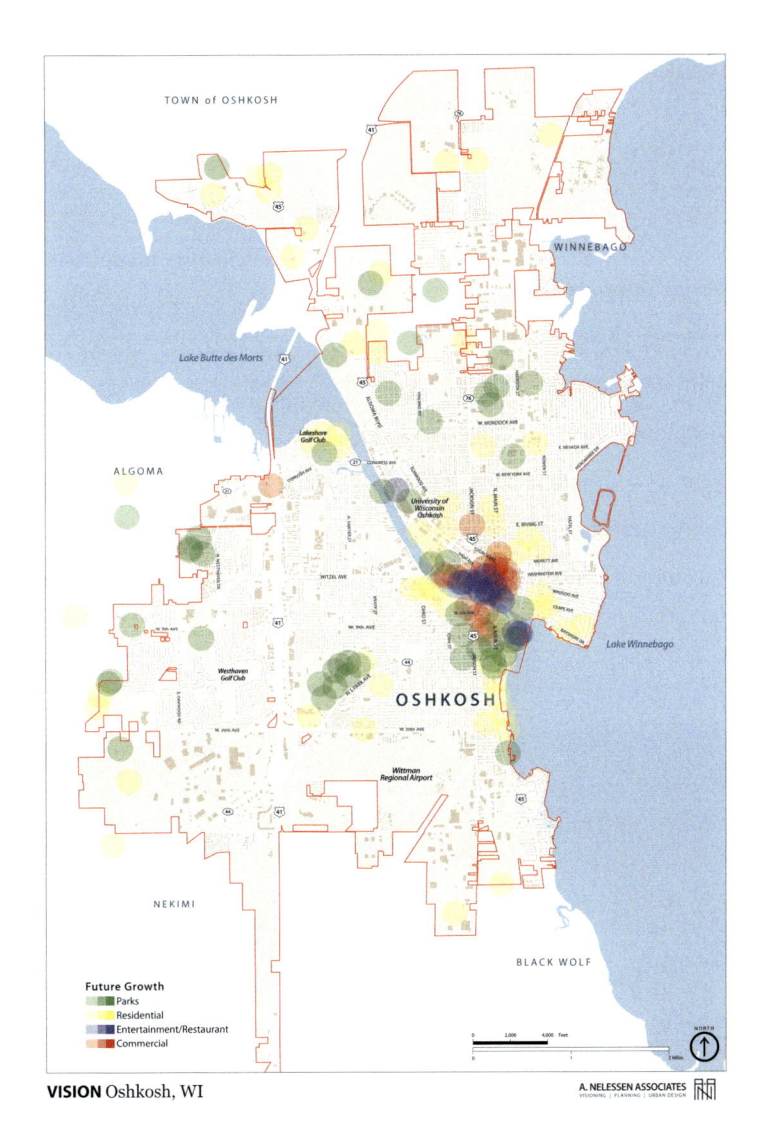

VISION Oshkosh, WI

A. NELESSEN ASSOCIATES
VISIONING | PLANNING | URBAN DESIGN

The "Vision Oshkosh" Recommended Community Vision Plan

The Vision Oshkosh, Wisconsin Plan is the synthesis of the response values from the VPS and the 26 community planning and design teams.

Comment and design response: The Community Vision Plan locates where future development, redevelopment, and infill should be located. The red is commercial, focusing on the downtown. The blue is entertainment/restaurants; the yellow is a range of residential buildings; and the green are parks, plazas, and open spaces.

It is remarkable that people want most future development to be concentrated in and around the old downtown, not along the highway, as has happened in the last several years. This is a remarkable turnaround and would revitalize the town, but it is not what the people of Oshkosh are getting. The trajectory is more sprawl along the highway, but there are hopeful signs for the downtown, with some street closures and new businesses opening. Whether the political leadership will move in this direction and or the zoning will be amended, only the future will tell.

Vision Plan Implementation—

Metuchen, New Jersey

Comment and design response: It has all the positive characteristics generated from multiple visioning sessions for small towns. The parking building in the background has a liner of one-story retail with a green roof. The plan and final architectural forms meet most of the consensus visions for small downtown infill and the desire for an active public space. It is a transit-oriented development in that it is located adjacent to the train station on a lot previously used as a surface commuter parking.

Most fascinating about this project is that it was envisioned nearly 40 years earlier, albeit on a smaller scale, in one of the first downtown community visioning sessions. That Vision Plan recommended a plaza on the same corner, mixed-use housing, and a mixed-use parking structure, which speaks to the long-term power of community visioning.

View from the corner of New Street and Pearl Street.

PIAZZA    9

Rendering of the New Downtown Infill Project, Metuchen, New Jersey

This project was constructed on a municipal surface parking lot and portrays mixed- and multiple-use housing, with retail on the ground floor, fronting onto a new public plaza.
Source: Metuchen web site

Main Intersection Adjacent to Plaza

Pavement extends from the plaza across the inter-section, an excellent urban design feature.

New Mixed-use Parking Building

Located adjacent to the regional train station for commuters, it replaces the large surface parking lot with mixed and multiple uses. It provides parking for resident, merchants, and downtown shoppers.

Vision Plan Implementation—

Collingswood, New Jersey
This small town is a success story for infill and rehabilitation of their downtown core.

Enhanced Facades and Streetscapes

The entire Main Street has been upgraded, with streetscape and façade improvements, making it a popular destination.

New Development Engenders Additional New Development

New developments are being built on adjacent lots previously used as surface parking.

New Mixed-use Infill Building

New mixed-use infill building on the previously va-cant lumberyard lot has shops on the ground level with housing above and embedded parking.

Comment and design response: Facade and architectural design vocabulary of the new mixed-use retail and residential buildings enhances the character and scale of the existing Main Street and responds well to the vision set forth in the VPS and the VTW.

Consensus Vision Preferences for Small Towns

Planning and design standards for small towns must emphasize the downtown core as a priority pedestrian experience while focusing on the maintenance and enhancement of the existing surrounding neighborhood housing stock, quality streetscapes, extended bicycle lanes, and possible on-demand transit. The scale and character of existing and new infill buildings, along with the character and functions of streets, should be in conformance with the Infill Development Diagram (IDD) and respond to the generic positive images and resulting recommendations for small towns from Community Visioning sessions.

When appropriate form and character are applied, implemention will contribute to the success and sustainability of the small town.

- Reinforcing the town core should be first priority by infilling empty, underutilized buildings and surface parking lots with as many mixed-use residential buildings as possible.
- Determine the five-minute walking distance from various neighborhoods centers and designate community on-demand bus/transit stops.
- Next, where possible, design and build the bike lanes radiating out 2 ½ miles from the center.
- Provide a central public gathering place, plaza, or market with other public spaces of smaller scale.
- Provide wide and well landscaped and furnished pedestrian realms.
- Build or rehabilitate mixed-use buildings with continuous retail fronting on the primary pedestrian realms (sidewalks).
- Build multifamily housing within easy ten-minute walking distance of the core.

- Mobility options beyond walking must include, at minimum, bus, bicycle, and on-demand transit.
- Do not allow exposed surface parking except for on-street parallel or diagonal parking. Encourage parking behind buildings and out of the public viewshed. Encourage mixed-use parking buildings.
- Require maintenance of all structures, landscapes and public ways.

PLANNING AND DESIGN POLICIES Generated from VPS Questionnaires

76% to 83% either agree or strongly agree that the downtown CBD and surrounding neighborhoods of these small towns should become the **first priority for infill and redevelopment** of high-quality living, working, and education. Reinforce the town core by infilling empty lots, underutilized tired buildings, and surface parking.

Infill buildings can take multiple forms and character and height. Focus on the street wall context and pedestrian realm, not on density and height but consider the impact of sun and shade. but consider the impact of sun and shade. Mixed and multiple uses are most often preferred. The scale of infill buildings and streets should be built in conformance to the VPS positive recommendations for the small town to be as successful as possible.

74% to 84% support the policy that the small town should **adopt design standards** to achieve and maintain quality buildings, properties, streetscapes, and landscaping. An Architectural Design Vocabulary must be prepared in a visual form that illustrates the 20 basic details recommended for buildings and streetscapes. It is a critical section of a Form-based zoning code.

89% to 91% think that the small town should require/encourage property owners to improve the condition of buildings and landscapes that are in disrepair, poorly maintained or neglected. Adopt and enforce a property maintenance code.

12

Visions for Urban Cores of
Large Cities

The majority of future growth is projected to occur in urban areas. The most desirable and livable urban areas will be connected, sustainable, safe, walkable, healthy, and green, with interactive places and spaces that attract residential, corporate, and civic facilities. The task of the Community Visioning process was to determine the physical form and character of places and spaces that people feel are most appropriate for urban areas, based on many scenarios.

Of the multitude of downtown urban areas that contracted Community Vision, there are three that best represent the vision consensus: Milwaukee, Wisconsin; Midtown Atlanta, Georgia; and Journal Square, Jersey City, New Jersey.

The majority of the Vision Plans contracted for urban areas focus on the deteriorating centers of cities. The vision results are representative of the consensus on the desired character. Each of the subject cities completed the entire Community Visioning process with a resulting synthesized Vision Plan. The initial focus groups, Visual Preference Surveys, and Demographic, Market, and Policy Questionnaires were instrumental in establishing the preferences. It was the community input from the Vision Translation Workshop (VTW) that provided the Urban Design Plan and the recommendations for form-based zoning as well as the first-phase catalytic projects.

At the start of every vision process, a Susceptibility To Change (STC) map was generated by multiple teams of participants, identifying those areas considered the most and least susceptible to change in the future. The answers from the Policy Questionnaire were instrumental in reinforcing the preferences. In Midtown Atlanta, the two-dimensional STC plan was rendered in three dimensions to make it easier to understand.

Three-Dimensional Model of Areas' Susceptibility to Change

The Susceptibility to Change model generated for the second Midtown Atlanta Vision Plan.

Comment and recommendations: The red and light pink areas are those considered most susceptible to change. The building that are not susceptible to change are shown in three dimensions. It was amazing to realize the desired extent of the areas that participants considered susceptible to change, providing opportunities for redevelopment and improvement.

Simulated Images for Urban Cores

In every visioning process, there are one or more images, most often simulations, that characterize the desired urban character. The following is a pair of images using the classic **"before"** and **"after,"** portraying a place people know and use every day and simulate of the type and character of place they preferred and recommended.

Response Value −2(4)

**Existing City Center with Arterial Highway
BEFORE**

A six-lane thoroughfare passes through the center of this urban core. This street-form illustrates an engineering solution for rapid movement of vehicles at the expense of the pedestrian, bicycles, and urban character. With a response range of −6 to +1, a small number of participants thought it was positive or neutral. "Not that bad."

Response Value +5(4)

The Visioned City Center and Major Multi-modal Street

The simulation portrays the arterial converted to an urban boulevard (complete street) with high-rise buildings in the background, adjacent to the Port Authority Trans Hudson (PATH) rail station. It generated a response value of +5 and a range of +9 to +1. All participants thought this was positive and appropriate for the urban core of this dynamic and growing city.

Comment and recommendations: The simulation captured all the urban design features wanted in this urban core. The desired image is the reduction of the six-lane "freeway" through the center of this urban center to a four-lane boulevard with a light-rail; bike lanes; and wide, well-landscaped sidewalks. High-intensity development is shown in the core of the area and along boulevards. The urban design characteristics of this positive image reinforced the final recommendations generated by the VTW and into the Recommended Redevelopment Plan and ordinance.

Highest-Rated Positive Image

The Pedestrian Realm

When the Visual Preference Survey (VPS) of the Community Visioning Process is completed, find the highest-rated image and the category in which it was presented. This image is referred to as the the genius loci "spirit of place". It is the image that conjures the most positive sense of hopefulness, joy, happiness, pride, and safety.

Response Value +8(2)

The Ideal Pedestrian Realm

This character of this pedestrian realm is the highest ranking image what most people want in their urban core.

Comment and recommendations: Every detail in this image should be incorporated into all Vision Plans' Architectural Design Vocabulary, including the wide sidewalks, textured surfaces, demarcation of cafés, umbrellas and tables, discrete small signs, planters, mixed-use buildings, building wall of light colored materials that reflects sun light, tall ground floor, and decorative lighting.

Most Negative Responses

Places, Spaces, and Buildings

Many stores and residents in the urban core and surrounding neighborhoods left for the suburbs. To compete with this growing trend, city cores had to accommodate traffic flow and massive amounts of parking. Back in the 1950s, cars were king; streetcars were removed; and freeways were built in town, destroying neighborhoods and resulting in the domination of surface parking lots. Municipal officials thought this was the right approach, not realizing all the physical, emotional, financial, and social damage they would cause over time.

To comprehend what is wrong with many downtowns, one need only review the lowest-valued images and their visioning category. The location of the negative images corresponds to areas typically designated as highly STC by participants. Too many places in too many downtowns receive negative and unacceptable ratings. The most negative are typically in places people experience the most often: The Pedestrian Realm. Places and spaces that are unpleasant to walk, generate negative feelings, where a pedestrian feels unsafe, anxious, and disgusted, generating depression, hopelessness, and fear. These areas are typically poorly maintained and prime for upgrading, infill, rehabilitation, and/or redevelopment. They must be changed to enhance the visual and market appeal of the area.

Deteriorated Sidewalks and Building
Too many of the sidewalks and street walls have this negative feeling due to the lack of maintenance and removal of buildings.

Sidewalk Edged with Cyclone Fence
One of the sidewalks leading to the center of this urban area as it passes over the depressed train tracks and train storage area. No one wants to walk here if they can avoid it. When they have to, they become depressed. Imagine having these feeling at the start and end of every work day.

Comment and recommendations: This is the highest level of engineered safety, keeping pedestrians from either jumping off or throwing objects over. The concrete lane divider does not help. The lowest-rated images reinforce the desperate need for pedestrian realm improvements.

Comment and recommendations: There is no landscaping, and the surface parking lots are exposed. Only the implementation of new, more intensive, mixed-use infill buildings and positive streetscapes will change this perception and rebuild market and pedestrian confidences.

Surface Parking in Urban Cores Are Negative Everywhere

Surface parking prevent the full potential of urban experience from being realized.

"Surface parking areas are the urban land banks of the future".

Tony Nelessen

Every open parking area receives negative response values in every VPS for urban areas. There are so many locations in urban areas where buildings that were historically part of a positive street wall, accessed by walking and served by buses or streetcars, have been removed for surface parking. The historic urban fabric wasn't designed for modern, convenience-driven parking demands. Because of the lack of a coherent parking strategy in older urban areas, parking lots were located expeditiously to meet the vehicular demand, with limited, if any, design standards. A parking lot would generate more revenue than the building that was previously there. Having open parking lots in urban centers is how the urban center thought it would compete with open parking lots in suburban commercial areas. However, this destroyed the fabric and character of the core. It is estimated that nearly one-third of most urban cores are dedicated to parking. An extraordinary amount of land is being wasted on parking lots. According to the Research Institute for Housing America, there are between 3.7 and 27 parking spaces per household. Cities are not suburbs! Cars and parking lots should not be the predominant, reoccurring, sequential image of urban cores.

Response Value –7(3)

Off Street Surface Parking Lots

Each image of surface parking received similar negative responses. Too much downtown land had buildings removed for surface parking or squeezed this onto any available space, contributing to overall very negative, depressing feelings about these areas.

Comment and recommendations: Clearly these urban cores lacked a comprehensive parking strategy that must be planned and implemented. One can consider open surface parking lots, at best, a holding pattern that must be infilled.

Surface Parking Rated More Negatively

Response Value –8 to –9(2)

All the above parking lots were value rated even lower. Their dominant characteristics are on-grade, unkempt, asphalted lots and one-story strip commercial infill buildings with poorly designed facades.

Comment and recommendations: This visual character is not appropriate in urban cores. Litter and dirt reflect the lack of maintenance, characteristic of places in the bottom phase of urban evolution. These areas require a strong positive vision generated by the community in order to move into the next phases of rehabilitation, growth, and optimization.

Negative Building Types

The following images illustrate site plans and buildings that are unacceptable in any vibrant, successful urban downtown area. These are most appropriate along suburban arterials and highways. Even there, they are not positively rated by many.

Single-Story Restaurants with Surface Parking

The single-story fast food restaurant is set back with front and side yard surface parking. It received very negative responses. The adjacent pawn shop doesn't help either.

Comment and recommendations: This commercial retail building and the sense of place it creates is really disliked and should never be allowed, no matter how desperate the core has become. It violates all positive design characteristics for urban areas.

Comment and recommendations: They tried. The negative response value clearly indicates that people did not want this in their core areas. It belongs in a multi-use development in the auto-oriented suburbs adjacent to a highway arterial.

Negative Street Walls and Urban Form

> The character of the street/building wall plays an important role in negative or positive responses to places.

Response Value –6(5)

Suburban Big Boxes in Downtown

This single-story, flat-roofed, car-oriented "big box" has a partially covered and landscaped parking lot in front of the building.

Response Value –3(2)

Overly Wide One-way Street

All streets of this type in downtowns receive negative responses. The low negative response suggests that some participants are becoming conditioned on this form and character.

Comment and recommendations: The streets are too wide, many of them one-way, with ill-defined pedestrian realms and discontinuous building/street walls that have no visual and spatial continuity with the street. These streets should be converted to two-way, with the pedestrian realms widened and landscaped, a design vocabulary, and a form-based code for the street/building wall. As it is, people don't want to drive or walk along these streets unless they have to.

Response Value –5(4)

Corner Building Removed for Surface Parking

Too many buildings have been removed for surface parking, particularly on the corners, exposing the previously hidden facade of the adjacent buildings, which were never meant to be seen. No one wants to walk here.

Comment and recommendations: The lack of landscaping, street furniture, and building continuity in the pedestrian realm increases its negativity. When the city stops being a city in form and character, there are perception problems which send it on a downward spiral—all for a few parking spaces. This is a site that is highly susceptible to change and infill.

Response Values –4(3)

Single-story Retail with Corner Parking Lot

Many cities, out of desperation, accepted single-story strip commercial development with front-yard parking in their downtowns to compete with the auto-culture of the suburbs.

Comment and recommendations: This is value-rated negative in every urban downtown where it is present. It is unfortunate if it was approved and built under a current zoning ordinance. It is the antithesis of a downtown. Keep one-story, box-type retail with front-yard parking out of the city core.

Response Value –4(5)

Street with Overly wide Traffic Lanes and Narrow Sidewalk

This street was designed by traffic engineers to accommodate volumes of traffic to and from the city center. Little attention is paid to the pedestrian realm, which is so typical.

Comment and recommendations: Notice the light gray spaces between the parked car and the traffic flow, where either a bike lane could be located, or the sidewalks could be widened. Street standards need to be revised.

Negative Storefronts

Store fronts, display windows, sidewalk and streetscape are a formative part of the pedestrian experience. All must be positive to have a successful downtown.

Comment and recommendations: This store and adjacent storefronts have exterior security gates which portray negative conditions along the street. Participants gave this a –7 response value, with a range of –10 to –4. Everyone finds this unacceptable and does not want any more of the deteriorating and fear-generating ground-level facades in the downtown. Participants want this to be changed to a more positive look and feel that they want their downtown back. There are many types of positive store fronts, sidewalk treatments, and street landscaping that can be emulated.

Response Value –6(4)

Boarded-Up Storefronts

Boarded-up store fronts contribute to negative perceptions and the perceived hopelessness of the downtown.

Response Value –7(3)

Marginal Retail Frontage

This storefront with security gates and an ugly window display and facade screams out, "unsafe to be here."

Comment and recommendations: It is very detractive to the pedestrian experience and negatively impacts the market. Every effort must be made to prevent the boarding up of commercial frontages. It is the equivalent of saying, **"your body (the city) has cancer."**

Designing the Positive Downtown Experience

If cities want streets to regain a feeling of positive urbanism, they should approve and build continuous mixed-use building walls; widen sidewalks; enhance multi-modal movement; add bike lanes, landscaping, and street furniture.

Streets

Streets are a community's most imageable and significant public spaces. It is from the street that one's first impression of a place is formed. For all downtown vision plans, the primary structure of the plan is the **Urban Armature**, including the streets and blocks on which the pedestrian, transit, vehicles, and other infrastructure circulate, and onto which buildings are attached and public spaces are formed.

Extending the grid of streets, creating new blocks, widening or narrowing some streets, improving intersections, adding new streets and providing greater accessibility via transit and people walking is one of the first priorities to establish a dynamic Urban Armature for future development. Where streets have been removed for "super-blocks" or where freeways cut through the valuable fabric of the city, urban design vision plans recommend the removal and redesign of freeways into boulevards. Extend the grid of streets, where possible, to the shortest walkable blocks of 200 to 400 feet. These lengths will produce the greatest number of corners. New plans must be drawn that indicate the recommendations for new and improved streets and intersections. Specific recommendations for improvements to intersections, sidewalks, and locations for landscaping must overlay these maps.

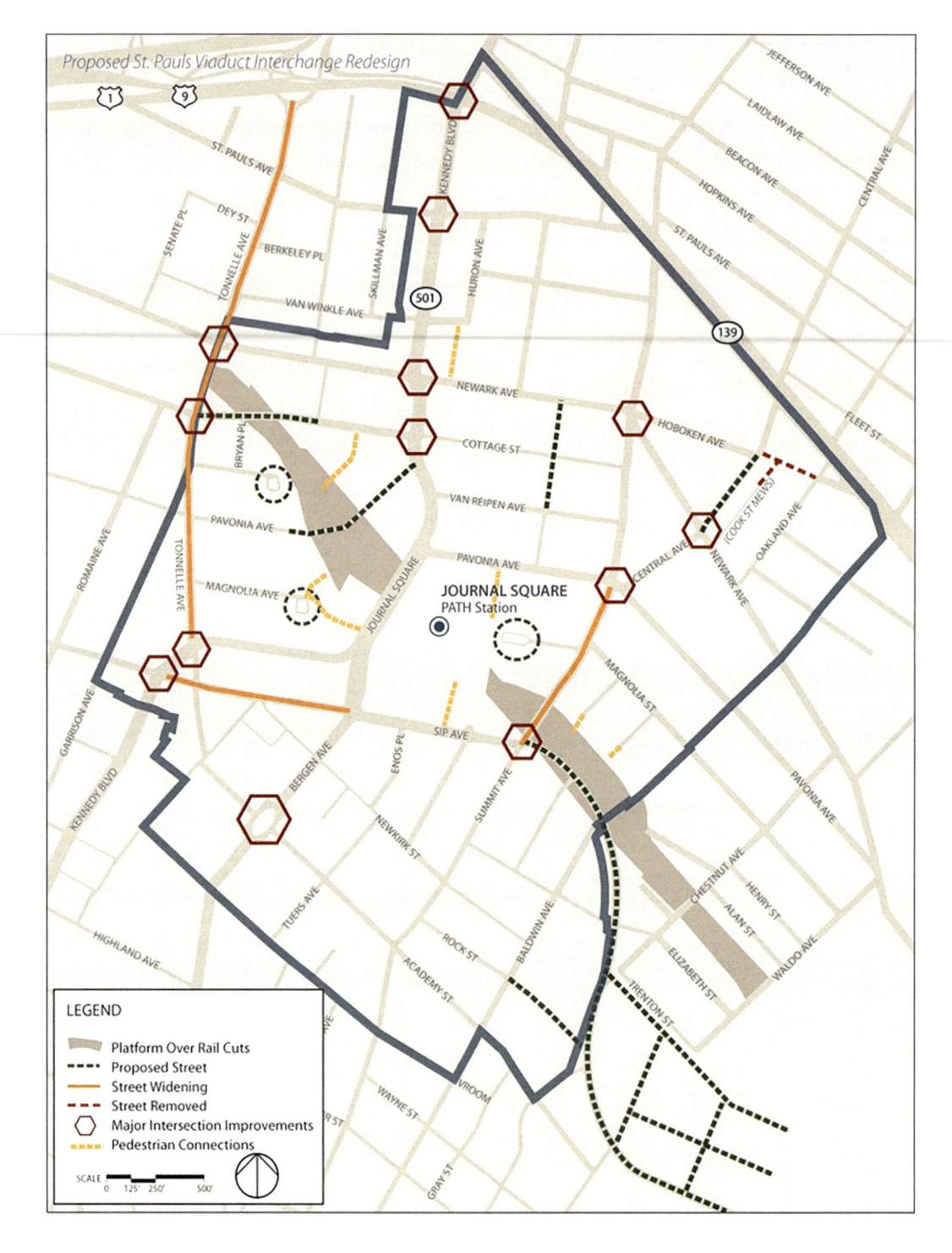

Map of Intersections Improvements

Pedestrian flows require that streets be crossed. Proper design of intersections for cars and pedestrians is mandatory. Intersections must be analyzed, and engineering solutions must be generated. Map the streets and intersection improvements that need to be reconstructed.

Map of New Streets and Street Extensions

Proposed new streets for downtown Milwaukee that will add new blocks and complete many grids.

The Pedestrian Realm (All Places and Paths Where People Walk)

The most successful downtowns are walkable, connected, with dynamic street activity.

The most positive and negative responses are typically in the Pedestrian Realm category. It is from the personal walking experience where these impressions of place are the strongest, because it is more intimate with a slower perception speed. A positive walking experience is critical to the upbeat feeling and success of urban areas. Highly valued pedestrian realms have mixed-use buildings, wide sidewalks, people walking and sitting, cafés, colorful umbrellas, interesting facades, decorative lighting, and light-colored masonry to reflect the light. They must have interesting, well-lit display windows complemented by street trees and furniture, and engaging street activity. The more continuous and concentrated the pedestrian flow, the better. Where these positive features of the pedestrian realm are present, people feel comfortable and safe. All street-walls and pedestrian realms must

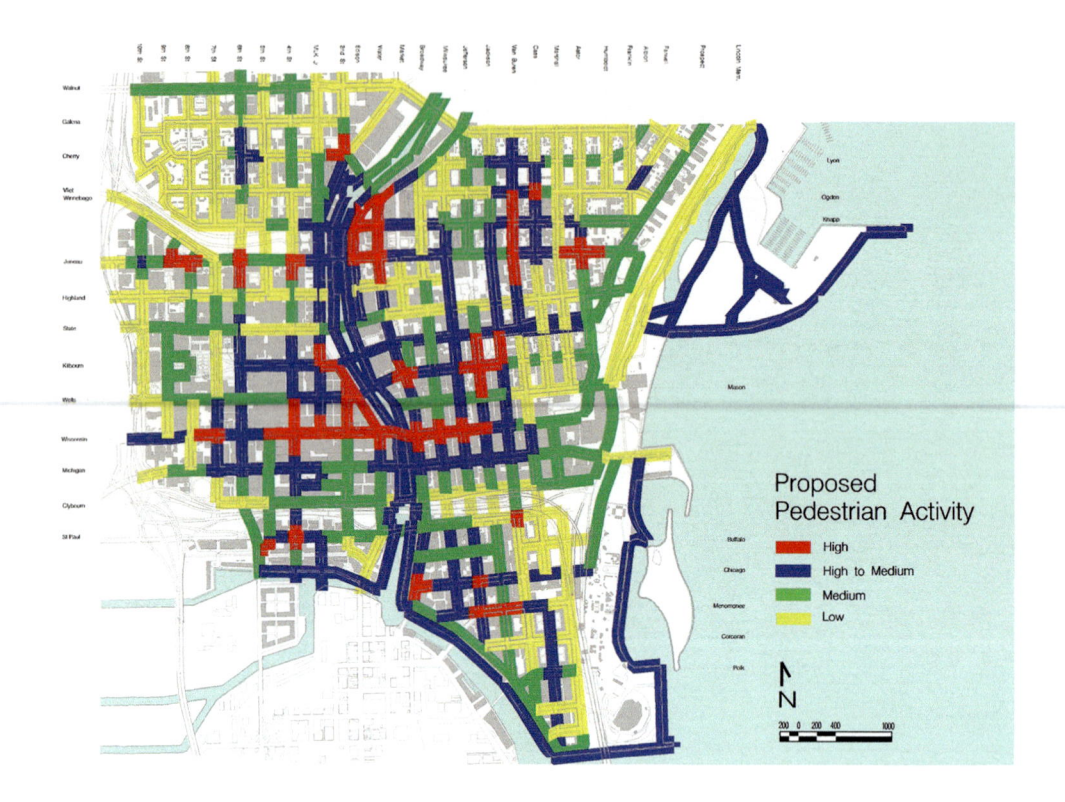

Map of Downtown Milwaukee that Classifies Pedestrian Streets by Activity

One of the many maps generated from the Downtown Milwaukee Community Visioning Process. It illustrates where the most pedestrian activity is located and determines the priority for streetscape improvements. The red streets and intersections should have the highest priority for enhancements.

periodically undergo maintenance, transformations, and upgrades. To achieve these positive preferences, many streets need to be redesigned, more for pedestrians and bicycles than cars. The positive images in the VPS clearly indicated the type and character of streets that people desire. If these features were present on any urban downtown streets, they would be positive and successful. People of all demographics and incomes have a strong positive preference for great streets with outside eating and building-edge activity. This has been true in the past and will be true in the future.

Comment and recommendations: The map above indicates that not all streets have high priority, focus on streets that will have the most pedestrian activity. The more positively a streets is perceived, the more people will use it. Map idea was generated by Rick Chellman.

Components for a Positive Downtown Experience

Promote Wide Sidewalks with Interactive Mixed-use Edges

Wide Sidewalk and Café

This pedestrian realm has wide sidewalks, with an active café edge and a deep building wall setback, combined with a leafy canopy from adjacent street trees.

Comment and recommendations: This is a perfect combination of urban design features, highly desired in any urban downtown. Great streets require welcoming sidewalks and building walls with interactive and visually engaging edges. The wider and more active the sidewalk, the greater the number of pedestrians and activities, the more successful the downtowns.

Response Value +5(4)

Retail Sidewalk

This commercial street wall has all the urban design characteristics that make in-store retail successful. The proportion of the pedestrian realm enhanced by the wide planting area, unique located signs, and lower display windows has a positive emotional and spatial impact.

Comment and recommendations: It has the positive response of a place where people feel comfort-

able and that they want to experience. Enhancing the experience are the facade overhangs, awnings, landscaping signage, and lights. Interesting shop windows pull the eye to the storefronts. Many are low to the ground, a successful display technique that matches normal eye scans. The level of transparency and night lighting of the store windows is also to be seriously considered. This image rated high in both the Pedestrian Realm and the Sign category.

Pedestrian-only Streets

An essential feature of urbanism for tens of thousands of years, this street type should be incorporated into all city urban cores.

Response Value +5(4)

Pedestrian Street

Pedestrian-only streets, where cars are banned, are becoming more popular and desired now that the "car and parking everywhere" phase in the cores is diminishing, and pedestrian intensity is increasing.

Comment and recommendations: Pedestrian-only streets can be relatively narrow, requiring a continuous ground surface treatment and retail frontages with activity spilling out into the street. Notice that this pedestrian street is visually terminated, adding to the sequential interest. The +5 response value with a range of +9 to +1 means that everyone thought this pedestrian-only street was positive and appropriate. Incorporating pedestrian only areas should be considered in every urban core, particularly where there is a concentration of retail and street activity connecting to public facilities, like a train/transit station, plaza, or major public space.

Comment and recommendations: The scale, proportions, landscaping, and architecture of this type of space always attracts a high number of pedestrians, as can be seen. For many years, this pedestrian-dominated marketplace was one the highest-grossing shopping areas by square footage anywhere in the country. It is emulated in many downtowns. The +5 response, with the range of +9 to +1, means that everyone finds this a positive and appropriate preference. If these urban design characteristics were emulated in more downtowns, these, too, would be more successful.

Pedestrian Realm in Urban Residential Districts

Response Value +5(4)

Pedestrian-Only Street/Plaza with Glass Canopy

This pedestrian-only street has retail, cafés, and restaurants spilling out into the public realm from the ground level of both facades. The exterior space of the old market buildings has seating area, tables, landscaping complemented by the glass awning, and continuous ground-level surface texture.

Being able to walk out of your apartment onto safe, well-designed and engineered, beautiful urban sidewalks contributes to the high quality of urban

living, particularly when easily accessible to retail, services, transit, and civic facilities. A continuous positive pedestrian realm is a true urban pleasure and a basic requirement for successful downtowns.

Comment and recommendations: Nature is being integrated into this residential district via the parkway with trees and plantings, complemented by the landscaped semi-public space. This is a highly desired residential pedestrian realm, including a passenger drop-off with the canvas canopy. This leafy street has design features that should be emulated in any high-density urban areas.

Response Value +8(2)

Residential Street with Stoops, Stairs, and Semi-public Edge

This street of lower residential density is also one of the higher-rated pedestrian realms. It has the ideal combination of sidewalk width, landscaping, semi-public front garden, stairs, and stoops.

Comment and recommendations: The building wall is three- to four-story attached townhouses. The sidewalk is separated from the front yard by a low decorative fence or hedge. Some of the front yards have trees, which are complemented by the street trees in the planter boxes. The plantings boxes in the sidewalk instill a sense of nature into the streetscape. This is a good example of ideal urban residential and streetscape design despite the dead tree which has not been replaced.

Response Value +8(3)

Sidewalk with Planted Parkway and Semi-public Space

One of the highest-rated VPS images in the urban Pedestrian Realm category portrays a sidewalk in a high-density residential district adjacent to the downtown.

Metrics for Walkable Downtowns—Sidewalk and Street/Building Wall

Sections for Positive Pedestrian Realms—Retail

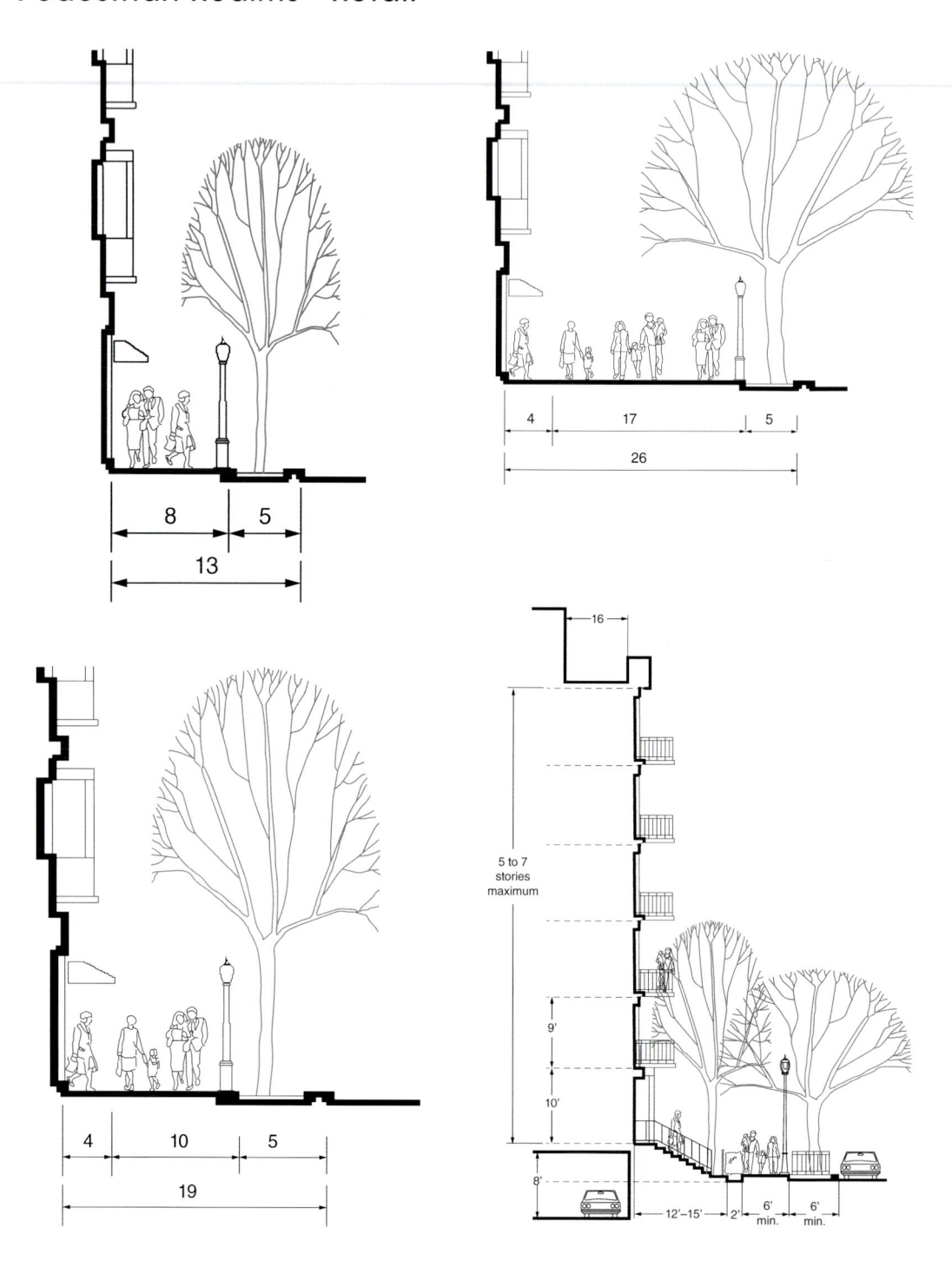

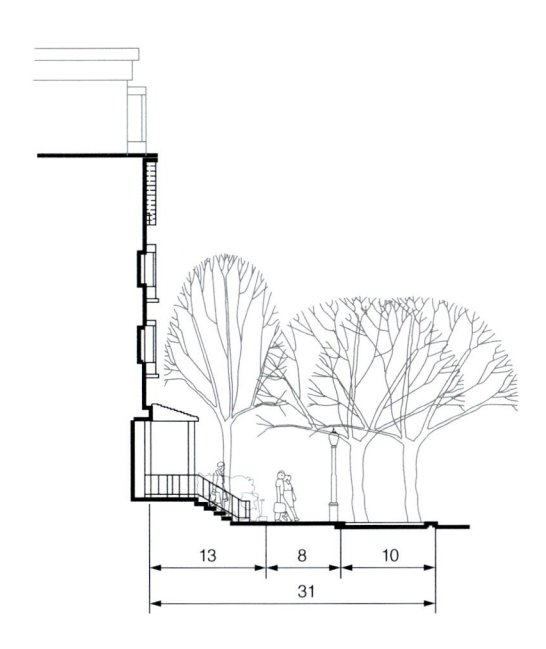

Sidewalk and Building Wall Sections for Various Locations in the Core

Here are the recommended sections through sidewalks and building facades. The first are three sections for retail frontages with the appropriate range of sidewalk widths. The wider sidewalk allows more active retail opportunity for cafés and outdoor displays. The two following sections are of a residential building with stairs, stoop entrances, and a semi-public front garden space. All should be incorporated into the Street Regulating Plan of the Form-based zoning code.

Downtown Riverfront Walkways,

One of the most popular pedestrian realms in urban areas. Where urban areas have rivers coursing

through them, the frontage along the edges provides an extraordinary opportunity to create a positive urban experience and enhance the value of place.

Response Value +7(3)

Riverwalk in Milwaukee, Wisconsin

Water views and pedestrian access along the open edges provide extraordinary m walking arketing and economic benefits for any downtown.

Riverfront walkways are a valuable investment in any downtown. They provide a very positive pedestrian experience for people visiting, shopping, living, working, and walking. They are the equivalent of a water-based open space park in the center

River Walk Plan

This plan shows the existing and the future expanded riverfront walkway. It also designates potential water taxi stops, using the river as another form of public transport.

of the core. They can function as a liner connection between several positive urban places and spaces. The light reflected from the river and the activity on the river adds to the positive ambience. Riverfront walkways can become an important catalyst for investments in housing, mixed-use buildings, offices, restaurants, and parks. Water views and pedestrian access along the open edges are a destination providing extraordinary marketing and economic benefits for any downtown. They need to be incorporated into the overall Master Plan.

Comment and recommendation: This plan was important as it ensured the continuity of a design that promotes a continuous positive walking experience with housing, offices, cafés, restaurants, and art exhibits along the entire length of the river through the downtown. The plan calls for a complete walkway network on both sides for the length of both rivers. As the plan is built out, water taxis will become an integral feature of multi-mobility in the core.

Urban centers must be walkable and connected to other cores and places of activity within specific time distance parameters. Maximizing the ability to walk safely and interactively to and from destinations on positive pedestrian realms must be the first priority of urban mobility. Minimizing private car usage and parking by walking and maximizing the use of easy, convenient public and private transit. Construct more usable, positive, and interactive street space sequences thereby promoting a higher quality of urban life. The primary mobility goal is to implement Transit Dependent Development (TDD) where the use of the private car is minimized, where walking and all forms of transit are preferred because they are so convenient. TDD is different than Transit Oriented Development (TOD) where transit and walking is suggestive but cars and parking still dominate.

The highest concentration of mixed-use buildings, public spaces, and pedestrian activities should be within a five- or maximum ten-minute walk to and from the core and/or multi-modal transit concentrations. Outside this primary walking areas, mobility plans must expand the walking range and positive experiences through the use of local transit modes and bicycles. Accessibility to a range of transit options is mandatory. Many urban downtowns are too long or wide to be able to fall within the desired five- to ten-minute walking times from origin to destination. Other transit modes are required to ensure easy multi-modal connections within and to adjacent locations.

Most successful urban downtowns and adjacent residential areas have the best pedestrian and multi-modal connections within short walking distances. This is the recommendation inherent in the Infill and Development Diagram (IDD) presented in the previous chapters.

One of the first requirements of understanding transit accessibility is mapping the isobar time-distance from the largest concentration of transit modes. Carefully review where and how far people walk and the quality of the walk. The following map illustrate a study area and the walking isobars surrounding a major multi-modal transit stop/station.

Comment and recommendations: Most proposed higher-density development must be within a ten-minute walk out from the core center. The majority of development, with a high Floor Area Ration (FAR) or unit density, is recommended within the five to six-minute area, with even higher FAR within a three-minute walk. This is a fundamental urban design attribute of decreasing intensity of development as one walks away from the center area or core. Notice that the walking distances are not shown in the typical, single radius circles or "as the crow flies." This was plotted first in Geographic Information System software (GIS) and then by actually walking various pedestrian routes radiating out from the center to determine the actual time-distance locations at different times of the day. Walking also provides the opportunity to analyze and photograph the visual, spatial character of the pedestrian realm.

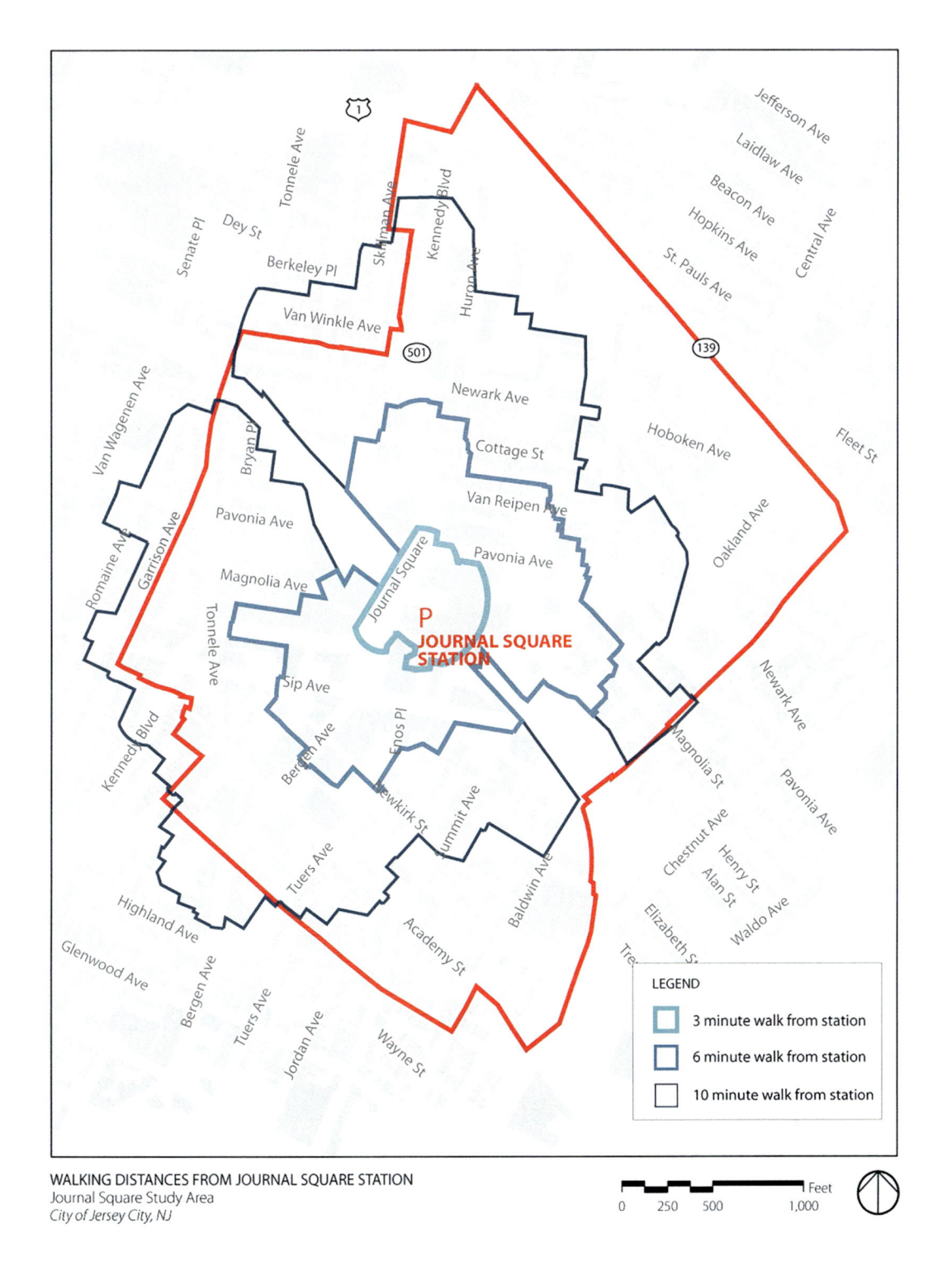

LEGEND

- 3 minute walk from station
- 6 minute walk from station
- 10 minute walk from station

Feet
0   250   500   1,000

Urban Core and Walk-Time Isobars

This map defines the three-, six- and ten-minute walking distances in isobars to and from the central transit station.

Most downtown streets are primarily devoted to the movement of cars. Vehicular lanes have been widened. Many streets have multiple lanes of fast-moving traffic. Sidewalks have been narrowed, and pedestrian flow has been restricted.

The car, not the pedestrian, is more important. Bus stops and stations are often designated to the most negative spaces and pedestrian realms. A very negative visual, spatial, and human experience has resulted. Alternative traffic patterns and pedestrian realms must be proposed and implemented.

Pedestrian Crossing on a Wide Side Street

The visual character and pedestrian experience crossing a side street in the urban core. It is impossible to cross in one cycle of the signal lights if you are a slow walker.

Comment and recommendation: When vehicular capacity is the primary design criteria, it is the pedestrian who must suffer the negative consequences. More emphasis must be placed on the capacity, safety, and accommodations of the pedestrian, particularity at intersections.

Response Value –4(6)

Existing Bus Terminal

This large, dark, and noisy bus station is rated as negative, unacceptable, and depressing by most participants. It has a response range of –10 to +1, few finding it minimally acceptable.

Comment and recommendation: Buses are an important public transit mode in this city center. It is intimidating to use this station. It is important that urban center bus stations not be perceived as negative and brutal. A more acceptable and positive station experience was highly desired by participants.

Heavy Rail/High-Speed Station

99% of participants prefer below-grade rapid transit with stations at convenient locations where urban uses are at their highest density, and pedestrian flow is at its most intense.

98% of participants wanted a positive, safe, and engaging walking experience to and from transit.

84% of participants support daylighting and refurbished the below grade station. (i.e. allowing natural light in, improving pedestrian circulation and the look and feel of the station).

42% would rank cafés as their first choice of station amenities.

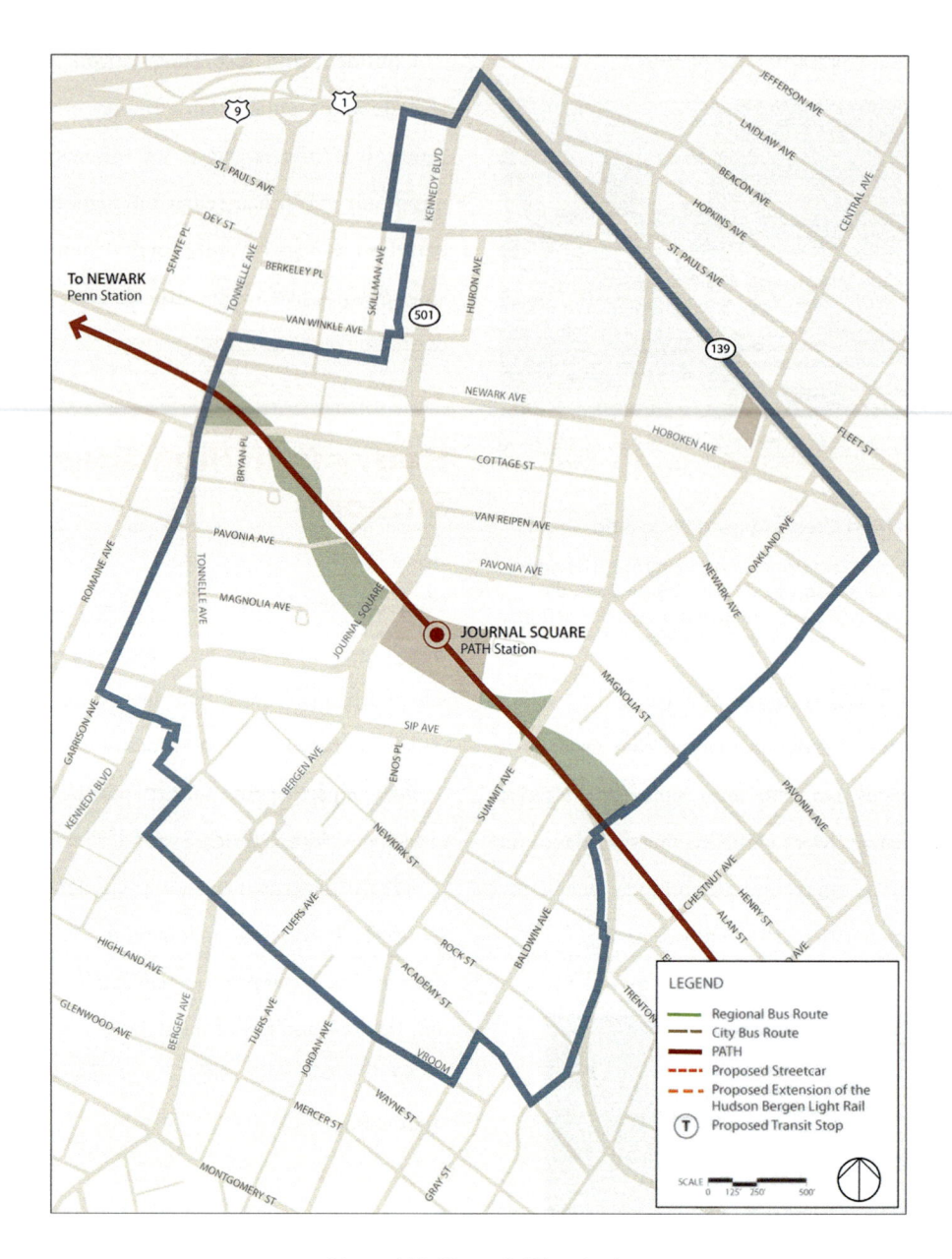

Map of Multi-modal Terminal

This map illustrates, with the red dot, the location of the highest concentration of transit modes, hosting local and regional buses, taxi stops, and jitney stops. The most important is the 24-hour heavy rail (PATH), shown with the red line, with its underground station under the red dot.

Comment and recommendation: Indicated in darker brown is the area of the above-grade plaza that currently spans over the below-grade station. The green indicates the proposed greenway, extending the existing plaza. It is designed in the vision plan as a central park, a continuous pedestrian and bicycle green-way that would span over the canyon and cover the train tracks. It would be new land in the high density core which will become invaluable in the future. The greenway would be an extraordinary pedestrian space, with walking connections to the entire core. Making the positive, safe, and convenient connection between various modes is fundamental to a successful and vibrant core.

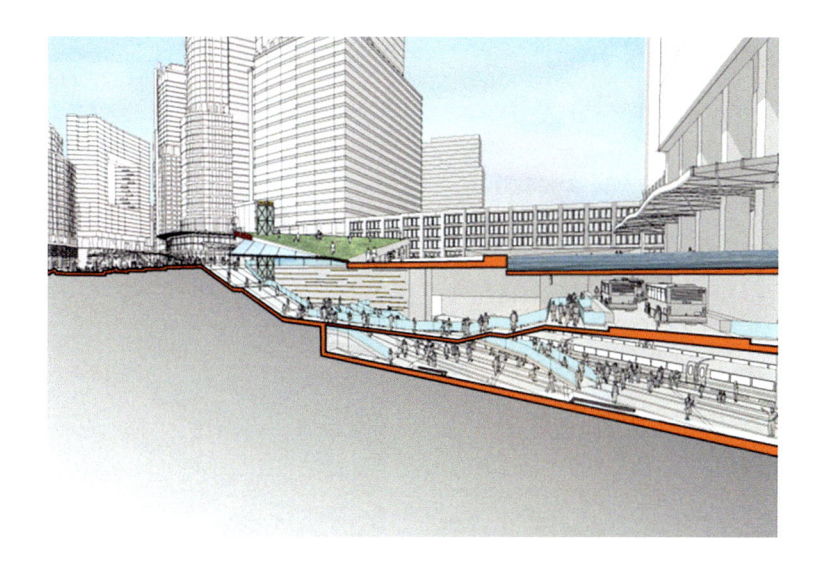

Section through the Proposed Upgraded Multi-modal Station in the Core.

This is proposed as a multi-modal transit station for Journal Square, Jersey City, NJ. It will become the focus of the development plan for the tallest buildings and most intense public spaces. This detailed section allows a view into the station and the plaza above.
Source: MHS Architects Hoboken.

Comment and recommendation: The tilt-up, grassed-roofed structure is the entrance to the station, centered in a large public plaza. The dark blue area is a glass-bottomed reflecting pool that lights the lower platform levels. Regional buses are located on the next level down, below the plaza and above the heavy rail. The PATH heavy rail station is on the lowest level, where it is currently located. The new station is designed with easy connections via ramps, elevators, and escalators to the other mode-shown in light blue. The upper-level is plaza.

The local bus would be just a short walk to the street level across the plaza, where taxis, streetcars, jitneys, and a great walking experience await. This induces high pedestrian flow, which is the sign of a more successful and active center.

A central pedestrian plaza is ideally focused around a multi-modal station entrance.

Proposed New City Center Public Plaza

The proposed plaza envisioned above the new multi-modal station. This rendering illustrates what the character, form, and design vocabulary of the plaza and station entrance, generated by the Vision Process, should look and feel like. The triangle pushing out of the ground is the new proposed entrance to the station. The plaza with a retail edge is full of pedestrians, retail, and services, complemented by urban landscaping in the proposed urban green-way.

Character of the Interior of the Proposed Station

A positive impression of a station and its entrance that is well designed, easy to use, and centrally located can only bring success to a downtown core.

The existing station and entrance received negative visual responses: it is connected directly to the World Trade Center which has the most extraordinary and beautiful station designed by architect Santiago Calatrava with very high positive response values. In contrast, the existing Station is not acceptable and will hurt the future image of core, if it is going to become a major world scaled urban center, which it has every potential of becoming. The station needs to be seriously upgraded. A new public/private financing strategy with private developers will have to be employed. The opportunity to build high rise, high density mixed-use buildings above the station, including a well designed upgraded station as proposed in the development plan is a likely path forward.

Interior View of the Proposed Station

Interior images of the proposed upgraded multi-modal station incorporate ramps and a glass ceiling (the underside of a reflecting pool at the plaza level) to bring natural light into the lower levels. The multi-level pedestrian circulation will keep the space dynamic and open. The PATH can be seen at the lower level.

Source: A. Nelessen Associates and MHS and Associates Architects

Ramp Leading to and from the City Center Plaza

The ramps allow easy access to the underground transit modes. Elevators are just adjacent.

Source: A. Nelessen Associates and MHS and Associates Architects

Urban Core Preferences— Urban Mobility with Streetcars

There is a growing desire for the re-installation of traditional streetcar lines to enhance the character, accessibility, and marketability of urban centers that want to be more pedestrian-oriented and have extended access to the core.

Streetcars Were an Essential Mobility Mode in City Centers

Historic research indicates that many cities had an extensive network of streetcar lines. These had stops in most higher-density urban neighborhoods, connecting to the heart of the city and to the primary stop/station. This was the golden age of city centers, seriously diminished when the streetcars were removed to accommodate private vehicles and additional traffic lanes. Now, people want to put them back.

The vision for many urban downtowns is the reintroduction of a streetcar or "trolley" line. The streetcar could assure multiple additional connections between outlying neighborhoods surrounding a major mixed-use commercial center. Each stop would be designed as a mixed-use sub-node, and ideally, the line would terminate at a mixed-use parking intercept. It would stop at all sub-nodes and directly in front of the main transit station. Each stop has a service area within a three- to five-minute walk.

During the initial phase, a dedicated rubber-tire bus could be used as funding and construction of a narrow-gauge streetcar occurs. All stops should be designated during the early bus phase and should remain permanent and substantial in nature. This will get riders comfortable with the stops and ensure a sense of permanence while transit-appropriate development is being built. All this is necessary in preparation for a permanent streetcar line. Narrow-gauge streetcars received the highest ratings in terms of preference. Their tracks are narrower than a conventional light-rail. They are a better fit in urban areas. They expand walking distances, replacing multi-lanes of traffic in city centers. A new streetcar line would have stops, three minutes walking time apart, all at secondary retail mixed-use nodes. They would provide easy connections to the heavy rail transit station. Ideally, trolleys would also link to major district intercept parking, keeping most parked cars out of downtowns.

Visioned Streetcar Line Mid-town Atlanta, Atlanta, Georgia

The map indicating the proposed streetcar line for Midtown Atlanta along Peachtree Street with its ten stops. The yellow circles are an approximate five minute walk. The location and stops are the synthesis of multiple design teams during the VTW. The streetcar lines start in downtown Atlanta and can extend to the Amtrak Station and Buckhead.

Streetcar Lines (light-rail) in Urban Areas

that it is a distinguishable feature of the area. The stops should incorporate new technology, including, but not limited to, heating and cooling, safety lighting, and GPSs (Global Positioning Systems) to indicate where/when streetcars will arrive.

Response Value +4(5)

Narrow Gauge Streetcar at Stop

This light-rail image always receives positive responses in urban Community Visioning sessions. This multi-car, narrow-gauge streetcar is new and modern. The track is located on the inside of the roadway. The stop is slightly elevated, with handicap accessibility and a small shelter.

Response Value +5(3)

Refurbished Older Streetcar

This simulation of a historic trolley/streetcar in the Milwaukee Downtown Vision process received a positive response. All participants thought it was appropriate, with a range from +8 to +2.

Comment and recommendation: This is an ideal linear mobility option for most urban downtowns, with dense adjoining residential neighborhoods that wish to become more sustainable and connected by an optimum five- to ten-minute walk to its stops. Where areas are out of the walking distance range, a bicycle network or an on-demand mobility service is recommended. The design of the stops should "fit in" with the visual character of the urban qualities and architecture of the center; however, each stop should be unique so

Comment and recommendations: The original trolley cars in Milwaukee were removed from service and disassembled in the 1950s as downtown started its downward evolutionary spiral, and the private car, new freeways, and parking dominated. The positive response to this simulation and other images of trolleys led to the recommendation of a new streetcar network, which was implemented 16 years after the completion of the Vision Plan for Downtown Milwaukee (shown later in this chapter).

Many cities, like San Francisco, have reintroduced older refurbished streetcars. The presence of rehabilitated older cars makes people smile.

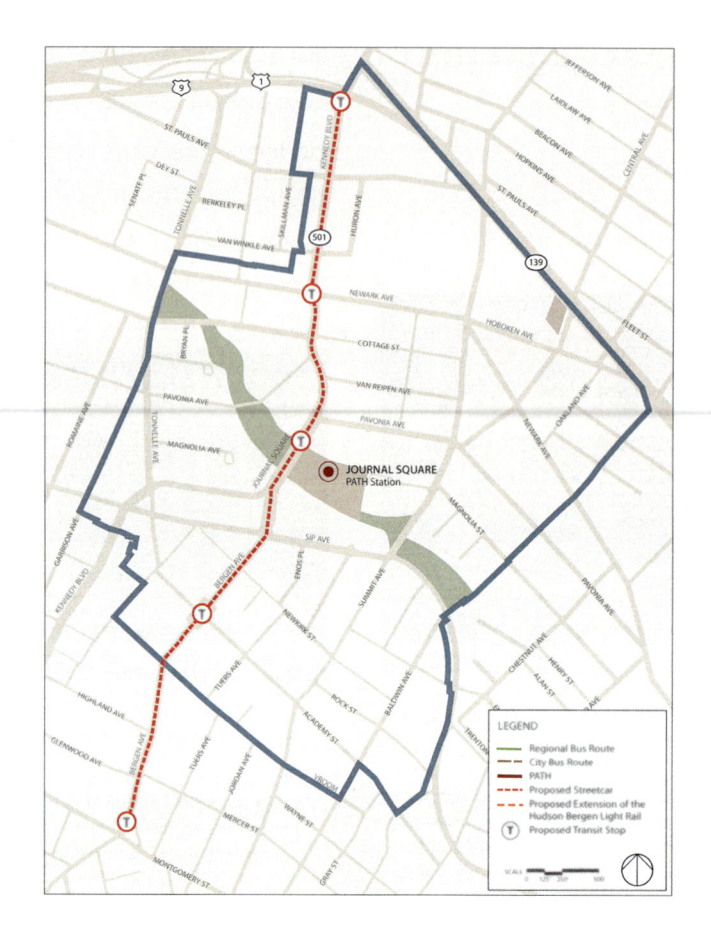

Proposed Streetcar Line

Journal Square, Jersey City, New Jersey

The proposed streetcar line for Journal Square in Jersey City, with six stops. It connects, on the top, to the proposed mixed-use parking intercept and in the center to the PATH station, and continues to a mixed-use residential, commercial area further south. It would travel back and forth at each stop every eight to ten minutes.

Response Value +5(4)

Comment and recommendations: The rubber-tired vehicle is flexible and has a traditional character. It is also the least expensive to purchase and operate. Initial route selection can test ridership before a more permanent light-rail, Bus Rapid Transit (BRT), or narrow-gauge trolley line and stops are constructed.

Rubber-Tire Trolley as the First Phase

The positive response to this rubber-tired trolley, with its response range from +9 to +1, suggests that participants like this form of public transit.

Street Car Stops

Quality designed streetcar stops/stations in the downtown area are fundamental to the success of the public transit facilities.

The following are images and renderings of a transit plaza and positive stops.

Modern Variation on a Traditional Trolley Stop

This image uses a traditional pitched roof form, benches, and lean-on circular supports for the waiting pedestrians.

Concept Design for a Modern Bus/Trolley Stop

It is more contemporary but still uses the pitched clear roof for rain/snow/sun protection. A unique feature of this shelter/stop is the motion-activated infrared heater used to deal with colder winter weather. Also included are other recommended street furniture, including streetlights, parking-signing, and way-finding in and around the stop. These must be included in the recommended Street Regulating Plan and possibly in the Design Vocabulary.

Rendering of Multi-modal Transit Plaza

Rendering of the transit plaza in the city core with stops for local buses, narrow-gauge light-rail, taxi, and jitneys. This is part of the large center public plaza. The street has been transformed to a large-scale shared-use street/plaza with light-rail line, bus lanes, and auto and taxi access, with the largest area devoted to the pedestrian realm. The visioned on-grade local transit plaza would be the major connector between the light-rail and the local buses. The regional buses and the rapid transit (PATH) would be a short walk away in a new underground station.

Comment and recommendations: Both young, old and parents with children will use it because it is conveniently located and well designed; however, each stop should be unique so that it is a distinguishable feature of the area.

Streetcar/light-rail lines and stops are major catalysts for positive streetscapes and infill development while encouraging healthy walking.

The following "before" and "after" images portray desired positive preferences. They illustrating transit's role in generating a positive response to negative places which can be accomplished by infilling mixed-use buildings on the existing surface parking lots; designing wide interactive sidewalks with street trees and textured crosswalks; and providing for a stop for the streetcar, as recommended in the VPS and the VTW.

Response Value −6(4)

Current Condition   BEFORE

The street in its current condition has four lanes devoted to vehicular movement. On the corner, there is an on-grade parking lot with a billboard. There are worn painted crosswalks and limited streetscape. The −6 response value, with a range of −10 to −2, is unacceptable and inappropriate now and in the future, according to everyone.

Comment and recommendations: The "before" negative image with a value of −6(4) can be transformed into a positive urban place, from depression to joy. The low negative value suggests that this is the perfect location for urban evolution using well-designed infill and street landscaping. As stated earlier, **"surface parking lots are the land banks of the future."**

Response Value +7(3)

Infill Development at Transit Stop   AFTER

The vision of what people want for this location in the future. The +7 response value, with a range of +10 to +4, means that everyone thought this the most appropriate for this location.

Comment and recommendations: The buildings, sidewalks, landscaping, and street wall/buildings edge contain all the urban features that were revealed as positive in the VPS. The streetcar lines are located in the center, with traffic lanes on the outside. Cars are able to use the center lanes when the streetcar is not present. The streetcar would stop at the intersection with a four-way stop. The defined pedestrian crossings, bollards, and café near the stop all reinforce the urban design. Streetcars and pedestrians get priority at intersection.

Response Value −5(4)

Existing Condition   BEFORE

This place has a collective negative response value. Notice that it is less negative than the parking lot with the billboard shown previously. It has a negative range of −9 to −1.

Comment and recommendations: Scanning the length of the sidewalk along the street, there is landscaping on both sides. Here again, the presence of the open paved lot, broken concrete, deteriorated curb, lighting poles, and painted peeling crosswalks contribute to its negative response. Perfect for infill, landscaping, and a trolley stop.

Response Value +5(3)

Revitalized Street   AFTER

The positive response to this simulation indicates the urban design features people want in this space and place to transform it from negative to positive.

Comment and recommendations: This simulation includes intensive new mixed-use infill buildings on both sides of the street, wide textured sidewalks, and an enhanced streetscape, including café/sidewalk displays, street crosswalks, new streetcar lines, and more pedestrians. Notice that the number of cars in the before image remains the same.

Urban Mobility—Buses, Taxis, and Jitneys

Local and regional buses will continue to be a major mobility mode in urban cores, typically made up of fixed routes on local streets, radiating out from the cores. A revitalized core must plan and design for bus lanes, stops, and stations, complemented by the other mobility modes.

Historic View of City Center

The heyday of Journal Square, as seen in this historic postcard of the "Main Street" of Jersey City circa 1935, before the 1950 car and highway explosion. The street is brick paved, which makes it look more like a plaza. It is full of pedestrian activity. The buses and people enlivened the center because the busy city bus station was in the middle of a wide boulevard, in the center of most commercial activity. All buses stopped here. It was a shared public plaza. The postcard provides a memory of the city center at its optimization phase, before auto-dependence and suburbia became manifest.

View of City Center Before Community Visioning Sessions

Above is the view from a wider perspective than on the postcard. You can orient yourself with the Loews Cinema building. Many buildings have been removed for parking. The brick plaza was paved over, transforming it into a six-lane arterial highway passing through the center. The buses were removed and put into a tunnel. New buildings were usually two or three stories. This was the suburbanization of this important city center.

The final Vision Plan for the area proposes the return of a central bus plaza, reducing the number of car lanes in the city center, which will allow all local buses to return to their original location. It would restore pedestrian activity brought by buses to the heart of the city center. This is partially a traffic-calming technique that makes the street more pedestrian friendly. Regional buses would be incorporated into the new redesigned multi-modal transit station.

Vision of the Future City Center—Focusing on the Multi-modal Pedestrian Plaza Design Contains: Local bus and taxi, covered waiting area; Streetcar; The raised triangle is the entrance to the PATH, connected to the greenway/plaza visually by textured walkways; Local bus stop.

Street Transformations— Bus and Taxi Ways

Preferences generated from the VPS and the VTW clearly recommended limiting the number of cars passing through the center and redesigning it as a more pedestrian-oriented shared-use space. To accomplish this, a section of a wide, multi-lane freeway passing through the most active retail street is envisioned to be reengineered in phases, similar to the successful bus street in downtown Denver.

Phased Transformation of a Major Arterial into a Phased Busway Shopping Street

When an important shopping street in the center of the urban core is unacceptable in its current form, with a negative response range of −8 to −2, transformation, sometimes called a "street diet" is required where sidewalks are widened, and lane width are reduced or eliminated.

Three phased simulations illustrate the potential evolution of this street as a dynamic shopping street, pedestrian plaza, and busway.

Response Value −5(3)

Existing Shopping Street
Currently, the street is a major arterial with little response to pedestrians.

Comment and recommendations: Traffic lanes were added, the original sidewalk reduced, and parallel parking removed on one side. This was reengineered as a major arterial at a time when car movement and surface parking were the predominant transportation policies that traffic engineers and planners thought would save downtowns. This policy of encouraging the automobile over the pedestrian and public transit was one of the major causes of death of this and other city centers that implemented the same policy. However, the center could easily be returned to a dynamic shopping street with an appropriate phased plan and leadership.

Phase One: Busway Transformation with Widened Sidewalks

This first simulation portrays a possible first-phase transformation, with an enhanced pedestrian experience, featuring the removal of one car lane, to be replaced with a widened sidewalk on one side of the street. Street trees, street furniture, signing, and awnings are added on both sides. Six lanes are reduced to five. This will benefit most of the merchants on this side of the street.

Phase Two: Busway Transformation with Center Pedestrian Plaza Walkway

The second simulation removes all vehicular traffic on this street except for bus lanes on both sides, with a textured center pedestrian way. Also, there is more intensive street landscaping and widened sidewalks on both sides, enhanced by additional landscape treatment. The busway would be delineated by a change in texture. Because of the intervals between buses, this design allows unrestricted, free flow of pedestrians diagonally across the street, enhancing the shopping experience. Existing and new merchants on both sides of the street would benefit.

Phase Three: The Ultimate Vision—Busway Transformation

This third simulation portrays the most positive vision for this section of the street with one bus lane, a larger public plaza, and an enhanced streetscape. Phase One could be implemented immediately; Phase Two or the ultimate evolution would depend on the introduction of the light-rail, remote parking, and a rerouting and reduction of traffic through the center.

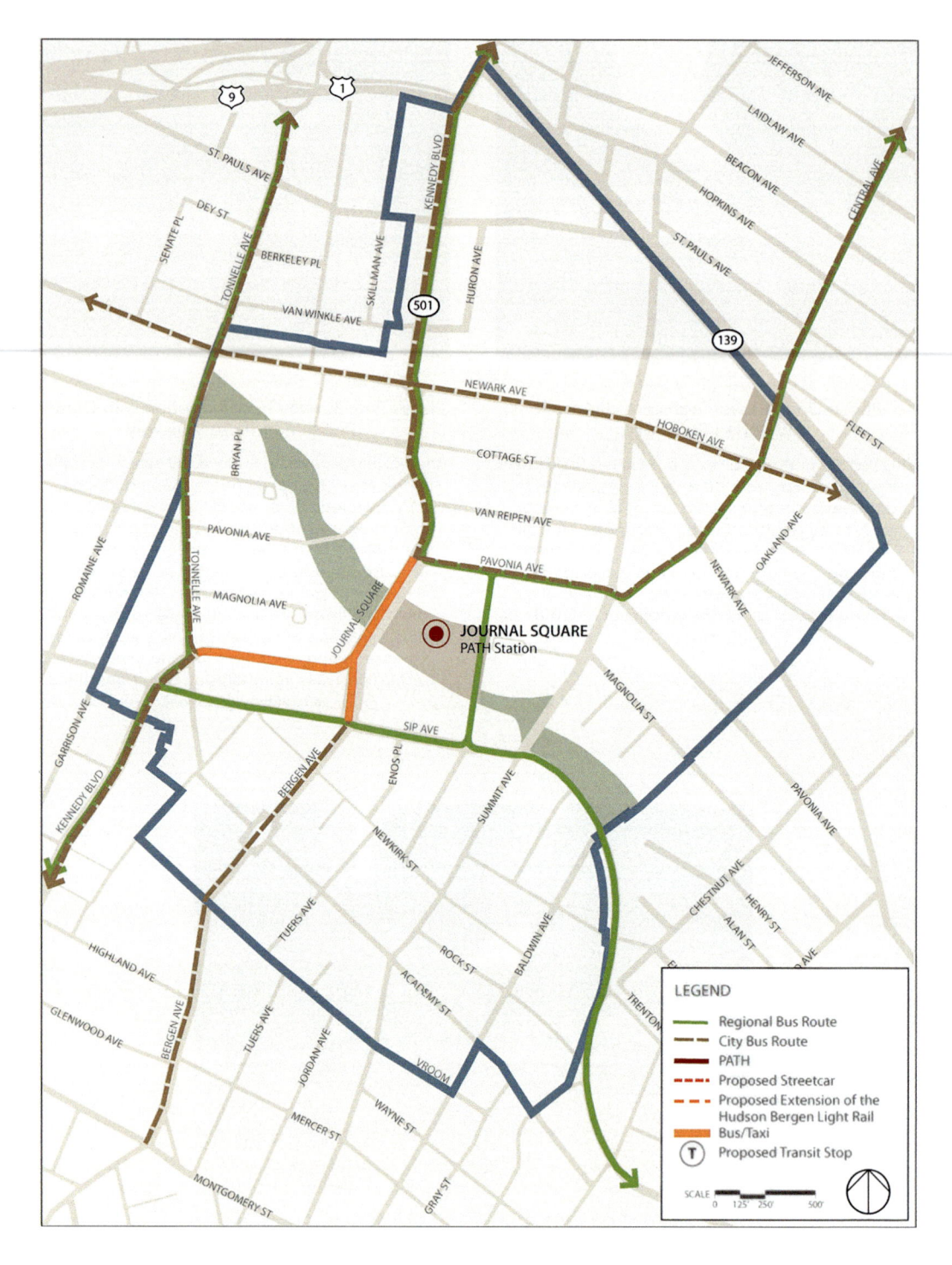

The Bus, Taxi, and Streetcar Lines

This map illustrates the recommended transit mobility network, including the streetcar, bus, taxi, and regional bus routes, and the pedestrian bike greenway. Of particular significance is the orange line that indicates the proposed bus-/taxi -only lanes.

A Complete Bicycle Network

A bicycle plan must have an interconnected network of lanes and paths. 69% of participants believe that defined bicycle paths and lanes should radiate out two miles from the core.

New bicycle lanes and increased bicycle, scooter, and other small electric vehicle usage are an important new development in many American urban areas. Such uses will reduce pollution; improve sustainability; and enhance livability, market appeal, and public health. A network of paths and lanes must be designed to encourage cycling and other low impact modes within the right-of-way on designated lanes. Cycling should be an easy, safe, and fast way of traveling to and from adjacent neighborhoods, retail shops, offices, light-rail stops, plazas, transit stations, and institutional and civic buildings, as well as through parks and plazas, in essence safe and easy connections connecting to everything. The most sustainable urban city centers will put a greater reliance on pedestrians and other low impact modes. Recent studies have shown that 40% of all trips are less than two miles in length, making bicycling a reasonable alternative to driving if it is safe, easy, and convenient. Bicycling adds to the positive perceptual value. Places with bicycles have higher response values. Transit Dependant Development (TDD) relies on rapid transit, buses, trolleys, taxis, and light-rail, and must incorporate bicycle and pedestrian flow as the key to sustainable neighborhoods and downtown development. A bicycle network plan with bicycle parking locations should be included in every urban design plan. A bicycle plan should, at the minimum, have two basic types of bicycle lanes and paths: striped on-street bicycle lanes and multi-use paths through the parks and plazas. Each bicycle lane configuration must be wide enough (4 feet) to accommodate at least one cyclist, comfortably safe from traffic, and must be well demarcated. Where there are on-street bicycle facilities, there must be proper striping, asphalt color, and pavement signage to ensure the safety of cyclists, pedestrians, and motorists alike. Paving should extend through every intersection in order to alert drivers to cyclists' presence and to direct cyclists.

It is important to have proper signage and striping for safety and way-finding purposes throughout the bicycle network. Way-finding signage will include: Identification, route, crossing lanes, and pathways. In addition to the network of bicycle lanes and paths, bicycle parking facilities must be provided at locations throughout the site, particularly near major employment and retail areas, parks, plazas, and bus and transit stops.

A recommended set of "green" bicycle standards

Provide enough bicycle parking for a minimum of 10% of all tenants within commercial buildings and 20% of tenants in residential buildings. Locate bike parking facilities within the building. Each commercial building over 100,000 square feet or with more than 300 employees shall provide showers and changing areas, or be immediately adjacent to a health club or gym paid for by the employer.

Response Value +5(5)

Shared Street with Bicycles

This image of a narrow street with parking spaces for bikes received a positive response value. Some found it a little too tight. It is a street form and character that should be highly considered.

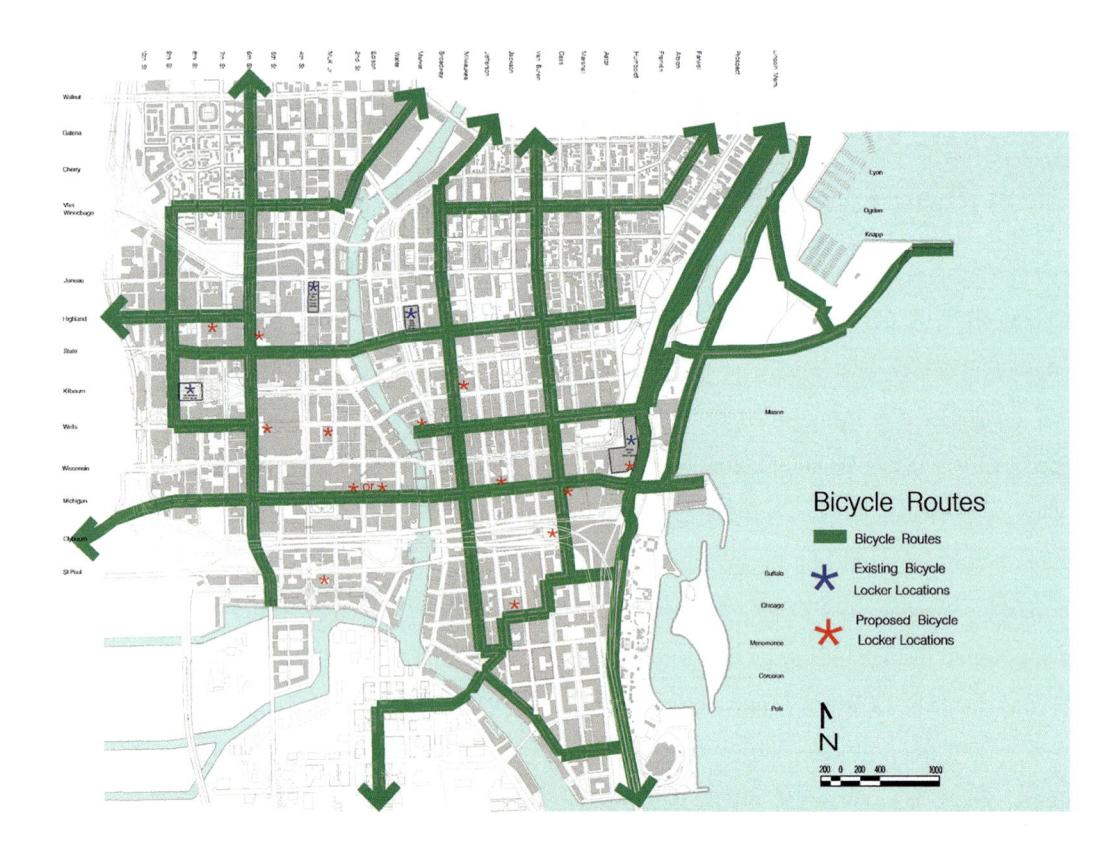

Bicycle Plan for Downtown Milwaukee

The bicycle routes recommended for downtown Milwaukee, with the proposed locations of bicycle lockers. The primary network does not incorporate every street and block, but a continuous grid bicycle network is required. On these streets where the primary bicycle path is recommended, specific street sections must be included in the Street Regulating Plan. On some streets, the car/traffic lanes may need to be narrowed, or parallel parking must be removed on one side.

Comment and recommendations: The width of the street and the building wall make the street feel very comfortable. It is a true multi-modal shared street, with pedestrians, streetcars, bicycles, cars, and bikes as well as parking for bikes and cars. To make short-term car parking more visible, regard the parking sign. Notice that the spaces for short-term parking for cars have been reduced to accommodate more bicycle parking. Even with narrow sidewalks, this street is very popular.

Response Value +6(3)

Security on Bicycle

Security on a bicycle is highly desired by participants. It brings the police and security personnel in close contact with the pedestrians, with back-up by car or motorcycle if necessary. It is friendlier. Community policing on a bike is less intimidating.

Comment and recommendation: People need to feel safe in urban areas. Humanizing security is critical. It is difficult, if not impossible, from a police cruser or security vehicle. All cites need this type of less-threatening security.

Three Preferred Bike Lanes

Design bicycle paths in urban cores that connect to surrounding neighborhoods

Response Value +4(4)

Most Protected Bikeway

This bike lane is adjacent to the sidewalk between the parallel-parked cars.

Comment and recommendations: This is one of the preferred urban bikeway. The location and width makes this one of the safest bikeways. It is two-way and protected from moving cars. Bicycle rider feel comfortable here. There is much controversy about its location. American drivers are used to parallel parking next to the curb and not having to take into consideration the moving bike to get to the sidewalk.

This type of bikeway is perfect in locations where bicycles and scooters are a prime mobility mode or where the intensity of bicycle use is high. It still allows parallel parking while making the bicycle and pedestrian experience more pleasant.

Response Value +5(5)

Partially Protected Bikeway
This bikeway received a slightly higher response value. It is one-way and well-marked.

Comment and recommendations: It is a separate one-way bike path protected by a wide exterior curb from the moving auto and truck traffic. It is parallel to a heavily planted center boulevard, which increased its response value.

Response Value +5(5)

One-way Painted Bicycle Lane
This is the most common painted-on, one-way bike lane, located between parked cars and traffic lanes.

Comment and recommendations: Notice that the parking spaces are wide enough for the out-swing car door, thereby minimizing potential impact on a moving bike. From the edge of the curb to the edge of the painted bike lane is 15 feet. The bump out helps delineate the edge of the parking and potential pedestrian crossings. This is the minimum accepted bicycle lane.

Quality Urban Neighborhood Streets

The neighborhood streets surrounding an urban core must also be transformed when they are perceived as negative. To improve the marketability and livability of the entire downtown, **large-scaled developments in the center must support the improvement of adjacent neighborhoods' infrastructure and landscaping**. Improvement cannot just be confined to their lot or the front sidewalks of their new high-rise buildings. The city core could be beautiful, but if the surrounding neighborhoods are negative, the area will never reach its maximum positive response values and market-value potential. By assisting and improving the surrounding neighborhoods the approval process will be easier, with less objections by neighbors.

Existing Condition   BEFORE

Existing negative condition of a typical local residential/neighborhood adjacent to the proposed revitalized urban core.

Comment and recommendations: With a response value range of –9 to –3, everyone thought this neighborhood street was negative and unacceptable in its current condition. This neighborhood had to accommodate private cars and parking, and thereby lost its charm. As the core is redeveloped to be shinny and new, these adjacent neighborhoods need upgrading to increase the value and appeal within the five- to ten-minute walk and the 2½-mile radius of the core center.

Response Value +4(3)

Proposed Street with Improvements   AFTER

A simulation of this same local street after transformation.

Comment and recommendations: The value increased from a –6 to a +4, with landscaping and infrastructure improvements, which include a paved and textured cartway, removing some asphalt for a landscaped parkway, and street trees while retaining the existing parking; extending the pavement texture into the front yard; and providing new curbing, streetlights, and banners. Unseen in this image is the need to replace the aging sewer, water, and storm water pipes. In order to do this, the street needs to be ripped up and repaved. For an urban area to be ultimately successful, the entire area within the five- to ten-minute walk must be enhanced and improved, and, ideally, spread to the area within the 2½-mile bike ride.

These improvements could be paid for with a Density Increase Bonus (DIB) that would apply to all new buildings that exceed a base height limit of, e.g., 5 to 12 stories. The district for the application of the DIB would be the area within a five- to ten-minute walk from the center of the urban core.

The Density Increase Bonus (DIB)

As buildings are allowed to increase above a certain specified height or number of floors, an impact fee would be extracted that must be used to improve the adjacent streets, infrastructure, and streetscapes. An additional bonus can be applied if workforce housing is provided, thereby, all areas within the district increased in terms of value and life quality, making the center more desirable.

Unfortunately, most developers are only concerned about the areas immediately adjacent to their building(s), with many getting tax abatements. They owe it to the community and themselves to improve the adjoining neighborhoods when increasing building heights above the allowed base height. **The fees collected can only be spent in the designated area and not deposited into the general fund of the municipality.** This will be objected to by some elected officials, not from the district who will think that they are entitled a portion of the fees. The DIB should only apply to the designated area. Other DIBs could be imposed in other areas.

Buildings in Downtown

The most successful urban cores have positive continuous building-walls of compatible and contextual buildings, creating sequences of well-proportioned, safe, pedestrian-oriented streets and public spaces. There are many lost spaces and underutilized lots and buildings that are ready to be infilled and re-purposed

to the highest possible density and positive contextual relationship.

A positive three- and-four-dimensional character of the urban streets generates legible, memorable, functional, feasible, implementable, beautiful, and well-proportioned building walls and spaces that people find positive.

The style, mass, facade, and materials that constitute the architectural character of each building can create a harmonious whole. Each must reference the architectural context/elements of adjoining buildings including materials, cornice lines, belt courses, base floor definition, color, and details. Using these, good architects can create positive building walls which frame the street, plazas, and spaces between the buildings.

Infill Plan for Journal Square

This map indicates in purple those locations recommended for new infill buildings that would create positive building walls and street spaces. The red dotted lines are the transit lines, including high speed transit (PATH), the proposed streetcar, and a new extension of the light-rail line.

Preserve Historically Significant Buildings and Facades

Historic building, details and workmanship are very difficult and expensive to duplicate. Preserve historic buildings and street wall facades wherever possible. Contextual sensitivity means that the new buildings complement the adjacent and adjoining buildings in form, color, floor heights, cornice lines, etc.

Response Value +7(3)

A Classic Well-Maintained Historic Building

Historic architecture captured in the Victorian, Italianate, and Baroque facades of many of the older buildings in urban downtowns received very high positive responses.

Comment and recommendations: Buildings of this historic nature must be preserved and incorporated into urban form where they are structurally sound. The details in this facade can no longer be replicated in their original materials, craftsmanship, and form. The play of light and shadow is extraordinary!

Response Value +5(3)

The Form and Character of Urban Residential

A high-value, high-density, residential infill building; modern, with traditional features.

Comment and recommendations: The building has a brick modulated façade with articulation at the fourth floor. The first floor is raised above-grade, with architecturally expressed entrances, giving it the appearance of a five- or-six-story townhouse-type building, although it is much taller. The downside of the facade is the "through the wall" air conditioning units for each apartment. The consistent repetition of similar window openings and styles give it an institutional look. Also, there is no modulation on the facade; it is a value-engineered building.

Design for Mixed-use Buildings

Mixed-use buildings have multiple uses in one building, e.g., commercial or service uses on the ground floor with housing and/or offices above.

Response Value +6(3)

Mixed-use Urban Infill
A contemporary building, with a two-story retail base and stepped-back upper floors that complement the adjacent and adjoining cornices and setbacks.

Comment and recommendations: The urban design of the street wall and sidewalk enhances the positive response value. The building has identifiable building modules, a variety of window types, using consistent materials (brick glass and stone) as well as excellent street landscaping and furniture. Together, they create an interesting facade to experience. These are urban design characteristics that create great facades and street walls, and should be codified.

Response Value +6(4)

Mixed-use Residential Infill
A more classical residential mixed-use building in downtown.

Comment and recommendation: Most significant about this building is the modulation of the street-wall with an articulated base; a range of window types and sizes; staggered step backs; terraces; and the primary, clearly defined entrance on the ground level. The light and shadow on this building is extraordinary, as are the range of units, many with their own green terraces. The stepped-back lower levels is in context with the base height of the adjoining buildings. These architectural characteristics are appropriate for any urban downtown.

Building Types and Heights

The tallest buildings should be located in the downtown, within a three- to five-minute walk from the center focus. The more mobility modes that cross or transfer in the center, the higher the allowable FAR (Floor Area Ratio). In addition, any new tall building above a specified height must contribute to the DIB for the upgrading of infrastructure, with an emphasis on providing pedestrian amenities plazas/parks, and enhancement of adjacent neighborhoods and residential streets. Provision of affordable housing must also be included.

Three of the most preferred building types and heights for larger city cores are illustrated in the sectional axiomatic models that follow

These sections of models were designed to form the massing for various infill locations recommended on STC (Susceptibility To Change) maps and models. These prototypes have embedded parking, although they could stand alone if parking is provided off-site within a reasonable walk.

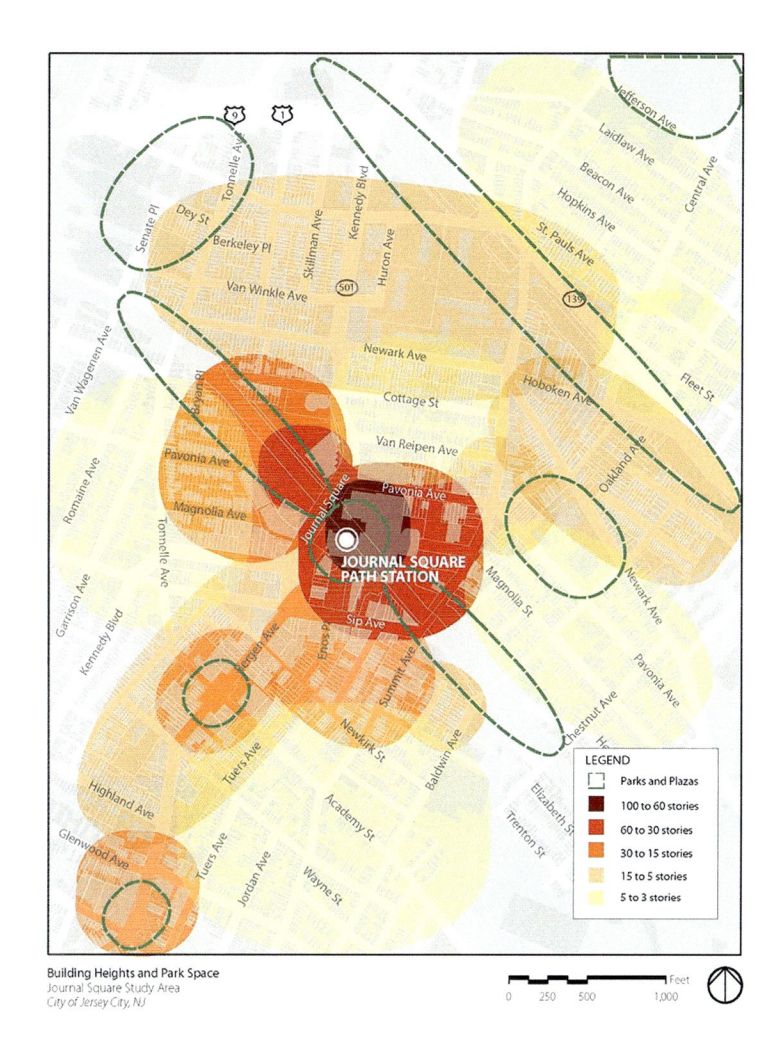

Building Heights and Park Space
Journal Square Study Area
City of Jersey City, NJ

LEGEND
☐ Parks and Plazas
■ 100 to 60 stories
■ 60 to 30 stories
■ 30 to 15 stories
■ 15 to 5 stories
■ 5 to 3 stories

Feet
0   250   500   1,000

Recommended Height Based on Community Visioning

Above, the map has the recommended allowable building heights. The tallest buildings in red (60 to 100 stories), with lower heights in the orange and yellow. The majority of the new buildings would range from 12 to 30 stories. The tallest buildings are located directly over or adjacent to the 24-hour PATH station. The heights were determined by participants in the VTW. This can be mapped for any downtown core in proportion to its size.

3D Model of the Urban Center—Core

This computer model illustrates the tallest buildings in the center, above the multi-mode transit center. The buildings decrease in height the further away one walks from the transit center. The recommended building heights by stories are: 70 to 100 stories, 60 stories, 30 stories, 15 stories, 6 stories, and the lowest at 3 stories. The buildings step-down in height, with one focus/landmark building at a recommended 100 stories. A landmark building(s) creates a strong visual impact seen from anywhere in the region, identifying the location of the core in the region.

Illustrated Sectional Model of 30+ Stories

This narrow section through a 30+-story tower, has four stories of embedded parking above-grade and one below. It has an articulated four-story facade along the pedestrian realm, with retail, offices, or housing enclosing the parking. Notice that the building is set back from the front street facade and that it has a community garden on the top floor and a green roof above the parking.

Illustrated Sectional Model of 15+ Stories

This section through a 15-story mixed-use building set back at the third story from the street wall/ facade. It has retail and/or offices on the first four floors. It has one story of parking underground and three stories of embedded parking. This building works well at 16 stories—15 stories plus a penthouse which is setback from the main facade.

Illustrated Sectional Model of 6 Stories

This six-story building has mixed-use, double-loaded corridors. It also has a bonus penthouse and terrace. Notice that the facade of this building rises directly from the sidewalk edge. The first floor is retail/service. It has a facade shift at the fifth floor and a setback for a terrace at the penthouse level. The building has half a level of underground parking and one floor of above-level embedded parking with a green roof.

Sectional Model of the Front Facade and Parking.

This three-dimensional section, through a mixed-use building, has design features that are recommended. The ground floor is retail with a mezzanine. Housing or offices could occupy the next two upper floors. It has a stepback at the fourth level to respond to the pedestrian context and scale, creating a terrace for that home. The building above is set back and has a double-loaded corridor. Each unit has a balcony along its facade. It has multi-levels of embedded parking attached in the rear, with a green park on the roof. Notice the wide sidewalk which locates it on one of the major pedestrian streets and will allow retail to spill out onto the pedestrian realm.

Milwaukee Redevelopment Plan

3D Model by A. Nelessen Associates - 1998

Recommended—Entire Block Infill

A computer model of a building prototype for a five- and six-story mixed-use, residential, urban infill building. The center of the block is a rooftop courtyard over parking. The buildings are typically 60+ feet in depth. They are divided into discrete Individual Building Modules (IBM), which make them appear like separate attached buildings, modulating the facade. The building form can accommodate a range of unit types from through-building lofts to units along a double-loaded center corridor or a grouping of several units served by individual elevator and stairs. This type of development can easily be built in phases. Retail is located on-grade on the corners, with the residential units raised above-grade with stairs and stoops. The corners have been emphasized by corner chamfering, complemented with an architectural emphasis: a tower/landmark.

The Retail Shopping Experience

An urban downtown Community Vision session can determine where retail shopping experiences are best located and what form and character it should take.

One of the overlays in the VTWs asked, "Where are the appropriate locations for various types of retail?" and "What are the appropriate pedestrian realms and mobility connections?" These have to work together to achieve ultimate market/customer success. It is even more important, with the advent of online retailing, that shopping be a positive place of social interaction, a memorable experience. It has to have multiple use, with restaurants and services in the mix. Shopping places must not generate a neutral or a negative experience.

Retail is divided into three basic categories:

- **Signature high-end retail on signature streets**
- **Community retail**
- **Neighborhood retail**

Signature and Community Retail stores have larger footprints and provide broader community needs, whereas Neighborhood Retail has a smaller footprint, providing every day local needs, accessed by an easy walk.

Signature Retail on "Signature Streets"

Signature, high-end retail shopping belongs on the most important and well-designed streets and pedestrian realms.

This type of retail is a challenge in many of the downtown areas that have succumbed to online shopping or are in the early deteriorating phase of the urban evolutionary spiral. Most of this type of shopping is targeted to specific consumers, mostly in suburban high-end mall locations, or well-established and designed urban streets, and now online. Nonetheless, it is always a strong desire of participants to have it, along with other retail stores, restaurants, and services to serve adjacent residential, and offices.

Positive-rated street facades along signature streets are composed of beautiful, architecturally rendered wider and narrower store facades, with both small and larger footprints, and complemented by attractive and compelling store display windows, interesting entrances, great street landscaping, and discrete and well-designed signing. All these are fundamental urban design characteristics, intended to produce positive sequential pedestrian experiences.

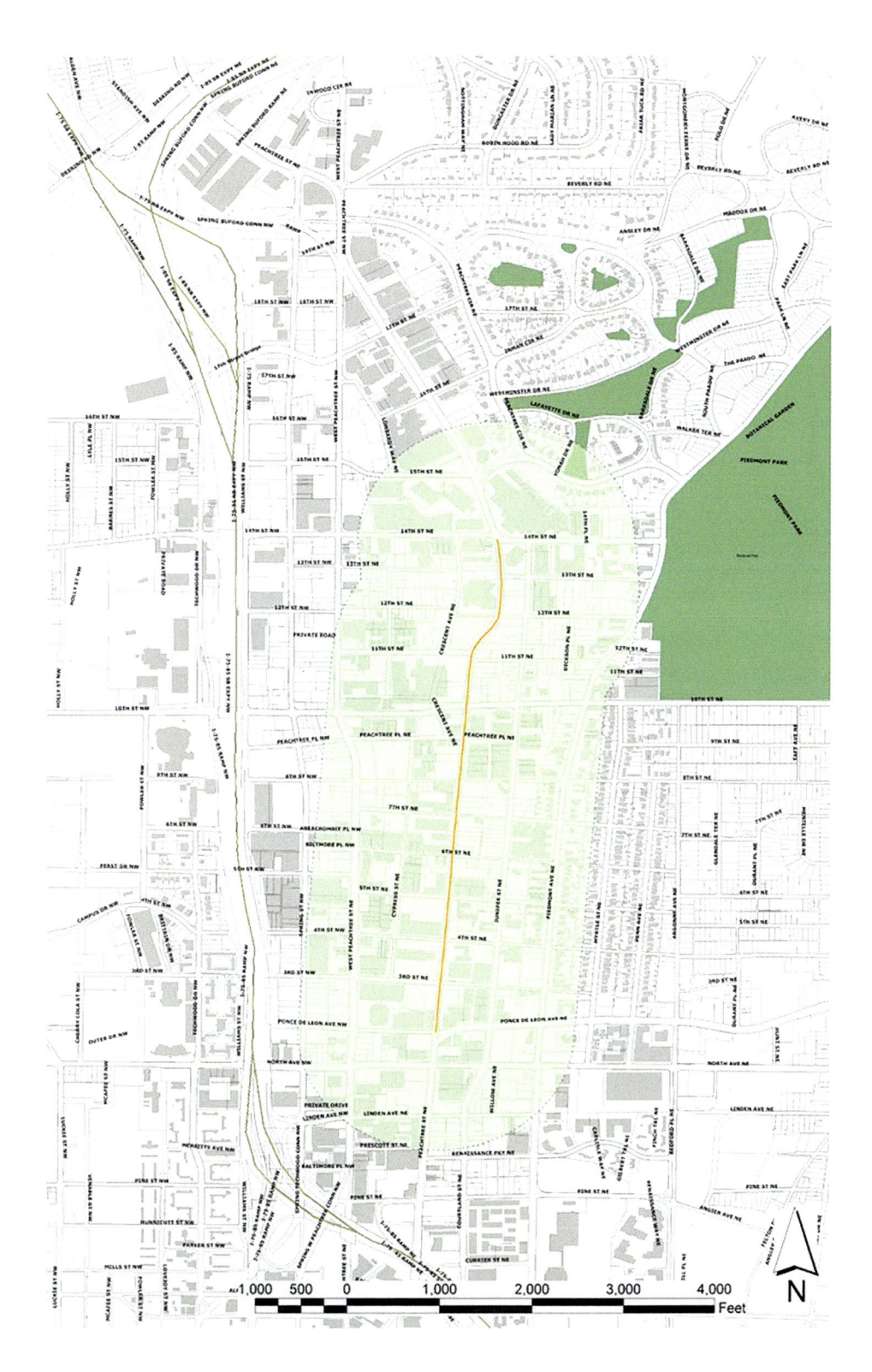

Map Locating Signature Shopping Street

The location and length of the signature street is illustrated by the yellow line/street frontage.
This assumes continuous multiple signature retail frontages along a ten-minute walk, end to end.
The light green overlapping circles on the map indicate the walking distance relationship to the
street. The light green area defines the three-minute walk.

Signature Shopping Street Facade

This retail facade received very high preference ratings.

Comment and recommendations: This facade design and retail establishment is very appropriate on a signature retail street. It has wide sidewalks, top-notch landscaping, and street furniture. It also has good transit access and parking. The building is mixed-use, with the entrance on the predominant corner. It has a chamfered round corner, maximizing the space for the pedestrian on the corner and capturing pedestrian flow from two directions. The window display and views to the interior of the store enhance the pedestrian experience.

Design the Store Types and Facades to Fit the Context

The following portrays the types of retail, and specifics of the building design desired.

Which of the following two images are more appropriate for an urban core location? The images tested the desired character using a retailer with suburban and urban building formats. The suburban store type received a value of –6(5). In an urban setting, This store format would be totally unacceptable.

Response Value –6(4)

Suburban Store Front

With a –6 response value with a range of –10 to –2, the above brand-name, one-story retail location with front parking lot would be unacceptable and inappropriate for the urban shopping experience.

Comment and recommendations: This facade and site design belongs, at best, in a suburban large lot setting.

Response Value +4(5)

Urban Store Front

There is a positive response to the same brand name in a two-story building on an urban corner.

Comment and recommendations: Its positive value of only +4 can be attributed to the unimaginatively designed facade. It is not mixed-use, nor does it have a green roof. It has a square corner. Had it been in a mixed-use building, and multi-storied, to meet the context of the adjacent buildings, the response values would have been higher. Still, the improvement from –6 to +4 is notable. **Keep urban cores urban in context and character. No suburban interventions!**

Quality Pedestrian Realms

The shopping experience can be enhanced by building quality pedestrian realms. The pedestrian realms that generate very high positive response values contain Urban Design standards to be emulated.

Response Value +8(2)

Highly Desired Urban Sidewalks and Building Edge

With a response value of +8 and a range of +10 to +6, this image is one of the highest-rated pedestrian realms.

Comment and recommendations: It has a wide sidewalk, approximately 18 feet wide from the public property line, as well as various retail facades, quality streetscapes and furniture, interesting, and discrete signing. The value of the location is enhanced, with a deep and overhanging setback for the café. Notice the change in ground color and texture at the property line on which the café is located as well as the blue-painted light posts. This is a pedestrian realm that can be easily accomplished.

Response Value +6(3)

Urban Sidewalk and Building Edge

This sidewalk is very appropriate for commercial retail frontages in the core.

Comment and recommendation: Positive pedestrian realms must have deep front setbacks (18 to 30 feet) and a range of shopfront widths (12 to 60 feet) and window displays. This pedestrian realm has a dual path sidewalk with landscape islands between a wider story-front walkway and a walkway adjacent to the parallel parking. The awnings have the dual function of shade for displays and protection from rain and snow.

Community-Based and Neighborhood Retail

Residential districts in urban areas need local retail and services. Community retail stores generally have a smaller footprint and narrower storefronts. Community retail and service uses need to be located within a short walking distance of adjacent residential uses.

Community retail and services include groceries, hardware stores, cleaners, restaurants and café, daycares, banks, pharmacies, hair salons, consignment and specialty stores that could include a bike store, exercise studios, and bakeries. These stores are frequented most often by adjacent residents, supplying residents with most of their daily needs. Because of the optimum three- to five-minute walking distance from home to store, multiple locations are required. Urban residential densities have to be high in order to support these services.

Response Value +8(2)

Neighborhood Café, Coffee Shop, and Restaurant

This image is what many Community Vision participants envision as the perfect neighborhood retail. With a range of +10 to +6, it is one of the strongest neighborhood retail images.

Comment and recommendations: Located on the corners of local streets, these buildings are three and four stories: mixed-use, with retail on the ground floor and housing above. The corner café, the child on the bicycle, and the pedestrians increase the response value. Everyone wants one of these in their urban neighborhood.

Map of Retail Locations

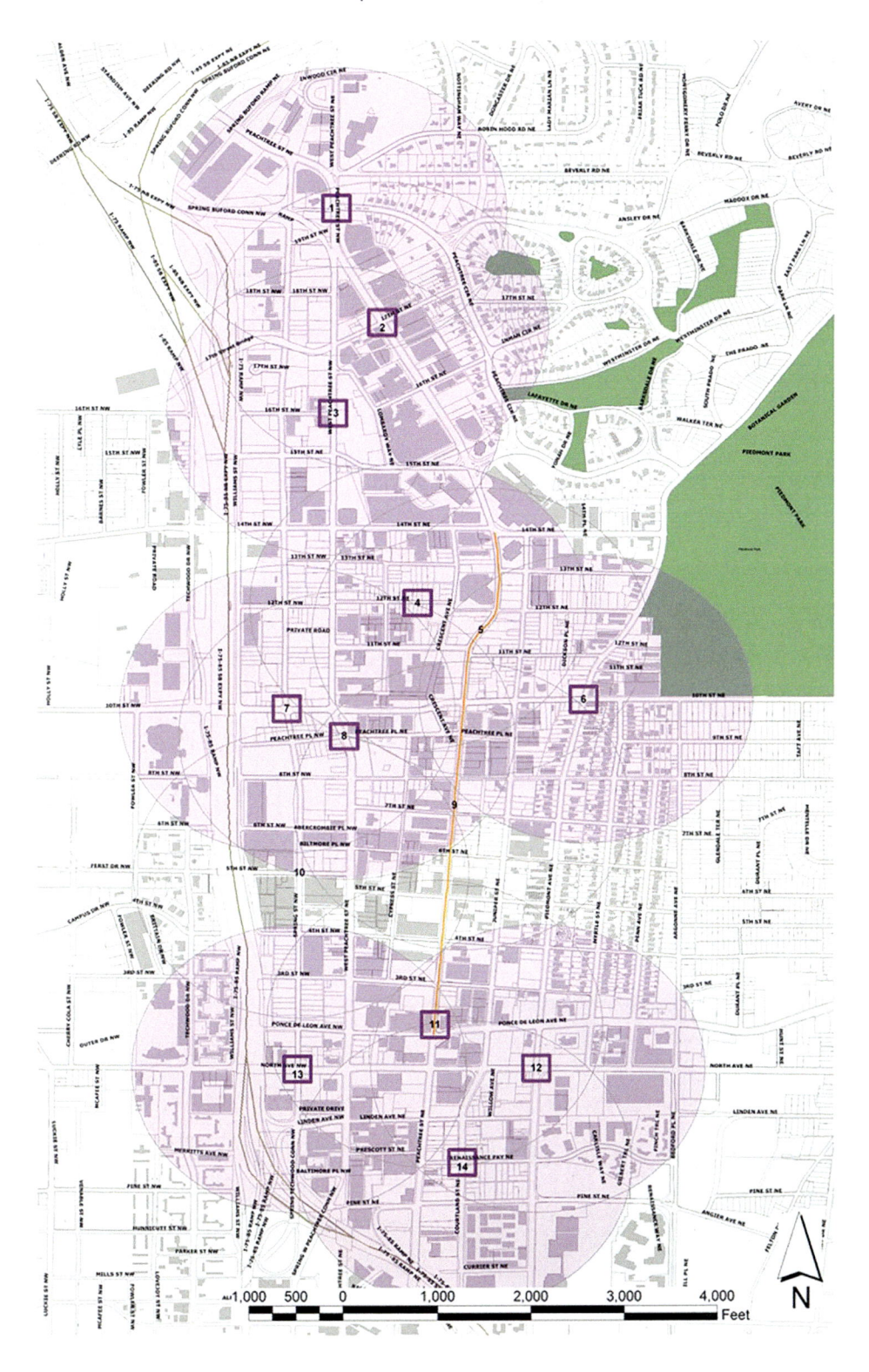

This map for Midtown Atlanta illustrates the recommended 11 locations for local and community retail in order to optimize the waking distance from residential concentrations. The purple circles represent a three- to four-minute walk. All are recommended on corners more or less in the center of an urban neighborhood.

Open-front Green Grocer in an Urban Neighborhood

Urban residents want to walk out of their apartment buildings and be within close proximity to goods and services. The response value of +7, with the range of +10 to +4, indicates that everyone finds this appropriate.

Comment and recommendations: A highly desired local retail location includes a grocer who sells locally grown vegetables and produce. Highly recommended are displays on the sidewalks in front of the building under a wide awning. Selling on the street gives it a "farmers' market" feeling. This type of retail makes urban neighborhoods more desirable while enhancing the character of the street.

Response Value +5(3)

Neighborhood Service Retail (A small hardware)

store and other local neighborhood service vendors are highly desirable within walking distance in urban residential neighborhoods.

Comment and recommendations: Retail and service uses that would be very positive in any urban neighborhood include a greengrocer, medium-sized food market, drug store, hardware store, local takeout and restaurant/café, fitness center, and daycare. They must be located where people are able to walk to them from adjacent urban residential neighborhoods, ideally passing it on the way to transit stops. It is critical that the residential density be high enough to support this retail. If not, locating them adjacent to transit stops might be a reasonable alternative.

Parking in Downtown

As long as there are motor vehicles, there will be a need for parking.

Every car in the United States today needs five to seven parking spaces somewhere. Most are used for a limited time duration, but nonetheless when you need it, you want one conveniently available. Most are empty the majority of time. Surface parking lots and singlefunction, value-engineered parking structures have been the killers of urban character. On a positive note, car ownership and the need for parking decrease with higher density and close proximity to transit. In addition, car hailing services have reduced the need for a car in urban areas.

There are more creative ways of dealing with parking, such as integrating it into mixed-use residential buildings; placing it underground or behind buildings, or in separate standing mixed-use structures or large remote parking interceptors connected by transit; as well as limited on-street parking. All these are appropriate for urban areas, provided they are in the "right" location. **Parking needs must be met within a reasonable two- to ten-minute walk or transit connection to destinations.**

Most urban areas have an excess of surface parking, receiveing the most negativing response values, represent a holding pattern in most urban areas that are in the downward phase of urban evolution. The foremost urban design priority must be the redevelopment and infill of urban surface parking lots, which are the land banks to accommodate mixed-use residential/ commercial/ civic development. **To the extent possible, the amount of parking should be limited in the core to the smallest ratio per unit or square foot and assigned to specialty/ priority parking only! In many core streets, private vehicles should be completely banned**.

Implementing the above policy will be difficult at first, given the years of accommodating parking in close proximity to where people live and work. **It must be removed incrementally**.

Alternatives can be implemented that are convenient; are easy to use; and expand the positive interactions with places, spaces, people, and activities. These interactions in a well-designed urban pedestrian realm will enhance personal health and exercise, the joy of living, working, and walking while improving the marketability of place.

There are four basic types of parking buildings/structures:

1. **Embedded**—where the parking is surrounded by other uses. It is not seen.
2. **Podium**—where the lower floor levels are designed as parking right to the sidewalk or property line edge. The ground floor could be retail, services, etc., which helps mediate the negative character. The upper levels exposed parking must be architecturally treated.
3. **Underground**—where parking is ramped below-grade with a building or park on top.
4. **Mixed-use**—where the ground floor along the pedestrian realm is dedicated to services or retail. The upper floors are parking, with flat floors and a facade that makes them indistinguishable from adjacent context buildings.

There are five different parking location options:

1. **On-street**—can be parallel, head-in, or back-in.
2. **In-building**—a half-level under low density residential, embedded, or podium (not highly recommended) with a green roof. Entrances and exits cannot negatively impact the pedestrian realm.

3. **Neighborhood**—in a mixed-use structure within a two- to a maximum of six-minute walk of residential units or neighborhood retail.
4. **Urban center**—an over ten-minute walk, with transit connections to the core of the urban area.
5. **Regional remote**—located several miles away from the center and adjacent to a freeway and toll ways, and connected to the urban core by rapid transit.

There is support for all the following structured public parking options. (Not including on-street parking.)

48% of all participants support regional remote parking.

50% support local parking in neighborhoods and urban centers.

58% of participants believe it is extremely appropriate to reduce the number of parking spaces required where buildings are closer to a transit stop or station.

69% support local parking within a two- to three-minute walk

81% of participants thought in-building parking is extremely appropriate or appropriate.

The above responses suggest that there is a full range of acceptable parking options for urban areas. All possible options should be explored to limit parking and auto movement in the core. All of the above, except for in-building parking, if implemented, would reduce or eliminate most auto traffic conflicts within the core pedestrian realms as drivers search for or access parking spaces. It is far better to use the lands normally dedicated to parking for other more productive human uses.

Urban Core Preferences— On-Street Parking

On-street parking will continue to play a role in most urban downtowns. It has been a high priority for auto-centric locations. Parking can be parallel, diagonal, head-in or back-in. It should be used primarily for short-term parking. It should be limited or eliminated on busy urban arterials with mixed-use edges in order to accommodate wider sidewalks, street trees and furniture, bicycle lanes, and transit.

Response Value +4(4)

On-street Parallel Parking with Bike Lane

On-street parallel parking adjacent to a bike lane is highly valued. This image has been used in multiple VPSs and in both the parking and mobility categories, and always receives positive response values.

Comment and recommendations: Parallel parking typically shields the pedestrian realm. Wherever possible, on-street parking should shield the bicycle path and the sidewalk. When the right-of-way is wide enough to accommodate a wide sidewalk and bike lane, parallel parking as shown is the ideal bike and parallel parking design. If a bike lane cannot be accommodated, parallel parking should be eliminated for a combination of alternative parking options. Without parallel parking, protect the sidewalk/pedestrian realm and bike lane using a wide exterior curb, planting area, or bollards.

In-Building Parking

There are multiple options for in-building parking. Underground parking is highly desired for limited urban parking. It removes the parked car from sight and eliminates the need for parking structures, which are generally negatively perceived unless they are well designed for mixed uses. In-building parking should be very limited at the lowest possible ratio if and when transit is available. The recommended standards are .25 parking spaces per unit for residential – and 1 parking space per 1,000 square foot of building occupied by offices or retail. The remaining required parking would be accommodated off site. Where parking can be accommodated underground, it is the most expensive to construct. Ramps are required for access, and these take up valuable surfaces. The larger the number of cars that access and egress; the greater the conflict with the pedestrian realm; the larger the pollution levels; and the more traffic, noise, and accidents occur on access streets.

Comment and recommendations: The ramps must be carefully designed and landscaped for safety and convenience. Great care must be given to where cars and trucks ingress and egress so as not to conflict with the pedestrian realm. Access should not be off of major streets by regulating access and egress to the lesser-valued streets with low pedestrian volumes.

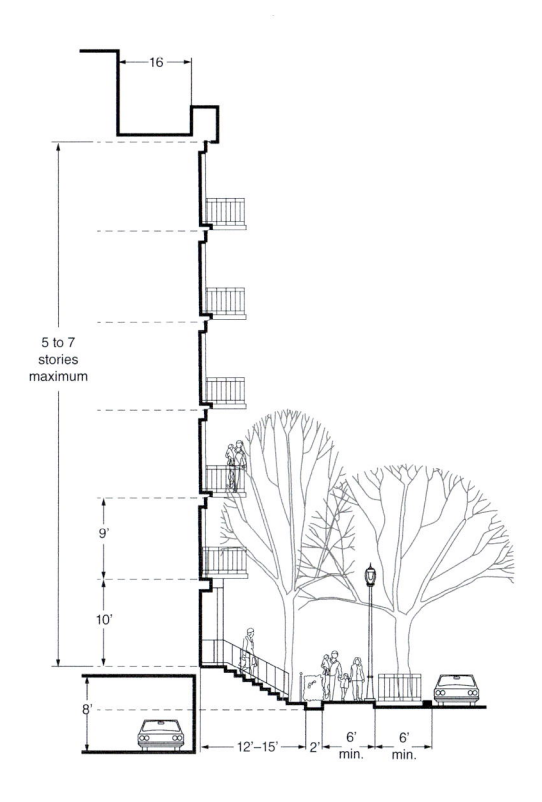

Section of Residential Building with Parking Under

One of the best ways to minimize the impact of parking and make it convenient is to park under the building, as shown in this section.

Comment and recommendations: When double loaded residential buildings are 60 to 62 feet in width, parking one level under the building is ideal since the foundation has to be dug and the first floor should be at least three to four feet above-grade. The design provides an economical accommodation of parking for residents

Response Value +5(4)

Screened Ramp to Under-building Parking

The most desirable parking is under the building or underground, with a screened ramp.

of the building. It is highly recommended for residential buildings of limited height.

Embedded Parking

Embedded parking is a structure in the center of a block surrounded by liner buildings which has a single-loaded corridor providing access to the units on the exterior of the building. Parking is not visible from any street except for entrances and egresses. The roof of the parking is typically a green park used by residents. These roofs have been designed for a range of activities, from putting greens, swimming pools, passive parks, and cafés to bars and other recreational uses.

Model of Building with Embedded Parking

Sectional rendering of a building with embedded parking. Called a "liner building," it has a single-loaded corridor along the edge of the parking structure on all sides along a pedestrian realm. At the level of the roof garden and above, the corridor is double-loaded with apartments overlooking the garden and the street. If the building is wrapped around the block, a mixed use along the primary pedestrian street edge is required.

The parking could also be located in a "podium" on the lower floors or even the ground floor. When parking extends to the facade of the structure, a screen is required because, without it, the parking would be exposed to the street, which is typically rated as very negative. Podium parking could also have retail on the ground floor along the primary sidewalk edge. If possible, avoid podium parking. A green roof above embedded and podium parking is a requirement.

Intercept Parking

"Park Once" Concept: The vision for all urban cores is to embed all new parking into mixed-use buildings, intercepting as many cars in remote parking buildings as possible; these are accessed from major highways and street/boulevards, leading to the core. After parking, people walk or are invited to take transit to their destinations. The concept is **to park once** and never have to get back into your car to access any other destination within the downtown core. This is dependent on a downtown multi-modality network including walking, scooters, and bicycles that interconnect all the major parking locations with popular destinations in the downtown.

There **are three types of intercept parking** that are appropriate for urban cores and the residential areas surrounding the core.

1. **Regional Intercept parking**
2. **Urban Center Intercept parking**
3. **Neighborhood parking**

All the Intercept parking concepts generate additional development opportunities because developers need only provide limited in-building parking and service access while reducing vehicular traffic in areas that are pedestrian oriented. Ideally, this is implemented by a Parking Authority or private entity that would administer and operate these facilities. The potentially positive visual and functional impacts on the center are enormous, as are the cost-benefits to the developers who can maximize the building FAR and height, by significantly reducing the amount of parking and number of floors devoted to parking

Zoning has to be modified and amended to allow developers to make a "payment in lieu" of on-site parking to provide the total parking requirement for the users of the building in off-sites locations within a short walk or transit ride, at much lower costs. If parking is to be built in the proposed building, the area for parking should be included in the allowable FAR.

Regional Intercept parking: This parking facility intercepts cars many miles away from the center. It is connected by rapid and convenient transit to the core. The vision behind regional intercept is a large, convenient, efficient, multi-level, multi-use parking building where commuters to the core buildings park in lieu of parking in the core, which has all the negatives associated with heavy traffic movement, pedestrian conflicts, etc. Removing as many parked cars as possible measures the success of any urban area that wants to be more pedestrian-oriented and green.

Regional remote parking intercepts are located off major freeways and arterials, in locations, where land is less expensive. Connections to the center by rapid transit, BRT, or some type of shuttle are required to make the system work effectively and conveniently. Structures can also be used for long-term parking for those that have a car but seldom use it as well as for car rentals, car sharing facilities, bus storage, fire departments, and public works.

Urban Center Intercept parking: Mixed-use urban center intercept parking structures are located within a five- to ten-minute walk to the destination on the periphery of the urban core. They must be accessible from major roadways and transit. They serve to entice cars to not enter the core area. These are mixed-use buildings with residential and retail/service immediately surrounding them. The central focus of the core area could be a maximum of a 10- to 12-minute walk from the Urban Center Intercept parking to the destination. If beyond a safe and pleasant walking distance, Urban Center Intercept parking structures should be connected to destinations by designated lanes for bikes, scooters, moving sidewalks, horizontal elevators, etc.

Moving parking to less valuable land, or not requiring parking to be constructed under or within buildings, allows greater use and intensity of development by not using valuable FAR or exceeding height limitations. In many jurisdictions, FAR does not include parking, which is a mistake. By including it, there is an incentive for removing parking from the site and locating it in one or more of the intercept locations. Relocating parking also eliminates the movement of vehicles where there is the greatest potential for pedestrian conflict. By providing parking within reasonable connecting distances, parking needs can be met, and the pedestrian experience in the core can be enhanced.

Identify potential locations and design for urban center parking structures.

Where possible, they should be located to allow access from a major thoroughfares and must have convenient transit connections, be that trolley, shuttle, jitney, bus, or light-rail. Where this is not possible, the parking should be embedded or underground but not at-grade. Large podium garages should be avoided because they bring more traffic into the center. A certain amount of immediately accessible or "orchestra" parking for a limited number of cars and service vehicles for each building should be allowed.

Response Value +3(3)

Urban Center Intercept Parking

The above is a simulation of an Urban Center Intercept parking facility of eight levels with mixed-use on the ground floor and a contextual setback at the fifth floor. It has a positive response value, with a range of +6 to +0.

Comment and recommendations: These can be large buildings, and every detail of the facade along the pedestrian realm must be carefully designed. It should blend and complement with the adjacent and adjoining buildings, with its entrance not unduly interfering with the pedestrian flow.

Neighborhood parking: These are smaller mixed-use parking structures within a **one- to five-minute walking distance of residential units along a positive pedestrian realm**. Optimally, these facilities should be located within a three-minute walk of the origins or destinations, but they can

be as little as one minute or up to five. By building collective parking, more land can be used for higher-quality designed housing. People will walk if the experience is positive and the distance is reasonable. It becomes more of an advantage if they live and work in the same area, and can access convenient transit. To the extent possible, entrances should be located on a secondary street. Neighborhood parking structures should be discretely located to encourage a minimum of or even no parking in residential buildings. They should be indistinguishable in facade treatment from the adjacent or proposed/future architectural context. Careful design consideration must be given to the sidewalks, retail edges, safety concerns, and landscaping of these facilities. Where possible, the ground floor should incorporate retail or service uses along pedestrian edges. Car-share programs and/or rental car locations are highly encouraged in these types of facilities.

Response Value +4(5)

Neighborhood Parking

Neighborhood parking in a mixed-use building within a one to a maximum of five-minute walk to and from all residential and commercial uses.

Comment and recommendation: The structure should respond to the context in scale, materials, and fenestration, with retail and or services on the sidewalk edges. Notice that this building is three stories to respect the neighborhood scale.

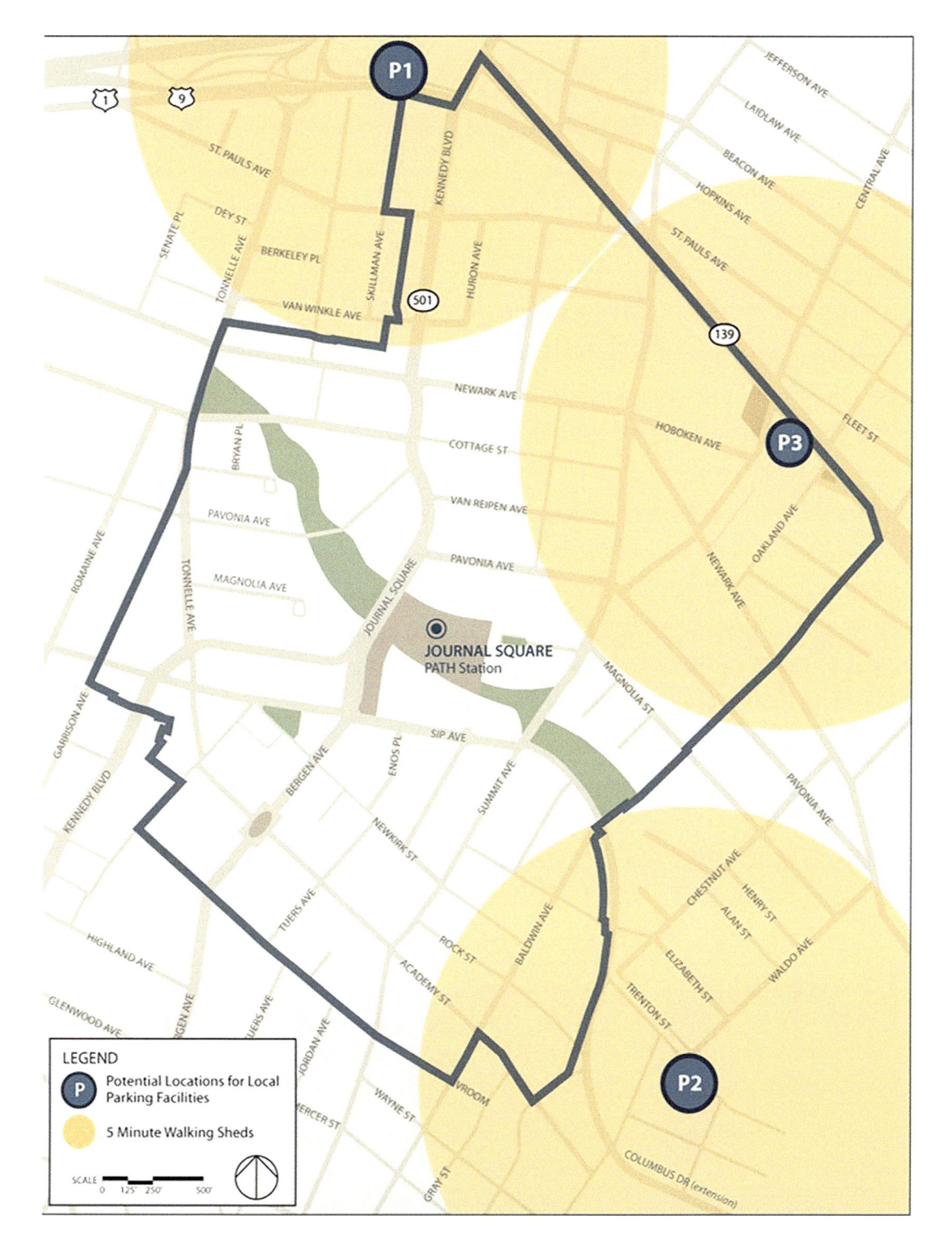

Map of Potential Locations for Urban Center Intercept Parking

The map above illustrates potential locations for urban center intercept parking with the five-minute (roughly ¼-mile) walking shed depicted for each potential site. Each location is adjacent to or on an existing or future transit stop that connects to the center.

Parking Standards

Design for Parking Structures

All parking buildings should be as efficient as possible. To the extent possible, parking floor plates should be flat, not sloping to encourage reutilization as the need for parking is reduced in the future. A horizontal floor is easier to retrofit. Parking should be located in mixed-use structures that incorporate incubator, market retail, offices, and services on the ground floor along a positive pedestrian realm, with parking located in the back of shops and upper levels. Openings should look like windows. The efficiency of the parking layout will be maximized when designed using 60-foot bays, two or three across, from 120 to 180 feet and optimally 240 feet long. This is the most functional and least expensive of all multi-level parking structures. If not well fenestrated on the outside wall, or embedded with liner building surround it, it will most likely receive a very negative response value.

Parking Ratios

A consistent parking standard must be applied to all redevelopment parcels. Traditional suburban auto-oriented design standards (e.g. one (1) spaces per bedroom or four to five spaces per 1,000 square feet of retail or commercial) must not be used in urban centers and urban neighborhoods that meet the recommendations herein. If those standards are still used, they must be amended to one space per unit and no more than two spaces per 1,000 square foot of other uses.

In the past, many successful urban centers have limited parking by lowering parking ratios. In order to implement a remote parking strategy and limit traffic congestion, parking ratios need to be reduced directly inside or under an urban building. The Vision Plan recommends that parking needs be met using a combination of on-site and intercept parking, as previously stated. For example, a parking ratio of one parking space for each new residential unit could be achieved by supplying only .25 spaces per unit on-site, **with the remaining .75 accommodated in a walkable parking facility a short distance from the residential development**. For offices and retail, provide 1 space per 1,000 square feet and all other parking accommodated in intercept parking facilities. All parking could be located in one or more intercept parking facilities. By limiting in-building parking, more land and building volume can be dedicated to productive uses while reducing congestion in the immediate area and improving the pedestrian environment.

Sustainability, Environmental Responsibility

Sustainability will become the hallmark of any progressive and world-class city or town in the future. Some of the highest rated VPS images suggest that green technology, such as solar panels, wind generators, and green roofs, is highly appropriate and desired. Ninety percent of participants think that rainwater collection, grey water collection, and recycling are extremely appropriate.

Sustainable technology should be incorporated into all buildings, thereby increasing the marketability and appeal of the area and reducing energy costs and the heat island effect.

Environmentally responsible technology is what people want. They should be mandatory on every building and redevelopment plan. Environmental sustainability is to everyone's benefit.

Response Value +8(2)

Green Roofs

Green roofs and terraces typically receive the high positive response values. People want to see more green roofs in urban areas. They are more usable surfaces, reducing heating and cooling costs, and absorbing rainwater.

Response Value +7(4)

Solar Collectors

Solar panels are becoming more efficient and less expensive. They can be mounted on roofs and facades of buildings. Combined with new battery and green building technology, solar panels allow new and retrofitted buildings to approach net zero.

Response Value +6(3)

Wind Turbines

Vertical wind turbines can be mounted on the tops of buildings, in parks, and in plazas.

Comment and recommendations: The three images, with their very high response values, portray the most desired technology for urban areas and must be incorporated into building design. The green roofs returned the highest response values and are highly recommended on every available urban rooftop. Other technologies include but are not limited to grey water recycling and dynamic energy production.

Although it is highly desirable and acceptable by all participants, there will be a reluctance to install by many developers due to the increased initial costs. The smart developers know better and understand that the benefits from the market and longer-term sustainability perspectives must be considered as they offset the initial costs and generate greater retuned and profit. Prices on all these technologies continue to decrease and become more efficient as production increases, and the market responds to demand.

Parks and Plazas

Parks and plazas enhance the urban experience. They are important gathering places that activate urban settings, responding to the fundamental human need to socialize and

be in nature. Parks need to be accessible to people within a short walk from offices and residences.

- There is a strong demand not just for parks and plazas but also for planting beds and pots, street trees and sculptures, and decorative and key lighting.
- Landscaping must be integrated into the urban fabric, with a green open-space network that is continuous, connecting parks, plazas, and playgrounds throughout the urban center to the surrounding neighborhoods.
- Continuous tree planting in the parkway along streets is an ideal connecting mechanism. Multiple seating areas and other special landscape elements will provide a unique character.
- Cities must also include public restroom facilities.
- There must be zoning and incentives that induce developers to set aside land to construct public parks and plazas.
- A detailed Landscape Plan must be one of the overlay maps in any urban design plan.

Park in the Center of an Urban Area

This image is consistently one of the highest-rated parks in urban visioning sessions. It contains every characteristic that people love about urban parks.

Comment and recommendation: It is the center of a high concentration of mixed-use buildings. It is heavily treed, forming a canopy and cooling shade. It has defined pedestrian paths and areas for activity, extensive green ground cover, sculptures, kiosks, and fixed and movable seating. It is a respite from the intense activity of the surrounding urbanity. It is a required de-stressor in urban cores.

Response Value +7(3)

Park in the Center of an Office District

Urban Parks are successful and well utilized, particularly during lunch hours when they are designed for maximum use and located in highly concentrated office areas.

Comment and recommendation: This park has wide curvilinear sidewalks which are both open and partially covered as they circle the open lawn area in the center. There are many places to sit with movable chairs, tables, and fixed benches. It is important for worker morale and productivity to have some possible exposure to green parks within easy walking distance to help them recharge on their lunch hours.

Response Value +6(4)

Urban Plaza

This paved plaza has many of the features that people love, including movable and fixed seating, water features, trees, and a steady flow of pedestrians to watch. The edge of the plaza has many restaurants.

Comment and recommendation: It contains almost all of the recommended features recommended in *Social Life of Small Urban Spaces* by William Whyte, including places to sit, sun, trees and shade, water, activity, and food. All must be present for a successful urban public space. Movable chairs are mandatory for successful personal interactions and the positive life of the plaza.

Response Value +6(4)

Park/Plaza in an Urban Setting

This park is in the center of a major urban concentration of mixed-use buildings and housing. It has been redone several times with this on grade solution being the most successful.

Comment and recommendation: All the positive design features of urban parks and plazas are here, including places for people to sit and see other people, a water feature, the grouping of trees, and street vendors all at-grade and not enclosed.

Response Value +6(4)

Fountain as Focus of a Park

A publicly accessible private park that focuses on a fountain with seating areas around it.

Comment and recommendations: Water in fountains or pools is one of the important features of highly desirable parks. Sights and sounds of water are a benefit for all. As people become more stressed out, these are important places for rest and contemplation.

Response Value +6(4)

Park above Underground Parking

This park eliminates the negative visual impacts of parking and fulfills a dual purpose of park and parking.

Comment and recommendation: This is a desired option for parking and an optimum solution for a park. The benches adjacent to the entrance driveway to the underground parking suggests that car speed is compatible with the pedestrian. This design option is highly recommended.

Public Place Making

When a new plaza or pedestrian experience is wanted, the VPS and specifically the VTW reveal places where new public plazas/gathering places should be located. Closing certain streets to traffic in or near the center where there is the largest concentration of pedestrians, in a series of phases, has been recommended in multiple visioning sessions, suggesting that pedestrians are more important than cars.

Response Value −2(3)

Existing Condition BEFORE

This six-lane boulevard is negatively perceived. It is pedestrian-, bike-, and bus-unfriendly. It is the site recommended for an urban plaza. The planted boulevard improves its negative value with a range of −5 to 0.

Comment and recommendations: As the core is developed, there is a greater need for more pedestrian places. Most through traffic will be phased out or relocated, or just disappear as more people become pedestrian once the "park once" concept is implemented or enough people live within walking distance of the core and transit. The following computer simulations portray one street near the center of the urban core that participants recommended be converted in phases to a pedestrian plaza in the later phase of redevelopment.

Response Value +4(3)

Simulation One—Phase One

In Phase One, one half of the street is removed for a plaza and light-rail line.

Comment and recommendations: This simulation of a street transformation is designed to make the center more pedestrian active and transit dependent. Implementation depends on increased pedestrian flow and the reduction or rerouting of traffic through the center with the implementation of the bypass and the construction of one or more remote parking facilities. This portion of the plaza could accommodate the proposed narrow-gage street car.

Response Value +5(4)

Simulation Two—Final Phase

At buildout, the traffic lanes on the left side are removed/relocated. A new complete plaza is realized that promotes street activity and maximizes the pedestrian realms, with street furniture, planters, and cafés, which, in turn, attract more people. It is also the location were a farmers' markets and entertainment venues can be staged.

Comment and recommendations: The more areas are devoted to the pedestrian, the more the quality of urban life improves. After years of auto-dominance, the new order will have more pedestrian places and spaces without the noise, pollution, and accidents associated with the private vehicle.

Greenways

Greenways are landscaped pedestrian priority corridors passing through the city, some have bicycle paths.

This linear experience is extraordinarily popular, particularly in high density areas.

The New York City Highline is one great example. The proposed greenway through Journal Square in Jersey City could be another.

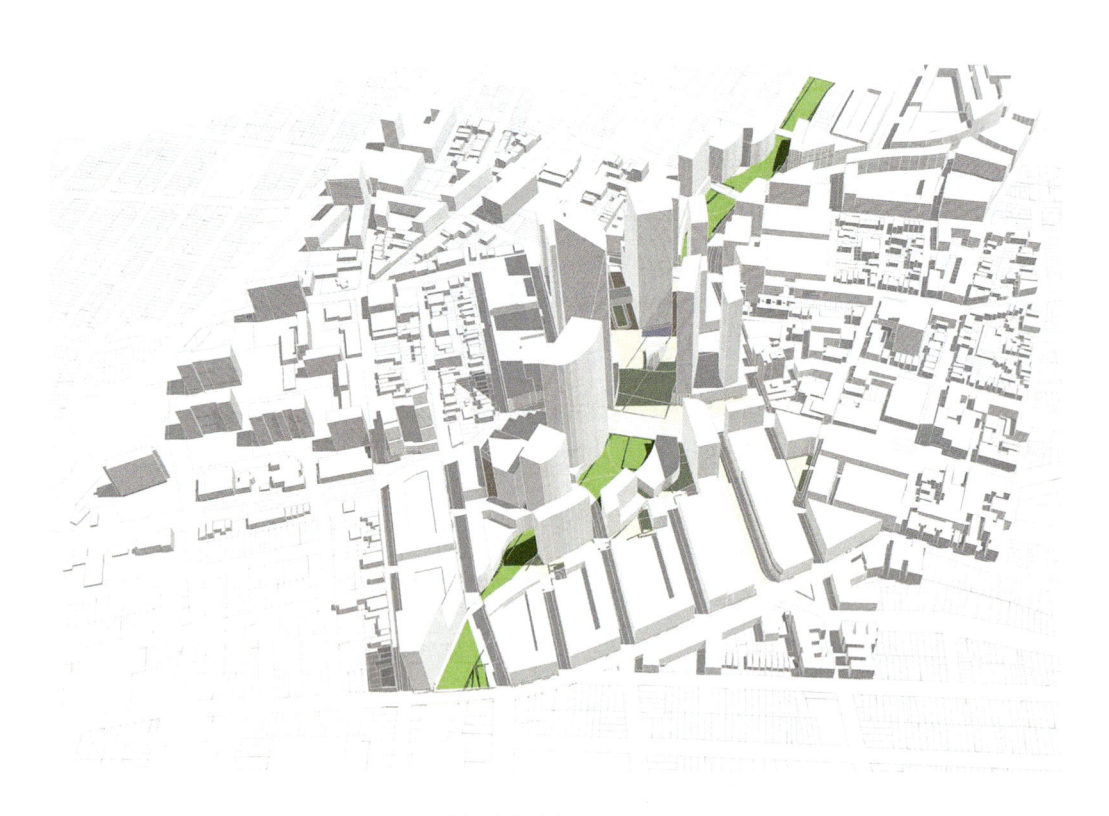

Model of Greenway

The green color in the model of the center illustrates the extent of the proposed and visioned greenway as it treads it way through the downtown. In this design, it is located over the tracks of the PATH, which are in a cut 30 feet below-grade. It functions as a major park, activity center, and connector to the major multi-modal transit terminal. Multiple activities are recommended for this park area and its edges. Notice that the buildings are on the edges of the cut and not in the center, thereby reducing costs and not disturbing the location of the tracks with building support columns.

Visions of the Urban Greenway

Visions of the Greenway Park

The rendering of the greenway as it approaches the city center where it crosses the multi-modal pedestrian plaza on the surface light-rail. It is busy and active, a major urban gathering place. The curves and crisscrossed pedestrian paths provide sequential interest and create meeting points and special seating areas.

Visions of the Greenway as it Evolves into a Plaza

The rendering of the greenway as it passes next to the entrance of the multi-modal underground transit station. The trees, planters, and pavement treatment ensure the continuity of the greenway.

Street Tree Landscape Plan for Downtown Milwaukee

Milwaukee has a large continuous park along the lakefront and several internal parks, including the walkway along the waterfront. The street tree/landscape plan for downtown linked all these together into a green network. Milwaukee already has an intensive tree planting program. This Landscape Plan enhances their effort and create more positive streetscapes for the downtown.

Street Tree Landscape Plan for Journal Square Urban Core

This map portrays the recommended planting of street trees forming a network of continuous green. This green/tree network links every "parkway"— (planting area along the pedestrian realms with trees) — with the recommended parks, plazas, and greenways providing a continuous positive green walking experience. The highest valued streets have trees planted on both sides.

Planted Urban Street

This street is a good representation of using tree planting and other landscape features to create a green network.

Street trees are mandatory. Urban street trees must be planted adjacent to the curb at close intervals to form a continuous green network which connects every street to larger and smaller parks and public spaces.

The space in which they are planted is called the "parkway," green trees connecting to green parks.

Summary Recommendations for Urban Areas

Planning and design standards for urban centers must reinforce the expressed need for the most interactive, highest-density, green, pedestrian and transit-dominant places and spaces. Negative places, spaces, streets, and buildings must be identified, and a plan for their transformation into

positive places, spaces, and buildings must be completed. A Density Increase Bonus Impact Fee not tax abatements should be initiated to ensure a positive public realm for the entire core area and surrounding neighborhoods, thereby increasing value for all.

Urban design features that must be incorporated includes:

- **Expand and enhance the pedestrian realm—** the spaces between the buildings to make city centers more walkable, safe, and interesting. The pedestrian must have priority over the car. Promote shared streets and pedestrian-only streets. Remove or reduce auto traffic in the center.

- **Expand the use of public transit options,** including below-ground rapid transit, streetcars, bus, bicycle, scooter-type vehicles, and cabs/Uber cars. Transit stops and stations must be well-designed, multi-modal, mixed-use, pedestrian-priority spaces. Design individual plans for each of the modes which overlay each other to create connected networks that make use of the car inconvenient. Connect transit to intercept parking.

- **Design buildings with the highest design quality and density in the center** with the largest "WOW" factor. Lower the building heights and density as one walks away from the center. Promote mixed-use buildings with retail and services on the lower levels along high-quality pedestrian realms, with residential or commercial units located above. Design residential buildings with semi-public yards along positive pedestrian realms. As one walks further from the one where the density is lower, promote stoops and stairs with semi-public front yards as entrance features.

- **Pay special design attention to the type and character of the proposed and existing retail uses.** In-store retail is changing. New retail use has specific standards for frontage and pedestrian realms, transit access, and parking. Do not allow any suburban/arterial strip commercial retail in the downtown.

- **Limit parking in the downtown in terms of location, number, and exposure.** Prevent conflict between pedestrians and access to parking. Intercept cars before they enter the downtown core as much as possible. Allow and encourage people to take short interesting walks to and from parking to residential and commercial uses. Do not permit exposed surface parking, except for on-street parallel or head-in parking. Encourage mixed-use local and urban center-oriented intercept parking buildings. Limit in-building parking. Promote regional remote parking.

- **Promote high levels of sustainability and energy efficiency** through green buildings, green roofs, solar panels, recycling gray water, and use of wind and other green technologies.
- **Integrate green and nature into the urban area** through the provision of landscaped public gathering spaces, parks and plazas, street trees, and other streetscape features, greenways, and green roofs. Design parks to be interesting and easily accessible. Promote water edge walking wherever possible.
- **Encourage the largest number and highest density of multifamily housing in the core and surrounding the core**, with local retail and services within walking distance.
- **Make the vision plan understandable through the use of graphically explicit plans, specific renderings, three-dimensional renderings, simulations, and videos.**
- Promote successes when elements of the vision plan are being proposed, at ground-breaking, and at openings.

13

Communicating
Vision Preferences—
Recommendations and
Realizations

In the new age of visualizations, planners and designers must use all the available media techniques to present what the envisioned places and spaces people want will look and feel like. Two-, three- and moving four-dimensional representations of the proposed development program and its context must be prepared and promoted with the optimum use of all new media.

Site plan computer models, renderings, and walk through videos with before and after simulations are extremely valuable in communicating community visions preferences. They present what specific urban design recommendations could look and feel like. To formulate a final Vision Plan and ensure it is understandable, the preferred positive images and synthesis of the Vision Translation Workshop must be translated first into two- (plan), then three- (axiometrics and renderings) and four-dimensional (videos and walkthroughs) representations. That is now the minimum expectation, given the advanced nature of media exposure. It is expected that a three-dimensional computer massing model will be "built" for the entire urban area as well as more detailed three-dimensional computer models for specific places and spaces which can be viewed in all directions and from various elevations. A printed three-dimensional model is also desired. New three-dimensional printers make this much easier than it was in the past. However, a three-dimensional printed model does not allow techniques like walkthroughs, video sequential simulations, or virtual reality. A combination of two would be best. All three-dimensional urban models, whether built by a three-dimensional printer or virtually on a computer, must start with a two-dimensional illustrated site plan generated from the consensus community visions. The plan will determine where new infilling buildings, green spaces, and mobility modes will be located. Each lot, street, and public space rated as **most susceptible to change** must be included. Multiple urban design alternatives can be generated from the Visual Preference Survey (VPS) and the Vision Translation Workshop (VTW). One or more design alternatives will be selected to be transposed first into a two- and then into a three -and a four-dimensional sequence to represent the generated development program.

Three examples will be presented in print form to represent the vision that was communicated to the community during the last step of the Community Visioning process. The first is Journal Square, Jersey City, New Jersey; the second is Downtown Milwaukee, Wisconsin; and the third is Mid-town Atlanta, Georgia.

Example One—Journal Square, Jersey City, New Jersey

The illustrated two-dimensional plan and the three-dimensional model for Journal Square represent the following DEVELOPMENT PROGRAM:

22,000 to 63,000 new housing units

2 to 3 new public schools

5,000,000 to 20,000,000 Sq ft of new commercial space

12 acres of new parks and public plazas

5,700 linear feet of new streetcar line

2.78 miles of urban bicycle paths

18,000 to 43,000 parking spaces

2,600 new street trees

What is the fourth dimension, and how is it best communicated?

Most people cannot mentally translate a two-dimensional plan into three and four dimensions. Renderings and models are required. When renderings and models are combined with the positive images from the VPS in a multi-media presentation, together, they become a powerful tool towards visual understanding and implementation. They solidify people's visions of place. Renderings are a must in all promo materials.

Renderings can be one of the most important final products of a visioning process. They assist in understanding of the three- and four-dimensional urban designs and program recommendations. A picture is worth 1,000 words. Site Plans are seldom printed in media, whereas renderings are printed frequently. The digital drawings become the public relations interface. They can easily be blown up for billboards or reduced in size for brochures. Preparing good renderings of a final composite vision is an art and a science—a critical work product that must be budgeted into any vision or media promotion of the consensus Community Visions.

A Two-Dimensional Illustrated Site Plan

In purple, the new infill building opportunities. The green represents parks, plazas, the greenway, and the landscaping along the street. The heavier dotted red lines locate exiting transit facilities. The light dotted line is the proposed streetcar line. The large purple building on the top center adjacent to Routes 1 and 9 is the proposed mixed-use urban center remote parking. The gray colored buildings will remain and might require rehabilitation.

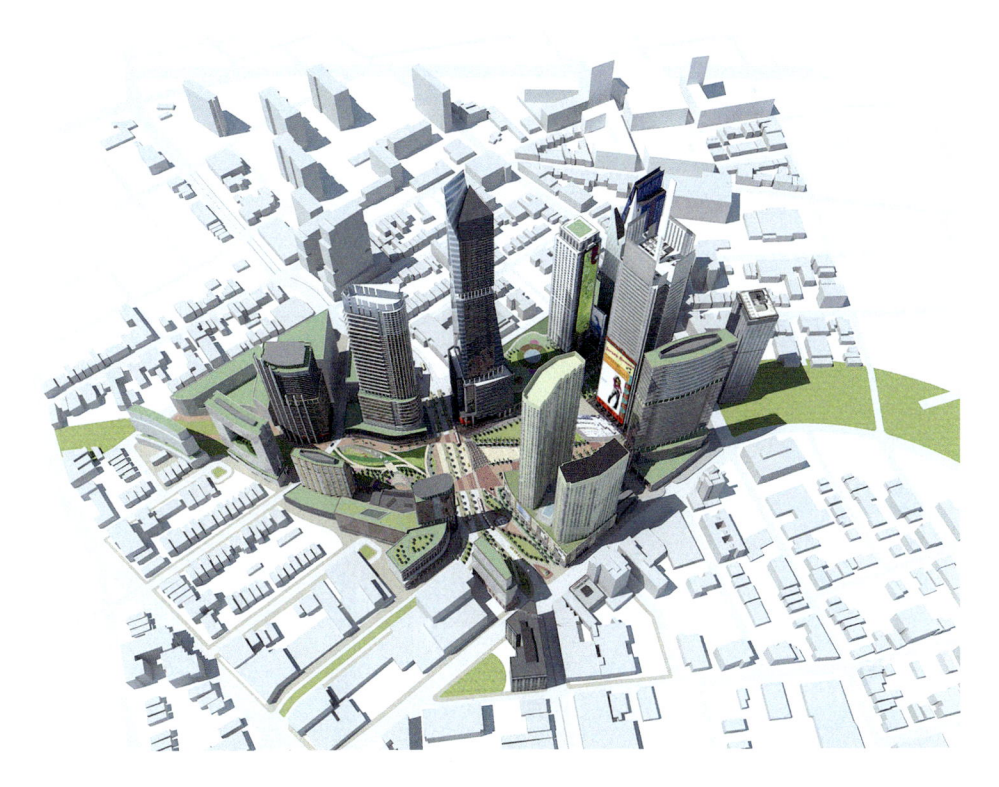

Three-Dimensional Model of the Central Core of Journal Square

This colored computer model of the city center generated from responses to the VPS and VTW illustrates the vision of a dynamic center core for this urban area. A new linear park, urban greenway is created, covering the "urban scar" of the below-grade rapid transit tracks. This linear park will become a major pedestrian connector within the core. The transit and pedestrian priority plazas are also shown in the center of the rendering. This three-dimensional model illustrates the highest buildings in a cluster in the center of the urban area, adjacent to the major existing and proposed transit line, public plazas, and greenway. On a computer or video, one can pan and move through the space with ease. In this image, one specific view point was selected from millions of possibilities. A video sequence was developed and used in the final presentations.

Rendering of Plaza and Greenway

This rendering depicts one "frame" of a video of the plaza and greenway looking towards the rapid transit entrance (green triangle) surrounded by the new mixed-use high-rise buildings on the edge of the greenway.

The fourth dimension allows participants to look around and walk through a model of proposed recommendations. Digital video visions created from sophisticated computer programs are used more frequently for presentations. This is currently being advanced by the "escape from reality" animation and video game industry, and supplemented by virtual reality headsets with advanced computer applications. These presentation techniques, and the ones that will follow as technology and programming become more sophisticated, are tools used to present

Early Phases of Realization of the Vision

The announcement of the first two high-rise buildings after the presentation of the recommended vision plan. These were the first major building to be built in Journal Square in 35 years.

and achieve "buy in" from the largest number of people. I hope that they will be used not just to "wow" clients but to provide hope and a new vision of positive designed places and spaces that meet citizens' wants and desires. The final presentation of the vision for the future of Journal Square used a combination of video flyover and walk through using Sketch-up and other simulations programs.

Example Two—Downtown Milwaukee, Wisconsin

Vision Plan

The synthesis of the Milwaukee Community Vision process produced 18 two-dimensional urban design overlay plans for the 837 acres in the downtown. The most effective way to present the comprehensive complex of the visioned recommendations was to generate several three-dimensional models of the Vision Plan that illustrated recommendations for infill on all vacant or underutilized lots, identifying the Susceptibility To Change Map prepared by participants. A sketch infill urban design plan was prepared for each potential infill site using the results of the VPS and VTW. Each sketched urban design plan was then transferred to the three-dimensional model of the downtown. This model demonstrated the extraordinary infill potential demonstrated by the development

opportunities program which expressed the fulfillment of the Community Vision as it was generated. **The vision process generated some extraordinary urban design interventions for downtown Milwaukee, including infill housing, removal of freeways, completion of the riverwalk, the downtown community market, continuous greenways and water edge walks, new high-rise residential and office buildings, new mixed-use buildings, a train station, a new museum, a sports venues, streetscape improvements, new streetcar lines, and parking intercepts.**

Recommended Three-Dimensional Infill Model

Areas with contiguous lots susceptible to change provide infill possibilities. The three-dimensional massing plan illustrates where infill buildings can be built. In dark pink are all those locations that were rated with a high or moderate susceptibility to change. The existing buildings that are not susceptible to change are shown in light pink and gray. Streets are shown in white and parks in green. The yellow areas are public venues. The larger grouping of new infill buildings is located at the proposed location for the removal of downtown freeways. There are also many scattered locations with smaller lots that will be infilled. The Park East freeway was to be demolished and visioned to undergo extensive redevelopment. The final plan, for political reasons, did not remove the other downtown freeway shown on the right of the model. The removal of the Park East freeway was a major victory for a more viable downtown and has been used as a model for other downtown freeway removal projects.

Development Opportunities—Milwaukee

Visions Plans projected the ideal vision over time using all available land and buildings deemed Susceptible To Change by participants. There are no remaining surface parking lots, vacant land, or in-town freeways at completion of the initial Downtown Milwaukee Vision Plan.

Development Program:

7,800,000 Sq ft	7,800 residential units
6,750,000 Sq ft	Mixed-use—residential/office
1,000,000 Sq ft	Office
4, 150,000 Sq ft	Retail
2,000,000 Sq ft	Civic
450,000 Sq ft	Industrial
10,300,000 Sq ft	Parks and Plazas
4,000,000 Sq ft	Parking Structures—mixed use
0 Sq ft	Surface Parking Lots
0 Sq ft	Vacant Land

In total, 36,450,000 sq ft of new construction was envisioned.

Infill housing is one of the most notable additions to downtowns, responding to the positive images of multifamily homes in the Visual Preference Surveys (VPSs), with locations generated in the Vision Translation Workshops (VTWs). The key to a successful urban area, at any scale, is the number of people living in and near the downtown within the 5, 10, 15 minute and 21/2 mile bike ride. An extraordinary range of new housing has been recommended and realized in downtowns after the adoption of vision plans. The range includes: Five story affordable, "four over one" with retail on the ground floor and housing above, six to 12 story residential with embedded parking, and mixed-use

Three-Dimensional Infill Model

The majority of mixed-use residential infill is five to six stories, which are portrayed in this computer rendering.

and residential slabs and towers with heights ranging from 18 to 60 stories. The following images represent some of the housing that has been built after the adoption of the vision plans.

and pedestrian realms are demanded. Access to parks within short walking distance is fundamental to the quality of urban living and the market value of the new housing.

New Housing—Five Story Mixed-use

This new mixed-use residential infill building is a "four over one" with a lower level of retail and embedded parking. This form reflects the existing massing and material used on facades in the adjacent historic district. The building facade is divided into distinctive modules defined by color, window treatment balconies, and building extensions. It has retail on the sidewalk level that complements the desired pedestrian realm.

New and rehabilitated parks are a requirement when new housing is constructed. To attract new residents and businesses, inclusion of new green parks, plazas, waterfronts,

New Parks Complement New Housing

To build and market high-density housing, developers need to make substantial contributions towards or construct parks in order to make urban downtowns more appealing and livable. The low rise and high rise buildings that were built, contributed to the design and construction of the adjacent park which is heavily used, adding value to the buildings as well to the adjoining neighborhoods.

Catalytic Projects

The Community Vision contract for Milwaukee required the recommendation of a **series of catalytic projects for early construction that would begin to fulfill the vision of the participants and provide assurance that the long-term vision would be realized**. Catalytic projects were implemented early because of the leadership of Mayor John Norquist and Planning Director Peter Park, with special assistance and financing by the Milwaukee Redevelopment Authority, who were instrumental in their early realization. It is critical to the success of any Community Visioning Project that a number of catalytic projects envisioned by participants are realized early. Milwaukee far exceeded this recommendation. The following are a few examples of completed catalytic projects.

Catalytic Project— Removal of Downtown Freeway

The most extraordinary **catalytic project** was the removal of the Park East freeway. Initially, both downtown freeways were in the vision plan for conversion to boulevards, but, in the end, only one was realized. Even this is a remarkable achievement, which led to recommendations for the removal of downtown freeways in other cities in the United States.

Simulations combining the before and after vision of the area have proven to be a valuable planning and urban design tool. The *"before" and "after" simulations* were completed for the Park East Urban Design Focus Area in Milwaukee. The aerial image, showing the freeway before it was removed, was used as the base for the simulations.

Park East Freeway   BEFORE

Aerial view of the Park East Freeway was used as the base for urban design studies and simulations. Most of the area under and around it are surface parking lots and were deemed highly susceptible to change by participants. The resulting vision plan recommended that the elevated freeway be removed and replaced with the original grid of streets; bridges; and a new boulevard infilled with retail, housing, civic and institutional buildings, a new public plaza, a sports venue, and the continuation of the riverwalk.

Computer Rendering of the Potential   AFTER

One of the many computer renderings of a large public park/plaza surrounded by new mixed-use housing and a new hotel complex, anchored by a very large multi-media entertainment complex. This aerial view of a proposed Park East redevelopment plan has a plaza with higher-density, mixed-use housing/retail services on the river edge. The proposed hotel is on the left, with the large multi-media entertainment complex along one edge. Notice the streetcar line and extensive use in the rendering of the historic yellow "Cream City" brick common in Milwaukee. To be understood, the aerial view must be complemented with a ground-pedestrian view.

Alternative urban design plans were prepared and rendered in three dimensions, overlaying the aerial for review and selection.

proved valuable to envision the future.

One of early uses of computer rendering/visioning techniques. Since that time, more sophisticated programs are available with more refined results. This was just the start but

Computer Rendering of Plaza

This computer-generated, ground-level view portrays the entry and river edge portal to the new plaza, surrounded by mixed-use residential buildings. The focus building in the far edge is the mixed-use, multi-media entertainment complex with a possible new hotel off to the right.

Catalytic Project— Farmers' Market

Milwaukee Public Market

This new public market was a recommended catalytic project. It was built on an empty lot adjacent to the freeway. This is a modern version of the more traditional form in scale and detail. This is a wonderful building and an extraordinary addition to the downtown. It was one of the early recommended catalytic projects.

Catalytic Project— Riverfront Walkway Extension

Riverfront Walkway

This image illustrates just one small section of the extension of a riverfront walkway in the downtown. The riverfront walkway has been one of the great economic, market, visual, and spatial successes in the downtown. When used in several other community visioning sessions, it typically generated a value range of +5 to +7(3). It has become a destination walkway.

Catalytic Project— Downtown Pedestrian Realm

Commercial Sidewalk Upgrade

Streetscape improvements to the signature main shopping street were one of the earliest catalytic projects which included widened sidewalks; streetlights; awnings for weather protection; and, most importantly, redesigning the building to have display windows along the pedestrian street edge in lieu of a blank wall. This has enhanced this marginal downtown mall, which was previously interior focused.

Residential Street Upgrade

Streetscapes that extend parks and plazas into the fabric of the urban form by providing wide parkways (planting area for street trees) and wider sidewalks enhance the city walking experience every day. Much of the landscape plan generated from the Community Visioning has been implemented.

Catalytic Project—Civic Additions

New Train Station

A new regional train station in the downtown was proposed by the Community Vision and thus constructed. It is a multi-modal location for street-cars, local and regional buses, and taxis. It is also within walking distance of many residences. It has expanded train service between Milwaukee and Chicago, and other regional cities.

Catalytic Project—Reintroduction of the Downtown Street Car Line

This was one of the initial catalytic projects, which was first implemented using historic-looking, rubber-tire buses. Unfortunately, there were insufficient residential units and new business uses in the downtown at that time to assure its success. Many Vision Plans and their catalytic projects may take many years before becoming reality due, unfortunately, to political objections and financial constraints. Nonetheless, the vision can be strong enough to eventually become reality. This process teaches patience and persistence.

Harley Davidson Museum

The new Harley Davidson Museum attracts many visitors to the downtown. It is a Milwaukee institution. The industrial feeling of the building complements its many exhibits.

Street Car Become Reality

Many years after the vision plan was completed, the proposed downtown streetcar network in downtown Milwaukee has been realized. The first phase of the new streetcar was in its test runs in the fall of 2018, approximately 20 years after the vision plan was completed. This speaks to the longevity of a visionary master plan generated by Community Vision.

Example Three—Midtown Atlanta

Midtown Atlanta is a great example of a successful implementation of the vision recommendations, primarily because of the diligence and commitment of so many professionals, residents, and business people. According to the Midtown Alliance, Midtown, led by a visionary Master Plan, has become a "model of urban excellence."

The Midtown Alliance is a progressive organization which focused on the redevelopment of the Midtown area of Atlanta when it was at the bottom of the evolutionary spiral, with many empty lots and deteriorating buildings but an overwhelming desire to shepherd its revitalization as a premiere area to live, work, move, play, and learn. The alliance conducted not one but two Community Visioning contracts with Nelessen Associates under the direction of executive director Susan Mendeihm and her extraordinary staff and members. Blue Print I was the most extensive of the Community Visioning sessions, receiving coverage by CNN. Its final recommendations for housing, business, and streetscapes were implemented in a matter of a few short years—a remarkable achievement! Blue Print II was the first to use the internet and public meetings to conduct the VPSs and generate responses to the Demographic, Policy, and Market Questionnaire. Many intensive Community Vision meetings and VTWs were held. So many of the recommendations have been implemented and continue to this day. Midtown is a fabulous success story and deserves a book by itself.

From Blue Print II, the Susceptibility to Change map prepared by the many participants was reformulated into a three-dimensional model, revealing those buildings and spaces that could and must be preserved and those that could be infilled or redeveloped. The three-dimensional computer model of Midtown Atlanta illustrates the buildings to be kept (in the light tan) and the lots with a high potential for infill and redevelopment (shown in white).

Model of the Areas Susceptible to Change in the Future

The computer model illustrates the buildings (in tan) that will remain for the foreseeable future, as was determined by the Susceptibility to Change exercise used at the VTW. The remaining land is available for specified types of redevelopment or infill.

A three-dimensional model is a good graphic to use in communicating the potential for infill, development, and redevelopment. To accomplish this, each available or partially available lot shown on the Susceptibility to Change maps and model had a conceptual urban design and building massing sketched out and programmed into the computer.

Model of Future Infill

Above is the three-dimensional computer model of proposed infill for every lot susceptible to change. The light purple locations are for residential buildings, six stories and under. The light pink locations are mixed-use buildings, six stories or less. The darker red locations are mixed-use buildings, 12 to 30+ stories. The darker purple location represents mixed-use buildings 20 stories or taller.

The model has the following development program:

42,800,000 Sq ft	42,800 New Housing Units
10,500,000 Sq ft	Offices/Mixed-use
3,400,000 Sq ft	Retail
49,940 spaces	Parking Spaces

New streetcar line and enhancement to existing transit service, the Metropolitan Area Rapid Transit Authority (MARTA)

New parks, plazas, and streetscapes

Simulations lead to implementations.

The following images are but a few of the simulations that were commissioned after Blueprint Midtown II. These are a direct translation of the responses to the VPS, the VTW, and the extraordinary actions by the Midtown Alliance to present to the public the desired results, which were quickly implemented.

12th Street   BEFORE

Negative pedestrian connection.

Significant streetscape improvements have been constructed in Midtown, creating a tree-lined parkway connecting various parks, plazas, greenways, and natural areas. Miles of new streetscapes have been implemented after vision sessions and simulations were presented. Midtown now has beautiful landscaped streets with street trees, lighting, paving, seating furniture, art, and bike racks, which make up the visual and spatial character that people wanted. A limited number of images of completed projects follows.

12th Street   AFTER

Streetscape enhancements, which include paving, street lighting, and hedging.

10th Street at Piedmont   BEFORE

Negative-rated street with surface parking lots and no streetscaping or paving textures. The vision plan imagined this infilled with a new streetscape.

10th Street at Piedmont   AFTER

What the street could look like when infilled with new buildings, added streetscape elements, wide sidewalks, and paving.

Completed Streetscapes

Streetscapes include new street planting, sidewalks, and street furniture enhanced with semi-public landscaped setbacks. People enjoy walking here, which is a key to its success.

New High-rise Residential Fronting Along
Peachtree Street in Midtown

The above two images are completed street
scapes including new street trees, sidewalks, and
street furniture enhanced semi-public landscaped
setback. People like walking here, a key to its economic and visual success.

plays an important role in the realization and implementation of vision plans for urban centers.

An extraordinary addition to Midtown is multiple new mixed-use Georgia Tech University buildings, including academic, hotel, and retail structures. The new campus is across the freeway from the existing historic campus and is connected by shuttle bus and green bridges.

This was one of the first new infilled urban campuses and has been emulated by many other universities.

New mixed-use residential infill photographed
from a 15th floor overlooking Peachtree Street.
Thousands of new units have been constructed
since the first Vision Plan, Midtown Blueprint I,
and even more have been built since Midtown
Blueprint II! New offices, restaurants, entertainment
venues, and museums all add to the vitality of
remarkable Midtown.

New Georgia Tech Buildings Adjacent to the
Historic Biltmore Hotel

These new mixed-use university buildings were infilled with retail along a street that connects the new
development to the older university campus, across
a freeway. The transition is a green park/bridge.

Expansion of educational facilities

Streetscape Adjacent to New Georgia Tech Buildings

The streetscape is laudable, wide, and well land-scaped, with good street furniture and interactive retail windows/building walls. These make it a great place to walk and be a student.

using multiple techniques that facilitated implementation and realization. Professional leadership played a decisive role. The investment has been extraordinary, generating places and spaces which people love and cherish.

All three of the locations presented in this chapter took the recommendations generated from their Community Vision and communicated the positive visions

Due to publication limitations, only a limited number of illustrations from these three locations are illustrated, but many more could have been.

14

The Future of Planning and Public Engagement

Planning and designing for the positive future require compelling visions that people can believe in. Those visions must be taken seriously and marketed for they hold people's emotional and physical responses, tapping into their desires for real, positive, safe, interesting, and sustainable places and spaces to live and work. But these visions also must be financially feasible and generate the highest return on investment.

Professionals, whose livelihoods depend on the betterment of places and spaces, along with the people who want to live, work, and play in them, must become more public relations, media, and advertising savvy. Advertising is vision. Robert Geddes, in his last book, *Cities in Our Future*, stated, "a willingness to establish and work with a vision of the future, rather than a blueprint for it, are most likely to be assets in addressing unwieldy urban situations."

Media Is the Portal to the Mind

Media impacts what gets built and what products are sold. Today, most news coverage beyond politics focuses on negative stories, like number of infections, deaths, killings, fires, and crime—"If it bleeds it leads." Negative public opinions and preferences about poor infrastructure, lack of maintenance, poverty, crime, and unemployment fuel consumers' and workers' dissatisfaction, which seems to attract more viewers and listeners. Starvation and poverty are growing, as is fear. Wars are ubiquitously reported, along with mass migrations and political unrest in many countries.

Reporting is supported by the rentless advertising drugs and cars.

People are still dependent on drugs and cars, despite all the drawbacks. Too many people seem to be apathetic, programmed by the media and the motivation to comply based on the "personal freedom" they think they have. Too many people seem to be in a state of cerebral discontent and acceptance, particularly older generations. In the words of the Pink Floyd, they have become "comfortably numb."

One truth emerged from the many years of visual preferences: **Too many places and spaces to which most people are exposed are rated as negative or near neutral**. Progress in implementing people's positive preferences and vision seem, in retrospect, to be painfully slow, given the strong positive preferences of what so many seem to want for places they perceived to be neutral or negative. Over time, visioning has revealed, through shifts in response values, that people are not value rating negative images as negative as years earlier. I am afraid that they have reached a state of hopelessness and mistrust, becoming more acceptance of the negative or neutral places and spaces through continuous exposure and non-responsiveness of government. This is a very alarming situation. Participants would like to have their positive visions realized, having more faith in governments and institutions which could encourage and approve the building of positive places and spaces. They want their governments, to promote a positive sense of community and well-being, not accepting the mediocre and expedient, the neutral and negative; to promotion of health and welfare not reduce it.

Too many Americans accept what is, provided they are preoccupied with a multitude of diversions - the classic Roman "bread and circus," of today like sports teams, movie stars, rock stars, reality television, iPhone applications, video games, binge watching, digital purchasing, drugs and alcohol, etc. In a discussion of this idea, my friend Adam Resnic, an owner of several brew pubs, stated, "As long as there are parking lots and donuts, too many people will die fat and happy." In response I argued that we must build many more positive visual and spatial places and spaces. But now do we do that when there is so much mistrust? If we promoted the common vision in the many Community Visioning recommendations, a new mental and physical state would evolve over time.

Today, people need to be fed a constant stream of mostly negative visual and emotional stimulus in order to remain content. Too many are occupied with making ends meet and dealing with life's stresses. The ubiquitous voice of consumption makes them believe that they should have more while so many have less. People become unhappy and frustrated with not having what other people have. When this is compounded with negative living and working conditions, these people can become more financially and psychologically stressed, and even angry. Cerebral malcontent can become verbal dissatisfaction, which can erupt into protest, then action, leading to civic unrest. Add a major health crisis, increased financial disparity, very serious climate impacts, political division, unemployment and low income, and you have a formula for social, physical, and psychological disaster. Many are also painfully aware of the increased cost of living, flat wages, social inequity, and health and income disparities and the negativity of places.

My depression-generation father used to say, "The situation must get worse before it gets better," reinforcing the lessons of the urban evolutionary spiral, which demonstrate that, when places are rated as negative, descending to the bottom of the spiral, the next evolution will inevitably be redevelopment or will places stay at the bottom?. With a positive vision, these places, spaces, and the people who live and work in them can become more fulfilled and satisfied.

In most locations, the positive collected visions cannot currently be built because of restrictive zoning ordinances, conservative bank lending policies and practices, combined with the greed of some developers who want it functional, cheap and profitable. They assume that what was recently purchased and reflects the zoning is what people want - that is all they know and they are used to building this product. For many developers and financiers, there is over reliance on the idea "If you build it, they will come."

Based on what people really want in the places they live, work and play new investments in better urbanism, public spaces, and infrastructure to support a new sustainable, humane urbanism are possible. Building these quality places and spaces is not a financial gamble if the visions of what people want can be approved and constructed. When an area is built with the civic amenities people want, they will buy it and love it. A consensus, holistic vision of place takes away much of the risk when built in a timely manner.

It is critical that visions of possible new urban solutions based on growing understandable threats like the impacts of increased CO_2, ocean level rise, climate change, must be addressed now. Then there is racism, poverty, income disparity, slums, drug addiction. All these conditions could be addressed if there was a national consensus vison for the change generating more positive conditions in our cities and suburban sprawl areas. The above comments are desires and hoped for priority visions for national infrastructure and environment improvement and investment plan. Every positive vision must have the financial investment needed to implement the positive changes demanded. It must be proven that these investments will be paid back multiple times in societal satisfaction, market acceptance, tax generation, and profit.

Every new product, from cars, medicine, and personal products to cooking pots, advertise in order to move their merchandise. Good marketing and advertising agencies have understood and rely on positive and negative emotions to get you to want their products and then purchase them, spending billions every year to keep the consumer economy vibrant. In today's market, most things are sold as lifestyle: Products associated with youth, vigor, cool places, movie stars, professional athletes, rock stars, expensive homes, hot cars, etc. "You too can have this," media tells us. This is another example of the motivation to comply and normative behavior discussed in Chapter 4. Also, much publicity is based on fear like. "If you don't do/buy this you will..." ...get sicker, go to hell, not be happy, etc. Most advertising is carefully scripted, produced, and recorded, a repetitive illusion to keep people pacified. It also has the potential to fulfill a fundamental human need to improve quality of life and do less work. It panders to our sense of sexual and monetary desires, our fears and stresses, and motivates desires for control, power, and sense of belonging. We, as planners, designers, developers, etc., need to tap into the same emotions.

Planners, designers, and engineers need to begin to better understand the power of emotional content, not just functionalists projections. They need to go beyond PowerPoint with some bold new concepts.

They need to answer the following questions:

- What are the visual and spatial characteristics that excite people?
- How are these positive characteristics of place communicated?
- What emotions are most appropriate?
- Where is the money coming from to compete with other advertisers?
- How, when, and where is it broadcasted?

The first principal of advertising is **"products sell that will make life better."** Planners, designers, and engineers can produce "products," places, and spaces for a better life. They can plan and design great structures, infrastructures, places, and spaces. The planning, architectural and construction companies have great capability which can build the visions.

Previous chapters in this book have presented a process by which thousands of images and simulations of the short- and longer-term future were shown and numerically value-rated. A holistic set of positive images was synthesized into visions of the places and spaces that people prefer and despise. **These images hold the fundamental truth of place, proportions, and size, modified with inherent scale, form, character, place, time, proportion, color, and intensity that can be emulated or retrieved from other media sources**.

> # Currently, it seems like no real positive visions exist for a more hopeful, sustainable physical future.

Some professionals have asked, "Why do we need to sell places and spaces when we only supply professional services?" Professionals must be more focused on selling the positive contributions they can make rather than producing endless pages of text and tables, or obtuse articles in journals and glossy professional magazines. Positive digital videos, movies, commercials, and virtual reality are required in addition to the above old standards. Selling a positive physical future needs to be a major focus of planning, design, engineering, the building profession and municipalities interested in communicating a new vision. They must hire a communications and marketing team.

Participants want their positively rated images built, and the sooner, the better. They are ready to absorb a positive vision. They want negative places transformed. They also understand that there needs to be a market, knowing that redevelopment must be financed by those that hold power. Power is money. Power is political influence. But if this is the case, whose vision will be built? If it complies with the consensus vision, fantastic! If it does not, it is even more dependent on the power of public vision to present an alternative compelling consensus vision of what people want. Aha! But who pays for this? Who is the guardian of the public interest? Who is responsible for the **Genius Loci**, the impression that places and spaces make on the mind? If we want better places and spaces, we need better planning and design, new compelling visual techniques, and the money to broadcast the new vision.

Is it the older generations, the rich and powerful, who could determine a positive vision of the future, or will it be the millennial and X generations? The current leadership (in 2021) is primarily made up of the baby boomer generation, conditioned on the old land use and auto- and parking-dependent patterns. They were not born into the Internet generations who are more open to multiple alternatives. There is the growing crisis of "lack of trust" in older-generation politicians and "disinformation" on social media, though there are growing number of new users and platforms providing new media outlets and possibly fresh positive visions.

Instead of the evil and fear, killing, and mayhem associated

with negative places, perhaps laughter, delight, joy, beauty, and satisfaction could be linked to preferred positive places and spaces.

It is media that must, over time, promote and encourage places and spaces, buildings, and service facilities that respond to the positive images that people want; ideally with corporate support. The collective sense of time and place held by generations and cultures in their memory and genetic programming also play a decisive role in determining what people want and how they can achieve it. This need to be exploited.

Without a consensus community vision, there is little hope for improvement. Given existing land use regulations, changing the negative conditions is difficult. More than once I have heard the comment, "People are afraid of change." Nothing could be further from the truth. Change is ubiquitous like it or not.

In the late 2010's, the corporate/consumer economy was booming, with unemployment down to historic lows. This will undoubtedly change in the future and, in fact, did. In 2020, there was 15+% unemployment and the COVID-19 pandemic, which impacted everyone. Urban Design changed. Consumer spending and delivery changed due, partially, to advertising. This is the best example of the modification of normative behavior and the motivation to comply.

One Positive Vision of the Future Bayfront project

Rendering of a synthesis community vision for a new urban neighborhood with the emphases on walking, transit, great public places and spaces, and corner mixed-use buildings. Everything needed is within a 15-minute walk or a short bus/bike/transit ride. This rendering has been used in multiple magazines and advertisements. It finally started construction several years after the Community Visioning process was completed, and the form-based redevelopment code was adopted. Notice the emphasis on stoops and stairs and street view windows.

Younger millennial workers do not want to be stuck in the middle of nowhere in a traffic jams every morning and evening, having the same cafeteria lunch experience or having to drive for their lunchbreak. This became apparent in an early VPS from a series of sequential images of office parks. As the images were taken approaching the strip windowed, office building, the more negative the response value. It is reasons why remote working became so popular. Most millennials want to be where the 24/7 action is and where the jobs are located as well

as close to transit and in walkable, cool, safe, and interesting neighborhoods and cities, with wide tree-lined sidewalks and great public spaces. Most of this generation desires places that are affordable, visually appealing, safe, interactive, urban, green, reflecting most of the positive images contained herein. The younger generations are forcing change in the market by communicating their likes and dislikes to their friends and the world through new media. According to Strauss and Hall in their book ***Generations***, a new enlightenment will emerge as the cohort gains power.

Social media and new apps for the ubiquitous cell phones, laptops, tablets, and other advancing Artificial Intelligence (AI) devices connected to the Internet are everywhere, all the time. Computing power and communication bandwidths have been improving exponentially since IBM (International Business Machines) produced one of the first personal computers in 1981. The "Internet of everything" is here. It has proven to have both positive and negative impacts which will continue. It is and will be concerned with the future of everything for good and evil. This will be a major force in determining positive or negative visions for the future of humanity and the places we live in. The new tech-dependent generation will come into power, with the full realization that much of what has been built since 1947 is old, out of date, deteriorating, polluting, unsustainable, inappropriate, and less than positive. Many are looking for what could be as opposed to what they have been programmed to believe and have experienced. A new reality is emerging.

Most people in the world now have cell phones and access to the Internet or will have both in the short-term future. The global village predicted by Marshall McLuhan has become a reality. Personal mobile technology that includes more functions with AI support is likely to become the controlling devices in the future for those that can afford it. Online interactions are increasing with new tools, like CoURBANIZE, MindMixer, Civic Lab, Neighbor.ly, Civinomics, and Caltrics—and still more emerging. It is also clear that anything marketed and sold to the public as a "must-have" is powerful, particularly when these items enter the mind through advertising, commercials, peer group pressure, or implanted microchips. New images of urbanism and sustainability can emerge if more and more people can see and respond using personal mobile communication technology focused on a humanist's vision of the present and future. Using this technology to generate a consensus vision is an exciting prospect to prepare society for a new future within a global framework. The key to this and the rationale for this book has been the importance of positive images as a unifying element and translating those images into potential plan applications. Creating beautiful, rational public spaces and places is moral, sustainable, and soul-uplifting.

Three-, and now four-, dimensional visioning responds to the findings that most people do not understand nor comprehend when viewing two-dimensional drawings and desiring a visual experience. Positive places and spaces must be visually translated into three and four dimensions in order to reveal what is proposed, to which people can responded emotionally. It is reassuring that the new generation of city planners, designers, architects, landscape architects, engineers, and developers are beginning to use new visual techniques for the purpose of designing, approving, and building positive places of interaction and community.

We, the people—the planners, architects, engineers, and developers—know that we can design and build better places and mobility networks that people have revealed they want to live and work in. The new visual and graphic tools, including AutoCAD, Ryno, GIS, Google SketchUp, InDesign, PowerPoint, City Engine, and multiple applications of AI and virtual reality, have fantastic promise. Digital projectors; image and data storage on the cloud; and virtual reality, video, TV, cable, and digital production, etc. are advancing every day. Effective presentations of planning and urban design projects demand extensive, exciting visual representations. **When envisioned places and spaces cannot be built in the exact form portrayed, design and build places and spaces in form and character, incorporating the best of scale, proportion, mass, and details portrayed in the images valued most positive by Community Visioning**.

The ability to implement a vision of a compelling future depends on the acceptance of the visions by the community, planning, engineering, and public works departments as well as, foremost, the governing body. After of positive presentation with public affirmation, ask for a **non-binding resolution by the planning board and the governing body, accepting the resulting Community Vision**. This is ideal before the vision is translated to master plans and codes. It sets the framework for future implementation of short-term catalytic and long-term projects. The final presentation, visuals, and video should be repetitively broadcasted.

In the search of a regional, state or national positive consensus vision, given the impediments and changes, can only be accomplished one town or region at a time. Successful results require the use of every communications media, including public meetings, Internet, social media, television, movies, streaming services, phones, radio, billboards, newspapers, and magazines. A positive consensus vision, properly marketed, advertised, and repeated, will reach the public consciousness and thereby accelerate implementation. **Technology and science have made the world smaller and could make planning processes more responsive to people's wants and needs**.

15

Why I Am Hopeful and
Sometimes Not

Hope springs eternal …
a quote from Alexander Pope is my guiding mantra.

Being both hopeful and sometimes not is a stressful contradiction. I would like to believe that I fall into the "perceptive idealists" category. As John Reader states in his book *Cities*, "Urban planning has always been a fertile ground for argument between the dreamy idealists of society, the perceptive realists and the hard-core pragmatists."

I believe in the fundamental humanism of the vision process and the results it generates. I believe in the reality of the place choices people make and the belief that, if given a range of possible alternatives, they will choose the most appropriate for the time and place, improving the quality of their lives. The positive visions of what people want, combined with the negative responses which indicate what people want changed, generated from the Visual Preference Survey (VPS), combined with the plans and ideas generated from the Vision Translation Workshop (VTW), are extremely informative to help envision a positive future. If more positive visions of what people rated highly and the plans they generated were to be implemented, healthier, more sustainable, livable, and beautiful cities, towns, and countrysides would emerge over time. Those communities that have embraced their community vision, amended zoning, and have strong leadership that champions a collective vision are now better places to live, work, and play. They are environmentally and socially responsible. This is "Planning and Design by Democracy not Dictate." To achieve better, we must give people the opportunity to express their better visions.

Unfortunately, most communities do not give their residents the opportunity to visually express their preferences for changes. The current physical environments that come from hardcore pragmatists are uninspiring, mediocre, car- and parking-oriented, environmentally destructive, and chosen simply because they are the least expensive to construct; they are reinforced by the politics of existing zoning and probably have the lowest construction costs per square foot and the largest short-term return on investment. Again quoting John Reader, "prosperity and profit is deemed far more important that a congenial environment."

Citizen involvement is the most democratic, planning process, but it is threatening to the dreamy idealists and, particularly, to the hardcore pragmatists. I feel hopeful, despite ongoing negativity and fear. So many places and spaces, both new and old, are negative, essentially dysfunctional, value engineered, ugly, and poorly maintained; it is disheartening that these exist but hopeful in that most participants rate them negatively and want to see them changed. What is even worse is when more places and spaces of negative character continue to be built using existing zoning and codes, reinforced by the existing political structure and the incremental lot by lot response by developers. I feel frustrated and depressed, a sinking sense of hopelessness, due to the political and economic betrayal of the visions of what people preferred and the democratic design process I believe in.

Time tests emotional responses for everyone. I experience emotional swings between the elation of the positive and the depressions of the negative. Everyone responds emotionally to health issues, finances, family troubles, job stress, political upheavals, negative environmental conditions, greed, and the deception of corporations and politicians. Add to this the negative emotional responses to places and spaces experienced on a daily basis. This is an enormous additional burden for people to carry. Is it any wonder that so many people turn to drugs for escape? People want a positive, hopeful vision of the present and future. Can this happen, or will the negative win? To permit negativity is to empower it.

> **I believe that the inherent desire of most humans is to harmonize spiritual and physical culture, and to experience positive places and spaces whenever possible.**

The community vision plans and regulations that allow the building of what people prefer can be achieved. In many cases, they might be considered too comprehensive, idealistic, and expensive. The vision is torn by the pressures of the competitive free market and the realities of economic, (do it cheaply), political (they are my friends and supporters), and media (tell people want they want and need) programming. The fundamental pressure to conform to assumed **normative behavior (NB)** in a negative environment caused by outdated zoning, and our **motivation to comply (MC)** with standard personal programming **(NB + MC)** too often conflicts with the positive collective visions.

Positive visions for places and spaces versus the reality of the mediocre and the negative requires patience to hold fast to positive visions and potential implementation as time passes, waiting hopefully for a new opportunity to emerge. Visions, once implanted in the brain, remain.

There is always a time lag between vision and implementation because the general public and those in power have been conditioned by the status quo, small-scale interventions, and variances. Our records indicate that the longest time lag between initial vision and implementation was 42 years. Other vision plans have taken up to ten years to produce real results; the shortest time frame has been less than one year. Patience is required.

New Housing and Mixed-use Infill, Metuchen, N.J.

Nearly completed 42 years after initial community vision. This multi-use building and public plaza is built on a former surface parking lot in a small downtown.

Small interventions, called tactical urbanism, incremental interventions, or catalytic projects, have happened over one or two months. It is easier to implement these small-scale interventions, like inserting a bike path or trail, closing off a street for a day or more, or removing a parking space for a street park. This can be the first step in implementing a larger vision. If promoted by media, it can start the evolutionary spiral moving.

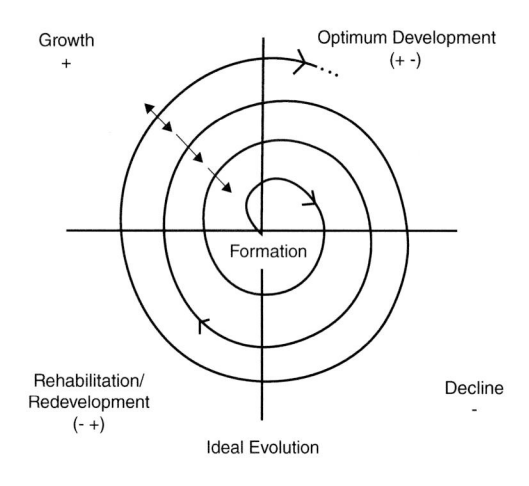

Urban Evolutionary Cycle

Throughout this book, I have referred to this Urban Evolutionary Spiral as a graphic, useful in illustrating and understanding the state of a place. Places are constantly evolving on this trajectory some faster, some slower. The spiral generates hope, patience, and understanding. Too many cities, towns, and suburbs are in the negative quadrants of urban evolution. Urban areas that are in the late stages of the decline/deterioration cycle, including their core and immediately adjacent neighborhoods, are more in need of redevelopment and rehabilitation than ever. Nonetheless, it may take time, but inevitably, change will come. In the meantime, those

negative places generate negative behaviors and that kills market potential—a vicious cycle.

Most zoning and master plans are still based on 1950s to 1970s engineering and planning, with possible new environmental and housing concerns. Many of the regulations are onerous, unfair, and out of date, directed by obsolete redevelopment plans, with staffs, politicians, and board members who have no positive public consensus vision to follow. These staffs, politicians and board members, are locked into the status quo attitude. "Let's keep what we have because new development will make it worse."

Too many approvals for new development are by variances, because the zoning is out of date. There are needless lawsuits between developers and municipalities over existing zoning which generate objections to site plans by adjacent residents and businesses. Those in power have focused on individual development parcels without consideration of the civic value of a positive holistic plan. As a result, plans are compromised to expediency, value engineering, auto orientation, and cheap construction on a smaller scale. The larger, more holistic the project, the more problematic the implementation. Market studies and zoning today are primarily rear-view mirror regulations, reflecting the past and not necessarily the future. It should be understandable, then, that much of the currently built results are rated neutral or negative. Our basic human desires for positive places and spaces have not been incorporated.

If Community Visioning results have not yet been codified in zoning, a positive technique is to have the vision results and plan adopted as a non-binding resolution by the city council or planning board. This is non-threatening and has no legal standing—but is still effective. The ability to build and improve, infill, and rehabilitate in phases, based on an "accepted" consensus Community Vision, voted by a resolution of the governing body, is the key to implementation. It takes time; a strong vision; leadership; and the understanding that there is a positive economic, social, and fiscal value. Implementation of a portion of the vision can change negative attitudes to positive.

People's positive visions respond in some respects to our historical human evolution where nature and community were foremost and conjoined. This memory of this evolution may have the key and provide appropriate instruction for a path forward. People, places, spaces, technology, and science have been continuously evolving, and humans have adapted. Looking to human accomplishments and buildings within the context of the previous 10,000 years of planning history, there are remnants of highly advanced cultures, with religious, social customs, architecture, agriculture, and technical achievements. During this time, great temples, cities, and towns were constructed. The advancement of technology and science paralleled great city plans and architecture, some which still stand and continue to be appreciated thousands of years later. Most have disappeared after descending to the bottom of the urban evolutionary cycle due to environmental, technical, and social/economic changes. Most have continued to evolve through new growth and optimization. The Renaissance and Age of Enlightenment period produced massive advancements in knowledge as well as multiple scientific

discoveries. The Industrial Era ushered in enormous technical advancements with a parallel increase in worldwide population and pollution. That expansion of knowledge, technological advancement pollution and population continues exponentially to this day. Future technological advancements could assist immeasurably in the evolution of positive urban form and character or destroy it. I believe that, if we harnessed the positive emotional power of the people with technology, science and our green past, the future could be positive and sustainable but requires financial and political will.

The population of the planet is increasing with greater disparity in incomes. The availability of resources will continue to decline. The quality of most new buildings, places, and spaces are becoming less positive, as is the existing infrastructure. Most place we build today will not last or be beloved. It seems that we, as a worldwide culture of Homo sapiens, in this current phase of evolution, seem to be on a parallel track of destruction in terms of our physical and emotional sense of place. The planet seems to be descending into an entirely unnecessary and negative phase of the evolutionary spiral. How far will it descend before it begins its revitalization? We must shake off the old and generate a new holistic positive vision for the future or leave it behind and fund new habitats.

The Power of Positivity

A positive consensus vision could be promoted as a vision of reason and delight from which all could profit. Media-promoted positive visual consensus could have a huge impact on societal programming, if it were allowed to be presented and assimilated. Positive visual consensus would have to be accomplished in smaller separate Community Visioning sessions in neighborhoods, towns, cities, and rural/natural areas, all connected as a large, ever-expanding worldwide database of value-based visions. To achieve this, many seemingly irreconcilable conditions would have to be considered, including the political, geographic, religious, and social differences; the realization of climate change; genetic engineering; and AI. All must be factors in future success and earthly sustainability. Greed, power, and influence must be factored in as well.

Rendering of the Consensus Vision for a New Bayfront Urban Neighborhood

Positive vision for a mixed-use pedestrian street in a new urban neighborhood. The opportunity to see and interact with other humans in a positive, safe, and healthy setting is a major recommendation of the Community Visioning process.

There are positive visions of the places and spaces in which participants in the Community Visioning Sessions want to live, work, play, shop, and transport themselves. What is even more important is when they realize **their personal preferences are part of a larger preference vision that are endorsed politically**. This is one of the great positive realizations in life. People who have experienced it know how rewarding participating in the planning of their own future can be. Armed with a positive vision, they strive to select feasible, enlightened options for the short- and long-term future and the leaders who will help them accomplish it. It is critical to remember that even with a majority consensus visions, there will be individuals and corporations who will fight it in court or in the public media.

There is enormous potential political and financial strength in collective visions. The proof is visible in observations and photographs of those towns and cities that have been able to implement their positive visions. They are great examples of prospering and living a fuller life. For those who live, love, work, and play in urban areas where they can walk and maintain a sense of community, with short connections to jobs, food, and family, a new character of urbanism is emerging and being recorded. More of these positive places, streets, neighborhoods, and towns are becoming reality. Unfortunately, there are not enough positive places to purchase, rent, and live in. Positive places tend to be more expensive. We simply must and can design, approve, build, rehab, and redevelop more, hereby **providing additional positive places and spaces that people want**. As more rural areas, suburbs, towns, and cities implement people's visions of the most appealing visual and spatial characteristics, a new sustainable healthy urbanism will evolve. That is one of the great hopes for the future.

Most Appealing Characteristics

- Urban places and spaces designed for people, by limiting the presence and impact of cars and exposed parking, are appealing, as are places and spaces where people walk.
- Places that take away fear are mandatory.
- Places designed in concert with nature, which make parks and green places part of our everyday positive existences.
- Places that are easily connected to one another by convenient transit, bicycles, and other low-impact vehicles.
- Places that provide delight and contentment are not only appealing but necessary.

Places containing the above appealing core urban design values, combined with a visual humanism, the correct human scale and street proportions, the right indigenous materials, appropriate light and colors, integrated with nature, dynamic activity patterns generating a positive sense of vitality on the streets and public spaces, and finally well maintained and cared for. These must be emulated and used as inspiration for any future designs. Many existing sites, particularly those built before 1945, are valued more highly. Most places designated as historic are viewed as positive. Much has been published about the ideal urban neighborhoods (Jacobs) and the specific characteristics of lively streets (Mehta 08), e.g. their scale, proportion, color, landscaping, dimensions, fenestrations, people movement, etc.

The positive visions and preferences presented in this book are reinforced by a growing number of professionals, organizations, and individuals, who have facilitated other vision processes, from which similar types of images and values have emerged. These have been used to build additional positive places that meet the challenges of walkability, human scale, greater exposure to nature, sense of community, preservation lands for growing food, and providing clean water. Implementation translates into greater sustainability and improved quality of life for the longest time possible as negative planetary environmental issues continue to proliferate. Hope for the future must be a committed positive consensus vision held by and communicated to the largest number of people. Richard Heinberg, in his book *The End of Growth*, stated, "life in an equilibrium economy can be superior to life in a fast-growing economy," and "Instead of more we must strive for better."

Human nature has conditioning and memory which respond to love, gratitude, joy, enthusiasm, hope, satisfaction, concern, generosity, empathy, a sense of well-being, and peace. At the same time, it has negative conditioning and memories that generate fear, stress, disappointment, anger, worry, despair, hate, greed, and war.

To proceed toward growth and optimization, positive visions should trigger a revolution of expectations. Exposure through multi-media is the portal to this accomplishment. To be realized, the future must incorporate a unified vision of new urbanism for development, redevelopment, and preservation for existing and future inhabitants of Earth. Implementation of the positive vision advances if there is enlightened leadership responding to a positive public consensus vision. Ignorance, fear, and government dysfunctionality, or a "that's the way we've done it in the past" mentality, will be condemning factors for urbanism in the future. Commonly held positive visions must be translated into three- and four-dimensional plans, movies, games, videos, and documentaries. Hopefully, zoning codes will be approved to accommodate this positive future vision for a more beautiful, sustainable, healthy future for everyone not just the wealthy on the planet. To achieve even a little of people's desired humanity of places and spaces is the key to future positive urban evolution. The future will be lived in by every single individual, all of whom have specific visual preferences. The realization that providing for human beings, as a pedestrian, living in a positive, working, and communicative environment, is the most important character of place to be achieved. It is more powerful if similar preferences are held collectively with many others or at least by a large consensus. But remember, not everyone will agree. Many people are negative all the time about everything. It is human nature. Although there is much negativity out there, when a desired positive character of place can be visualized, the positive aspirations of people can come true.

Positive images of place are powerful, more so once they are built. They reach people's life forces and become part of their imagination, inspiration, and thinking. It is my hope that politicians, developers, planners, architects, engineers, and those responsible for the short- and long-term future of places and spaces will use the recommendations thus far generated, and the Community Visioning process, the VPS, and VTWs to engage people in the planning and urban design of their future. **When a desired positive character of place can be achieved for many, the promise of the Community Vision to enhance successful urban evolution will be fulfilled**.

Afterword

Only a limited number of images are presented in this book, relative to the vast number of images that have been evaluated by groups all over the country. To keep the book affordable, many chapters, case studies, and images had to be cut, but the basics are here. The chapters on the "Visions for Cities and Towns Susceptible to Flooding" "Vision for Transit Dependent Cities" and the chapter on Historic Events and evolutionary influences that have impacts on urban morphological had to be eliminated. Many of the images are dated and not of the highest quality, reflecting the time at which they were photographed. Nonetheless, they hold the fundamental truth of place, proportion, size, scale, form, sequence, character, time, color, light, and intensity of use that people find appropriate. Implementing the spirit and intent of these value-rated images represents a promise of a better, happier future, with more humane, healthy, and safe livable spaces and places.

This is my last will and urban planning and design testament.

Many thanks for your concern.

Tony Nelessen.

Please feel free to use any of the images and values presented here to catalyze attitudes and thinking to achieve cumulative positive visual results and design inspirations. Please credit them to the author.

Community Visioning for Place Making: Visioning the Future-course syllabus available

This 12 week course will focus on the power of images to generate better, heathy, beautiful, and livable cities and landscapes in the future. It explores the powerful vision planning tool that has been used in 300 locations across North America and abroad. It will expose students to the recommendations produced through this visioning process and the documented results implemented through this planning and design process. It will expose students to incorporating the vision results into form-based zoning.

This course outline which has been tested at the undergraduate and graduate level is available for download. The course takes students through the Visioning Process from understanding the negative and positive characteristics of the places and spaces, sketch-overs, simulations, preparation of questionnaires, preparation of the Visual Preference Survey for the Internet, analysis of results, final presentations, and recommendations for policy and zoning changes.

Please contact Professor Nelessen:

tony@nelessen.com

Appendix I
Definitions

The following terms are used throughout this book.

Cartway: The road or street surface between the edges of the pavement.

Emotional response: A value given to an image or a stop-motion video based on an individual's emotional reaction. The value is expressed in numerical values from –10 through 0 to +10. The higher the value, the more positive the reaction. The lower the value, the more negative the reactions.

Genius loci: The reaction of the mind to the character of place. It also means "guardian of place."

Morphological consciousness: How structure or form impacts an awareness within oneself.

Parkway: That space between the curb and the sidewalk into which street trees are planted extending from the adjacent parks into the neighborhood.

Phenomenology: A philosophical movement that gives primacy to the impact on an individual's intellectual and bodily experience of the world.

Physical planning: The preparation of plans in two, three, and four dimensions for a wide range of development and redevelopment opportunities, land and building uses, transportation modes, and ecological settings. Physical planning is the art and science of pre-visualizing and graphically portraying site plans, graphics, and images for the preparation of Comprehensive Plans, zoning-/form-based codes, planning and zoning board applications, and construction documents.

Semi-public space: The lawn or garden area between the sidewalks and the house or residential building. This space is typically confined by a low fence, hedge, or wall at the side walk edge. It provides both security and safety.

Short-term future: From now to two generations in the future. In the span of the evolution of this planet, humans in their current form have existed for a very short period of time. When referring to the short-term future, based on the rapid evolution of technology, changes in the ecosystem, and societal and human adaption, we are in desperate need of sustainability for the future of humans and nature in the short term.

Two-, three-, and four-dimensional space: Two-dimensional space refers to spaces which are illustrated in two dimensions—typically flat plans or maps. Most people cannot "read" the spaces these flat plans represent. A three-dimensional plan is one where the buildings or topography are represented in the third dimension, where the buildings seem to pop out of the page using photographic or isometric techniques. This allows us to more easily visualize the spaces between the buildings. The fourth-dimensional space uses computer modeling techniques to move through or around a place or space as a pedestrian or drone flying over it.

Urban Design: The specific art and science of design and placement of infrastructure, streets, buildings, mobility networks, parks, plazas, and public landscaping in an urban (village, town, city) setting. Successful Urban Design is three and four dimensional, generating a legible, memorable, functional, feasible, implementable beautiful. Urban Design typically focuses on buildings that form well-proportioned three-dimensional streets and spaces cherished by pedestrians. Fundamentally, it is about the feelings and functions of the spaces between the buildings. By focusing on the spaces and activities between the building walls, Urban Design can promote a positive feeling about a place which is beautiful, feasible, healthy, and sustainable.

Visioning: A public participation process for planning and Urban Design in which a broad range of people from a community or region evaluate a range of visual, spatial, and functional images or videos using negative to positive numerical responses to generate a consensus vision

for the short-term future of their community or region. The process taps into the mental capacity to extract from experiences of place, imagination, intuition, and inspiration positive, negative or neutral emotional responses.

Through the evaluation and analysis of these responses, a consensus vision emerges that allows participants to translate those positive or negative preferences into two-, three-, and four-dimensional plans through a vision translation workshop.

Vision Translation Workshop (VTW): A public participation planning and design technique in which a group of participants, after expressing their visual preferences, locate on maps the best locations for these visions.

Visual Preference Survey (VPS): A planning and Urban Design application trademarked by the US Patent Office to Anton C. Nelessen in 1989. The process uses a range of digital still and video images of places and spaces in various categories and in various locations that are then evaluated by the public on a numerical scale of -10 to $+10$ based on their emotional and physical acceptability or unacceptability, as applied to present and short-term future development, redevelopment, or preservation. The VPS is central to the visioning process.

Appendix II
Communities from Which the Visions Were Generated

Community Participation Visioning

There are 397 communities in which some form of Community Visioning was completed: Either a fully facilitated Community Visioning leading to a vision plan or a Visual Preference Survey (VPS) only, with recommendations or an invited presentation in which a VPS was administered, and results were presented. All of the vision processes used typical place categories, and thus, many of the responses were similar across communities, although the images used were specifically from those communities. After reviewing most of the results, the images used in this book are typical.

The locations are only listed once, although there were several communities where multiple vision sessions were conducted over the years. Not included are the multiple vision sessions conducted as class/studio exercises. The list of communities was generated from Anton Nelessen Associates (ANA) historic archived files and is not complete, given the loss of documents due to flooding and several office moves. In addition, there are multiple locations from Vision Southern California which are not recorded here using *A Handbook, Methods to Present and Evaluate a Visual Preference Survey for the Local Government Commission, State of California* prepared by A Nelessen Associates, Inc.

A

Air Force Institute of Technology, Dayton, Ohio
Albany, NY
Alexandria, VA, Anchorage, AK, Ann Arbor, MI, Annapolis, MD
Appleton, Wisconsin Annual Environmental Congress of the Association for New Jersey Environmental Commissions, Ash Grove, MO, Ashland, OR, Ashland, VA, Athens, GA, Atlanta, GA, Atlantic City, NJ, Aurora, WA, Aurora, CO
Austin, TX

Harvard University Graduate School of Design, MA

Hempstead, MD, Highland Park, NJ, Hoboken, NJ, Hoffman, IL

Housing Scholars Training Course, Camden, NJ

Housing Scholars Training Courses, Focus on Newark, Howard County, City of Belle Air, and Hartford County, MD, Hyde Park, NY

I

Irvington, NJ

Ivy City, Washington, DC

J

Jacksonville, FL

Jefferson Parish, LA, Jersey City, NJ, Johnson County, KS

K

Kanata, Ontario, Canada

Kansas City, MO, Keiser, OR

Kenner, New Orleans, LA, Kent, WA

Kent lands, MD

King County, WA, King County, OR

Kitsap, King County, WA

L

Laguna Beach, CA

Lancaster County, PA

Lane Council of Governments, Eugene, OR, Lawrence Township, NJ

Leonardtown, MD

Lincoln Institute, Cambridge, MA, Little Rock, AR

Lockport, IL, Long Island, NY

Los Angeles Neighborhood Initiative Town Meeting

Los Angeles, CA, Louisville, KY, Loxahatchee, FL

M

Macon, GA

Macon-Bibb County, Macon, GA, Madison, WI

Manheim, Lancaster County, PA, Marathon, the Keys, FL

Markham Ontario, Canada Memphis, TN

Metuchen, NJ, Miami Valley, OH, Miami, FL, Middletown, CT

Midtown Atlanta, GA, Milwaukee, WI, Minneapolis, MN, Mission, KS, Montgomery, AL Montebello, NY

Moorestown, NJ, Morristown, NJ, Muncie, IN

Municipality of Verona, NY

N

National Association of Realtors, Washington, DC

National Transit Institute, New Brunswick, NJ, Navy Park -Baldwin Park, Orlando, FL, Newark, NJ

New Brunswick, NJ, New Haven, CT, New Orleans, LA, Newburgh, NY, Newport News, VA, Newport, RI, Niagara Falls, NY, Nicosia, Cyprus

NJ American Planning Association, New Brunswick, NJ

NJ Housing Scholar Design Workshops, Newark, NJ

Norman, OK, North Bend, WA

North Little Rock, AR, North Philadelphia, PA, Northfield, VT

Norwich University, Northfield, VT

Novello, NY

NYSACC – New York State Association of Conservation Commissions

O

Oakland, CA

Ocean City, MD

Oceanio, County of San Luis Obispo, CA, Ohio County, OH

Oklahoma City, OK

Olathe, Johnson County, KS, Olympia, WA

Ontario County, NY, Towns of Victor and Canandaigua, NY

Ontario, Canada, Orange County, FL, Orlando, FL, Oshkosh, WI

Ottawa, Ontario, Canada, Overland Park, KS

P

Palm Beach, FL

Parkville, MD, Pemberton, NJ, Phoenix, AZ, Pittsburg, PA, Pittsford, NY

Port Orchard, WA, Port Washington, WA, Portland, ME, Portland, OR

Prince George County, MD, Princeton, NJ

Providence, RI

R

Red Bank, NJ

Redmond, WA

Regional Transportation Authority Conference, Chicago, IL

Rehoboth, DE, Reisterstown, MD, Reno, NV, Reykjavik, Iceland Richmond, VA, Rochester, NY Rockland County, NY, Rockville, MD, Roseland, VA

Rosslyn, VA, Roswell, GA

Rutgers University, NJ

S

Sacramento, CA

Saint John, New Brunswick, Canada, Saint Louis County, St. Louis, MO, Saint Paul, MN

Salem, OR, Salisbury, MD, San Antonio, TX, San Benito, CA

San Diego, CA

Santa Domingo, Dominican Republic, Santa Fe, NM

Saratoga, NY

Sayreville, Sea Bright and Highlands, NJ, Scottsdale, AZ

Seaside, FL

Seat Pleasant and Capital Heights Prince George's County, MD, District of Columbia

Seattle, WA

Sheffield, CT

South Hampton, NY, South Padre, TX, South Walton, FL, Spokane, WA, Spring Hill, KS, Springdale, AR

State of Delaware, Wilmington, DE

Suffield, CT

Sumner, WA

T

Tacoma, WA

Talbot County, MD, Tallassee, FL

Tampa MPO, Tampa, FL, Tampa, FL

The Lincoln Institute, Cambridge, MA, Topeka, KS

Toronto, Canada

Town of Suffield, CT, Trenton, NJ, Truckee, CA, Tuxedo, NY

U

ULI Real Estate School, Reston, VA

Union League Club, Chicago, IL, University of California, Davis, CA, University of Hartford, Hartford, CON University of Kentucky, Lexington, KY, University of Maryland, College Park, MD, Vancouver, WA

V

Village of Culpeper, VA

Village of Sutton Bay, ME

Villages of Westhaven, Longwood, CA, Visual Preference Survey for Comprehensive Plan, Baltimore County Office of Planning, MD

W

Warwick, Warwick, NY

Warren Township, NJ, Washington Crossing, PA

Washington Township, Mercer County, NJ, Washington, DC

Wayne, NJ

West Baltimore, MD, West Little Rock, AR, Wheaton, MD, Wichita, KS

Wilmington Area Planning Council, Newark, DE

Wilsonville, OR

Worcester County, MD, Worcester County Planning Agency, Worchester, MD

Wright Pattern Air Force Base, Dayton, OH

Y

York, Canada

York, PA

Appendix III
Typical Responses from the "Book of Public Comments"

In the last pages of a typical Demographic, Market, and Policy Questionnaire, there is an opportunity for participants to write in their additional comments and responses to positive and negative images in the survey they have just taken. The following are typical responses.

About the Negative Images

Depressing Unsafe

It's frustrating

It's not some place I want to be

Dehumanizing

Confusing and chaotic

Auto-oriented

It's man destroying nature

If you feel bad, when you see this you feel worse.

It's ugly

I want to get away from it

It's harsh on the senses – stark, bare, non-human

Where there is ugliness there is ignorance

Where there is ignorance, there is ugliness

Repelling

It makes me feel bad

Shows that people don't care

Harsh on the senses

It's wasteful

About the Positive Images

Integrated with nature

Pleasing to be there

Safe

Secure

Interesting

Good

Beautiful

Beauty that inspires the human spirit.

Harmonious

Places you want to be

Appealing, not destructive to the environment

Places to enhance positive human integration and interaction

Places for people

Humanistic

Place to be proud of

Nice

Places you want to show your friends.

Places you are drawn into

Relaxed

Comfortable

Feels good

A beautiful place can lift ones spirit

Appendix IV
Bibliography

Alexander, Christopher. Neis, Hajo. Artemis, Anninou. King, Ingrid. *A New Theory of Urban Design*

Altman, Irwin. Wohlwill, Joachim F. *Human Behavior and Environment: Advances in Theory and Research*

Balula, Luis. *Urban Design and Planning Policy*

Beatley, Timothy. *Green Urbanism: Learning for European Cities*

Brambilla, Roberto. Longo, Gianni. *For Pedestrians Only: Planning and Design and Management of Traffic Free Zones*

Cadwell, William A. *How to Save Urban America*

Chakrabarti, Vishaan. *A Country of Cities: A Manifesto for Urban America*

City of New York. *Active Design Guidelines- Promoting Physical Activity and Healthy Design*

Cullen, Gordon. *Townscape*

Davies, Jahn K. Kelly, Michael P., edited. *Healthy Cities: Research and Practice*

Duany, Andres. Speck, Jeff. Lydon, Mike. *The Smart Growth Manual*

Felsenthal, Sandy. Newsweek *"15 Ways to Fix the Suburbs"*

Fishban, Martin. *Readings in Attitude and Measurement*

Gans, Herbert. *People and Plans: Essays on Urban Problems and Solutions*

Geddes, Robert, edited. *Cities in Our Future: Growth and Form, Environmental Health and Social Equity*

Gehl, Jan. Svarre, Birgitte. *How to Study Public Life*

Glass, Arnold L. Holyoak, Leith J. Santa, John L. *Cognition*

Gleick, James. *Chaos: Making a New Science*

Harari, Yuval N. *Sapiens: A Brief History of Humankind*

Hawley, Amos H. *Human Ecology – A Theory of Community Structure*

Heimstra, Norman W. McFarling, Leslie. *Environmental Psychology*

Heinberg, Richard. *The End of Growth: Adapting to Our New economic Reality*

Heinberg, Richard. Lerch, Daniel, edited. *The Post Carbon Reader: Managing the 21st Century's Sustainability Crisis*

Jacobs, Jane. *The Death and Life of Great American Cities*

Joseph, Frank. *Before Atlantis: 20 Million Years of Human and Pre-human Cultures*

King, Richard A. *Reading for an Introduction to Psychology*

Koeman, Jean B. *Everything Beautiful Is Far Away*

Kunstler, James H. *The Long Emergency: Surviving the End of Oil, Climate Change and Other Converging Catastrophes of the Twenty-First Century*

Lang, Jon. Mileski, Walter. *Functionalism Revisited: Architecture Theory and Practice and the Behavioral Sciences*

Lydon, Mike. Garcia, Anthony. *Tactical Urbanism; Short-Term Action for Long-term Change*

McLuhan, Marshall. *Understanding Media: The Extension of Man*

Mehta, Vikas. Journal of Planning Education and Research *"Determining Environmental Characteristics to Support Social Behavior"*

Morgan, Marlo. *Mutant Message Down Under*

Nelessen Associates, A. California Local Government Commission. *"Handbook- to Present, Score and Evaluate Visual Preference Surveys TM"*

Nelessen Associates, A. SG Associates, HNTB. Bergan County Department of Planning and Economic Development *"The Community Commuter – Transit for Suburban America"*

Nelessen, Anton. Cities and Counties of the Portland Metropolitan Region Metro and Tri-met. *Picture This – The Results of a Visual Preference Survey*

Nelessen, Anton. *Land Development: The National Association of Home Builders* "Flexible and Friendly Neighborhood Transit" Netherlands Foundation for Visual Arts, Design and Architecture *"The Timezones, 8 Limited 2008"*

Nelessen, Anton. *Visions for a New American Dream Process, Principles and an Ordinance to Plan and Design Small Communities*

Oakman, Johnathan R. Princeton University.: Woodrow Wilson School of Public and International Affairs *New Downtowns: The Future of Urban Centers*

Peterson, Martin C. *Metropolis Magazine* "The Green Movement: Tree Huggers Grow Up"

Pivo, Gary. Fisher, Jeffrey D. Real Estate Economics "The walkability Premium in Commercial Real Estate Investments"

Reader, John. *Cities*

Register, Richard. *EcoCities: Rebuilding Cities in Balance with Nature*

Steiner, Rudolf. *The Human Being, His Destiny and World Evolution*

Steuteville, Robert. Langdon, Philip. *New Urbanism: Best Practices Guide*

Strauss, William. Howe, Neil. *Generations: The History of America's Short Term Future 1584 to 2069*

Sullivan, Louis H. *The Autobiography of an Idea*

Suttles, Gerald D. *Planned Sprawl: Private and Public Interests in Suburbia*

Urban Design Associates. *The Urban Design Handbook: Techniques and Working Methods Volume 1*

Urban Land Institute. *Designing the Successful Downtown*

US Department of Transportation, and National Transportation Institute. FTA Livable Communities Initiative. Livable Communities: A Visual Pattern Book for the Rosslyn Metro Stations

Vahl, H. G. Giskes, J. *Traffic Calming through Integrated Urban Planning*

Winodrad, Morley. Hais, Michael. *Millennial Makeover: How a New Generation Is Remaking America*

Winogard, Morley. Hais, Michael D. *The Millennial Makeover: My Space, YouTube and the Short Term Future of American Politics*

Zelinnka, Al. Brennan, Dean. *SafeScapes: Creating Safer, More Livable Communities through Planning and Design*

Index